序 言

　　「高中英語聽力測驗①」出版後，深受許多高中英文教師的使用，練習題多，效果良好，提供給莘莘學子練習英文聽力測驗的良好教材。

　　在許多老師的要求下，希望可以有更多的練習，來應付更困難的英文聽力內容。因應此需求，學習出版公司再次推出「高中英語聽力測驗進階」，爲了給想要在英文聽力上，一舉獲得高分的同學。根據目前的評分方式，考試成績分爲四個等級：A（幾乎完全聽懂）、B（大致聽懂）、C（約略聽懂）、F（僅能聽懂少部分），一年有兩次機會報考，成績有效期限爲 3 年。5 成以上的校系，要求學生至少要有 B 級的成績。「繁星推薦入學」、「個人申請入學」及「考試入學」之招生檢定項目或納爲「個人申請入學」審查資料之一，許多大學也已經把測驗成績列爲入學標準，其重要性可見一斑。

　　「高中英語聽力測驗進階【詳解】」共十回，取材內容生活化，符合大考中心出題方向，題目眾多，內容多元，難度更高，適合要考高分的同學，或是想要增進英文聽力的學子。寫完題目，要把錯的題目，不會的單字片語完全搞懂，再聽一次。每題都有詳細的中文說明和註釋，方便同學複習常考的單字和片語。複習時，將不會的題目朗讀一遍，到眞正考試時就輕鬆了。

　　編輯好書是「學習」一貫的宗旨。本書在編審及校對的每一階段，均力求完善，但恐有疏漏之處，誠盼各界先進不吝批評指正。

編者　謹識

高中英聽測驗模擬試題 ① 詳解

一、看圖辨義：第一部分

For question number 1, please look at picture 1.

1. (**A**) Mr. Smith's eyesight is poor.　He needs a magnifying glass
to read a book.　史密斯先生的視力很差。他需要放大鏡來讀書。

　　* eyesight〔'aɪ,saɪt〕*n.* 視力　　poor〔pʊr〕*adj.* 差的
　　　magnify〔'mægnə,faɪ〕*v.* 放大　　***magnifying glass*** 放大鏡

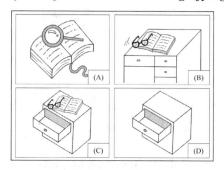

For question number 2, please look at picture 2.

2. (**D**) Jimmy has been a bad boy.　He's truly sorry for what he
has done.

　　吉米是個壞男孩。他現在對他所做的事真的感到很後悔。

　　　* truly〔'trulɪ〕*adv.* 真正地

For question number 3, please look at picture 3.

3. (**A**) Charlie is an accomplished chess player. He just took first prize in a local tournament. 查理是位技術高超的西洋棋選手。他才剛在當地的錦標賽獲得第一名。

> * accomplished〔 ə'kɑmplɪʃt 〕adj. 熟練的；技術高超的
> chess〔 tʃɛs 〕n. 西洋棋　　*first prize* 第一名
> local〔'lokḷ 〕adj. 當地的
> tournament〔'tɜnəmənt 〕n. 競賽；錦標賽

For question number 4, please look at picture 4.

4. (**C**) Mary isn't a musician, but she really enjoys listening to music. She's always wearing a set of headphones. 瑪麗不是音樂家，但她真的很喜歡聽音樂。她總是戴著頭戴式耳機。

> * musician〔 mju'zɪʃən 〕n. 音樂家　　*a set of* 一套；一組
> headphones〔'hɛd,fonz 〕n. pl. 頭戴式耳機

一、看圖辨義：第二部分

For question number 5, please look at picture 5.

5. (**B、C**) Which TWO of the following are true about the
picture?　關於這張圖片，下列哪兩項爲眞？

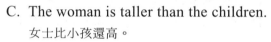

A. The dogs are sleeping.
狗正在睡覺。

B. The children are fighting.
小孩正在打架。

C. The woman is taller than the children.
女士比小孩還高。

D. The man is crying.　男士正在哭。

* fight〔faɪt〕v. 打架

For question number 6, please look at picture 6.

6. (**C、D**) Which TWO of the following are true about the
picture?　關於這張圖片，下列哪兩項爲眞？

A. The boy is riding his bike and his father is
concerned.　男孩在騎腳踏車，而他的爸爸很擔心。

B. The teacher is giving a lesson and the students
are sleeping.　老師在上課，而學生們在睡覺。

C. The girl is watching television.
女孩正在看電視。

D. It's nearly midnight.
現在時間將近午夜。

* concerned〔kən'sɝnd〕adj. 擔心的
give a lesson 授課
nearly〔'nɪrlɪ〕adv. 將近；差不多
midnight〔'mɪd,naɪt〕n. 半夜；午夜

For question number 7, please look at picture 7.

7. (**A、D**) Which TWO of the following are true about the picture? 關於這張圖片，下列 哪兩項為眞？

    A. The boy is selling fruit.
       男孩在賣水果。

    B. The boy is selling candy.
       男孩在賣糖果。

    C. The woman is thirsty. 女士很渴。

    D. The woman wants to buy some fruit.
       女士想要買一些水果。

    * candy〔'kændɪ〕 n. 糖果　　thirsty〔'θɝstɪ〕 adj. 口渴的

For question number 8, please look at picture 8.

8. (**B、C**) Which TWO of the following are true about the picture? 關於這張圖片，下列 哪兩項為眞？

    A. The man is reading a story to his children.
       男士在讀故事給他的孩子聽。

    B. The woman is preparing food for her children.
       女士在準備食物給她的孩子吃。

    C. The woman is wearing an apron. 女士穿著圍裙。

    D. The doctor is examining a patient.
       醫生正在檢查病人。

    * prepare〔prɪ'pɛr〕 v. 準備　　apron〔'eprən〕 n. 圍裙
      examine〔ɪg'zæmɪn〕 v. 檢查
      patient〔'peʃənt〕 n. 病人

For question number 9, please look at picture 9.

9. (**B、D**) Which TWO of the following are true about the
picture? 關於這張圖片，下列
哪兩項為眞？

A. The couple just met.
這對男女剛見面。

B. The couple just got married.
這對男女剛結婚。

C. They are riding horses. 他們正在騎馬。

D. They are posing for a photograph.
他們正在擺姿勢拍照。

* couple〔ˈkʌpl̩〕*n.* 一對男女　　just〔dʒʌst〕*adv.* 剛剛
get married 結婚　　pose〔poz〕*v.* 擺姿勢
photograph〔ˈfotə‚græf〕*n.* 照片

For question number 10, please look at picture 10.

10. (**B、C**) Which TWO of the following are true about the
picture? 關於這張圖片，下列
哪兩項為眞？

A. They are in a bank.
他們在銀行裡。

B. They are in a park.
他們在公園裡。

C. They are collecting butterflies. 他們在抓蝴蝶。

D. They are watching a film. 他們在看電影。

* bank〔bæŋk〕*n.* 銀行
collect〔kəˈlɛkt〕*v.* 收集；採集
butterfly〔ˈbʌtə‚flaɪ〕*n.* 蝴蝶　　film〔fɪlm〕*n.* 電影

二、對答

11. (**A**) Did you find what you were looking for?
    你有找到你要找的東西嗎？

    A. Yes, I did. 是的，我有。
    B. Yes, I will. 是的，我會。
    C. No, I won't. 不，我不會。
    D. No, I don't. 不，我沒有。【要改成 No, I didn't.】

    * **look for** 尋找

12. (**C**) Where's the leftover pizza from last night?
    昨晚剩下的披薩在哪？

    A. I'll eat it. 我會把它吃掉。
    B. My mom made it for me. 我媽做給我的。
    C. I ate it. 我吃掉了。
    D. I have nothing to eat. 我沒有東西可以吃。

    * leftover (ˈlɛftˌovɚ) adj. 剩餘的   pizza (ˈpitsə) n. 披薩

13. (**D**) How was your trip? 你的旅行如何？

    A. They were excellent. 它們很棒。
    B. There are some good ones. 有一些好的。
    C. We took a trip. 我們去旅行。
    D. It was very nice. 很棒。

    * trip (trɪp) n. 旅行   excellent (ˈɛkslənt) adj. 極好的
    take a trip 去旅行

14. (**C**) What kind of books do you enjoy reading?
    你喜歡讀哪種書？

    A. Words. 文字。   B. Liquid. 液體。
    C. Romance. 愛情小說。   D. Cold. 冷的。

    * liquid (ˈlɪkwɪd) n. 液體   romance (roˈmæns) n. 愛情小說

15. (**A**) Do you think it will rain this afternoon?

　　你覺得今天下午會下雨嗎？

　　A. Probably. 可能會。　　B. Excellently. 很棒地。

　　C. Silently. 安靜地。　　D. Questionably. 可疑地。

　　* probably〔'prɑbəblɪ〕*adv.* 可能

　　excellently〔'ɛksḷəntlɪ〕*adv.* 極好地

　　silently〔'saɪləntlɪ〕*adv.* 無聲地；安靜地

　　questionably〔'kwɛstʃənəblɪ〕*adv.* 可疑地

16. (**A**) Excuse me. I'm looking for a plunger.

　　很抱歉，我在找橡膠吸盤。

　　A. Plumbing supplies are on the second floor.

　　　 水管器材在二樓。

　　B. We don't make that. 我們不製作那個。

　　C. Try the vending machine. 試看看販賣機。

　　D. The electronics department is in aisle six.

　　　 電子貨品區在六號走道。

　　* plunger〔'plʌndʒɚ〕*n.*（疏通堵塞的水槽、浴缸等的）橡膠吸盤

　　plumbing〔'plʌmɪŋ〕*n.* 水管裝置

　　supplies〔sə'plaɪz〕*n. pl.* 補給品；生活用品

　　floor〔flor〕*n.* 樓層　　vend〔vɛnd〕*v.* 販賣

　　vending machine 販賣機

　　electronics〔ɪ,lɛk'trɑnɪks〕*n. pl.* 電子設備

　　department〔dɪ'pɑrtmənt〕*n.* 部門；（大型商店的）貨品區

　　aisle〔aɪl〕*n.* 走道；通道

17. (**C**) When will they announce the winner of the writing

　　contest? 他們什麼時候會宣布寫作比賽的獲勝者？

　　A. Yes, they will. 是的，他們會。

　　B. Most likely not. 很可能不會。

C. I'm not sure. 我不確定。

D. If they announce the winner. 如果他們宣布了獲勝者。

* announce〔ə'naʊns〕v. 宣布
winner〔'wɪnɚ〕n. 獲勝者；得獎者
contest〔'kɑntɛst〕n. 比賽
most〔most〕adv. 非常；極（= *very*）
likely〔'laɪklɪ〕adv. 可能地

18. (**B**) Do you have any allergies? 你有任何的過敏嗎？

A. Just be sure to bring it back this time.

這一次務必要把它帶回來。

B. None that I am aware of. 據我所知沒有。

C. Call me if you need anything.

如果你需要任何東西，打電話給我。

D. There may be another way around it.

可能會有別的方法能解決。

* allergy〔'ælɚdʒɪ〕n. 過敏症
be sure to V. 一定～；務必～
be aware of 知道；察覺到
None that I am aware of. 據我所知沒有。（= *Not that I know of.*）
around〔ə'raʊnd〕prep. 解決；克服

19. (**C**) How do you stay in touch with your family?

你如何和你的家人保持聯絡？

A. I have two sisters. 我有兩個妹妹。

B. We watch a lot of television. 我們很常看電視。

C. Mostly by e-mail. 大多是透過電子郵件。

D. Family is important. 家庭很重要。

* *stay in touch* 保持聯絡　　mostly〔'mostlɪ〕adv. 大多
e-mail〔'i,mel〕n. 電子郵件

20. (**D**) What happened to Larry's brother?

賴瑞的弟弟發生了什麼事？

　A. Yes, I met Larry's brother.

　　是的，我遇到賴瑞的弟弟。

　B. Sure. There's Larry. 當然。賴瑞在那裡。

　C. That's strange. Larry has a brother.

　　那很奇怪。賴瑞有個弟弟。

　D. I don't know. Ask Larry. 我不知道。去問賴瑞。

三、簡短對話

For question 21, you will listen to a short conversation.

　M：Is there someplace nearby where I can send money

　　overseas? 這附近有什麼地方可以讓我把錢寄到國外嗎？

　W：You could try the bank on Second Avenue.

　　你可以試看看第二大道上的銀行。

　M：Great. Could you tell me how to get there?

　　太棒了。妳可以告訴我如何去嗎？

　W：Sure. Just keep walking straight until the next

　　intersection. You'll see it on the left.

　　當然。只要一直直走到下一個十字路口。你就會看到銀行在

　　你的左手邊。

　　* send〔sɛnd〕v. 寄

　　　overseas〔'ovɚ'siz〕adv. 向海外；向國外

　　　avenue〔'ævə,nju〕n. 大道；大街

　　　straight〔stret〕adv. 直直地

　　　intersection〔,ɪntɚ'sɛkʃən〕n. 十字路口

　　　on the left 在左手邊

21. (**C**) Q : What does the man want to do? 男士想要做什麼？

    A. Find an ATM. 找提款機。

    B. Mail a package. 寄一個包裹。

    C. Send money overseas. 把錢寄到國外。

    D. Buy travel insurance. 買旅遊險。

    * *ATM* 自動櫃員機；提款機 (= *automated teller machine*)
       package (ˈpækɪdʒ) *n.* 包裹   insurance (ɪnˈʃʊrəns) *n.* 保險

For question 22, you will listen to a short conversation.

W : Does the 33 bus go to the zoo? 33 號公車有到動物園嗎？

M : No. You want the 15 bus. 沒有。妳要坐 15 號公車。

W : Does the 15 stop here? 15 號公車有停這裡嗎？

M : Yes. It runs every 20 minutes. 有。它每二十分鐘一班。

    * zoo (zu) *n.* 動物園   run (rʌn) *v.* 通行；往來

22. (**D**) Q : Where does the woman want to go? 女士想要去哪裡？

    A. To the library. 去圖書館。

    B. To the bank. 去銀行。

    C. To the post office. 去郵局。

    D. To the zoo. 去動物園。

    *library (ˈlaɪˌbrɛrɪ) *n.* 圖書館   *post office* 郵局

For question 23, you will listen to a short conversation.

M : You're soaking wet and sweating like a slave, Jane.
    What happened?

    珍，妳全身都濕透了，而且汗流浹背。發生什麼事了？

W : I ran all the way home from the bus stop.

    我從公車站一路跑回家。

M : Was somebody chasing you? What's the big rush?

　　有人在追妳嗎？妳在急什麼？

W : I wanted to get home before the mail came. I'm
expecting a package.

　　我想要在郵件來之前回家。我在等一個包裹。

> * soaking〔'sokɪŋ〕adv. 濕淋淋地　　***soaking wet*** 濕透的
> sweat〔swɛt〕v. 流汗　　slave〔slev〕n. 奴隸
> ***sweat like a slave*** 像奴隸一樣流汗；汗流浹背（= *sweat a lot*）
> ***all the way*** 一路上　　***bus stop*** 公車站
> chase〔tʃez〕v. 追　　rush〔rʌʃ〕n. 匆忙；緊急
> ***What's the rush?*** 急什麼？
> expect〔ɪk'spɛkt〕v. 預期；等待　　package〔'pækɪdʒ〕n. 包裹

23.（**C**）Q : Why is the woman wet? 為何女士濕答答的？

　　A. She is under a lot of pressure. 她有很多壓力。

　　B. She forgot her umbrella. 她忘了帶雨傘。

　　C. She ran home from the bus stop.
　　　 她從公車站跑回家。

　　D. She didn't arrive in time to receive the package.
　　　 她沒有及時到達收包裹。

> * pressure〔'prɛʃə〕n. 壓力
> ***in time*** 及時　　receive〔rɪ'siv〕v. 收到

For question 24, you will listen to a short conversation.

W : We've got a problem. The car won't start.

　　我們遇到問題了。這車子無法發動。

M : That's odd. Did you remember to get gas last night?

　　真奇怪。妳昨天有記得去加油嗎？

W : No, but the gauge said there was a quarter tank left.
　　沒有，但是油量表顯示油箱還剩四分之一的油。

M : Give me the keys. Sometimes the ignition is a bit tricky.
　　I'll give it a shot.

　　鑰匙給我。有時候要發動引擎有點棘手。我會試看看。

> * **have got** 有 (= *have*)　　start〔stɑrt〕v. 發動
> odd〔ɑd〕adj. 奇怪的 (= *strange*)　　gas〔gæs〕n. 汽油
> **get gas** 加油　　gauge〔gedʒ〕n. 計量器；油量表
> say〔se〕v. 寫著；指著；顯示
> quarter〔'kwɔrtɚ〕n. 四分之一
> tank〔tæŋk〕n. 油箱；（箱或桶等）所裝之物；一箱的量
> left〔lɛft〕adj. 剩下的
> ignition〔ɪg'nɪʃən〕n. （引擎）點火裝置　　**a bit** 一點點
> tricky〔'trɪkɪ〕adj. 棘手的；難以處理的　　**give it a shot** 試看看

24. (**B**) Q：What is the man going to do next?
　　　　　　　男士接下來要做什麼？
　　A. Go to the gas station. 去加油站。
　　B. Try to start the car. 嘗試發動車子。
　　C. Perform a magic trick. 表演魔術。
　　D. Take a shot of whiskey. 喝一杯威士忌。

> * **gas station** 加油站　　perform〔pɚ'fɔrm〕v. 表演；做
> magic〔'mædʒɪk〕n. 魔術　　trick〔trɪk〕n. 把戲
> take〔tek〕v. 吃；喝　　shot〔ʃɑt〕n. （威士忌酒等的）一杯
> whiskey〔'hwɪskɪ〕n. 威士忌

For questions 25 and 26, you will listen to a short conversation.

M : My students were so quiet today. Nobody wanted to
　　participate. 我的學生今天真安靜。沒人想要參與。

W : Same with my kids. But you know, it *is* Monday and this weather is simply depressing. 我們班的孩子也是。但是你知道的，今天是星期一，而且這樣的天氣真是令人沮喪。

M : You may have a point. It *has* been raining for almost a week straight. 也許妳說的對。已經連續下雨快要一週了。

W : I'm feeling a little blue myself. A little sunshine would do me good.

我自己都覺得有點憂鬱了。有點陽光會對我比較好。

　　* participate〔par'tɪsə,pet〕*v.* 參與　　　***same with*** ⋯ ⋯也一樣
　　simply〔'sɪmplɪ〕*adv.* 的確
　　depressing〔dɪ'prɛsɪŋ〕*adj.* 令人沮喪的　　***have a point*** 有道理
　　straight〔stret〕*adv.* 連續地　　　blue〔blu〕*adj.* 憂鬱的
　　sunshine〔'sʌn,ʃaɪn〕*n.* 陽光　　　***do sb. good*** 對某人有好處

25. (**C**) Q : Who are the speakers? 說話者是誰？
　　　　A. Lawyers. 律師。
　　　　B. Accountants. 會計師。
　　　　C. Teachers. 老師。
　　　　D. Students. 學生。
　　　　* lawyer〔'lɔjɚ〕*n.* 律師　　accountant〔ə'kauntənt〕*n.* 會計師

26. (**D**) Q : What does the woman say? 女士說什麼？
　　　　A. Her color is fading. 她的臉色越變越白。
　　　　B. Her students are unruly. 她的學生很不聽話。
　　　　C. The man shouldn't wear blue-colored clothing.
　　　　　　男士不應該穿藍色的衣服。
　　　　D. The weather has affected her mood.
　　　　　　天氣影響了她的心情。

* color〔'kʌlɚ〕n. 臉色；氣色　　fade〔fed〕v. 衰退；褪色
unruly〔ʌn'rulɪ〕adj. 不聽話的　　blue-colored adj. 藍色的
clothing〔'kloðɪŋ〕n. 衣服【集合名詞】
affect〔ə'fɛkt〕v. 影響　　mood〔mud〕n. 心情

For questions 27 and 28, you will listen to a short conversation.

W : Does the library have free wireless Internet access?

圖書館有免費的無線網路嗎？

M : It does. In fact, there is a campus-wide wi-fi network.

有的。事實上，整個校園都有無線網路。

W : Wow. Is there a password to get online?

哇。要有密碼才能上網嗎？

M : Yes, it's your student ID number.

是的，密碼是你的學生證號碼。

* library〔'laɪ,brɛrɪ〕n. 圖書館　　free〔fri〕adj. 免費的
wireless〔'waɪrlɪs〕adj. 無線的
access〔'æksɛs〕n. 接近或使用權
Internet access 網路連線　　*in fact* 事實上
campus〔'kæmpəs〕n. 校園　　campus-wide adj. 整個校園的
wi-fi〔'waɪ,faɪ〕n. 無線傳輸系統；無線網路（= *Wi-Fi*）
network〔'nɛt,wɜk〕n. 網路　　password〔'pæs,wɜd〕n. 密碼
get online 上網　　*ID* 身份（= *identification*）

27. (**D**) Q : Who are the speakers?　說話者是誰？

　　　　A. Co-workers. 同事。

　　　　B. Technology consultants. 科技顧問。

　　　　C. Factory workers. 工廠員工。

　　　　D. College students. 大學生。

　　　* co-worker〔'ko,wɜkɚ〕*n.* 同事
　　　technology〔tɛk'nɑlədʒɪ〕*n.* 科技
　　　consultant〔kən'sʌltn̩t〕*n.* 顧問
　　　factory〔'fækt(ə)rɪ〕*n.* 工廠　　college〔'kɑlɪdʒ〕*n.* 大學

28. (**A**) Q：What does the woman want to use?
　　　　　女士想要使用什麼？
　　　　A. The Internet. 網路。　　　B. The bathroom. 浴室。
　　　　C. The teacher. 老師。　　　D. The telephone. 電話。
　　　* bathroom〔'bæθ,rum〕*n.* 浴室

For questions 29 and 30, you will listen to a short conversation.

M：I'm telling you, that was one heck of a game!
　　我跟妳說，那真的是場精彩的比賽！

W：Whatever. You're just gloating because your team won.
　　或許吧。因為你的隊贏了，所以你就沾沾自喜。

M：No, I am not. It was a genuinely exciting game to watch.
　　Don't be a poor sport, Sarah. You can't win them all.
　　不，我沒有。這真的是一場值得觀賞的刺激的比賽。不要輸不
　　起，莎拉。妳不可能樣樣勝利。

W：Just drop it, Brad. The game is over. Talk about
　　something else, OK?
　　別說了，布拉德。比賽已經結束了。講講其他的事情，好嗎？

　　　* **I'm telling you** 我可以肯定地說；我跟妳說
　　　a heck of a【用於強調】很嚴重的…；非常的…
　　　whatever〔hwɑt'ɛvɚ〕*pron.*【用於回應，表示不在乎或不感興趣】
　　　　或許吧；無所謂
　　　gloat〔glot〕*v.* 竊喜；沾沾自喜　　team〔tim〕*n.* 隊伍
　　　genuinely〔'dʒɛnjuɪnlɪ〕*adv.* 真正地

exciting〔ɪk'saɪtɪŋ〕*adj.* 刺激的；令人興奮的

sport〔sport〕*n.* 爽快的人；隨和的人；樂於助人的人

a poor sport 輸不起的人

You can't win them all. 你不可能樣樣勝利。

drop〔drɑp〕*v.* 掉落；停止　　***drop it*** 算了；別說了

29. (**A**) Q：What happened in the game? 比賽發生了什麼事？

　　A. The woman's team lost. 女士的隊輸了。

　　B. The man's team played poorly. 男士的隊打得很差。

　　C. The game was postponed due to rain.
　　　　比賽因為下雨而延期。

　　D. The man played well. 男士打得很好。

　　* lose〔luz〕*v.* 輸　　poorly〔'purlɪ〕*adv.* 差勁地
　　postpone〔post'pon〕*v.* 延後；延期　　***due to*** 因為

30. (**B**) Q：Which description matches the woman's attitude?
　　　　哪個描述符合ㄈㄟ十的態度？

　　A. Complacent. 自滿的。　　B. Irritated. 被激怒的。
　　C. Confident. 有自信的。　　D. Excited. 興奮的。

　　* description〔dɪ'skrɪpʃən〕*n.* 描述
　　match〔mætʃ〕*v.* 符合　　attitude〔'ætə,tjud〕*n.* 態度
　　complacent〔kəm'plesṇt〕*adj.* 自滿的
　　irritated〔'ɪrə,tetɪd〕*adj.* 被激怒的；不耐煩的
　　confident〔'kɑnfədənt〕*adj.* 有自信的
　　excited〔ɪk'saɪtɪd〕*adj.* 興奮的

四、短文聽解

Questions 31 and 32 are based on the following report.

　　Flying may be the safest form of transport, but many
of the three million people who take to the air each day are

terrified of crashing. Now more than ever, though, it's
possible to survive a plane crash. Most people believe that
if they're in a plane crash, their time is up. In fact, the truth
is surprisingly different. In the U.S. alone, between 1983
and 2000, there were 568 plane crashes. Out of the
collective 53,487 people on board, 51,207 survived. The
advances in science and technology now mean over 90% of
plane crashes have survivors.

　　搭飛機可能是最安全的運輸方式，但是每天有三百萬人搭飛
機，他們之中有許多人害怕墜機。然而，現在比起以前更有可能
自空難中生還。大多數的人相信，如果他們發生空難，他們必死
無疑。事實上，令人驚訝的是事實並非如此。單單在美國，1983
年至 2000 年間，有 568 起空難。總共有 53,487 人在飛機上，有
51,207 人生還。現在在科學和科技上的進步，表示會有超過百分
之九十的空難會有生還者。

** ─────────────────────

fly〔flaɪ〕v. 搭飛機　　form〔fɔrm〕n. 形式
transport〔'trænsport〕n. 運輸　　***take to*** 到；去
the air 空中　　***take to the air*** 飛行
be terrified of 害怕　　crash〔kræʃ〕v. n. 墜毀
though〔ðo〕adv.【置於句中或句尾】然而（= *however*）
survive〔sə'vaɪv〕v. 從…中生還；存活
plane crash 空難；墜機（= *air crash*）
*one's **time is up*** 時間到了；期限已到　　***in fact*** 事實上
alone〔ə'lon〕adv. 單單；僅僅　　***out of*** 在…之中
collective〔kə'lɛktɪv〕adj. 集體的；共同的；總的
on board 在飛機（船、火車）上
advance〔əd'væns〕n. 進步
technology〔tɛk'nɑlədʒɪ〕n. 科技
mean〔min〕v. 意思是；表示　　survivor〔sə'vaɪvə〕n. 生還者

31. (**A**) What is this talk mainly about? 這段談話主要是關於什麼？
    A. General airplane safety. 一般的飛行安全。
    B. The odds of being in a plane crash. 發生空難的機率。
    C. How to overcome a fear of flying.
       如何克服搭飛機的恐懼。
    D. Why people survive plane crashes.
       人為何能自空難中生還。

    * mainly ('menlɪ) *adv.* 主要地   general ('dʒɛnərəl) *adj.* 一般的
    odds (ɑds) *n. pl.* 可能性；機率
    overcome (ˌovəˈkʌm) *v.* 克服   fear (fɪr) *n.* 恐懼

32. (**D**) What does the speaker say about flying?
    關於搭飛機，說話者說了什麼？
    A. 90% of plane crashes do not have survivors.
       百分之九十的空難沒有生還者。
    B. No one can survive a plane crash.
       沒有人可以自空難中生還。
    C. If you're in a plane crash, your time is up.
       如果你發生空難，你必死無疑。
    D. Flying is the safest form of transport.
       搭飛機是最安全的運輸方式。

Questions 33 and 34 are based on the following report.

    The recent controversies over the government's move to raise electricity and gasoline prices have underscored the fact that our country lacks a clear energy policy. The President has justified his swift decision to "normalize" energy prices to cover the huge losses of the utilities by claiming that if we don't endure the short-term pain now, we will suffer more in the long run. What does his assertion really mean or imply? Is he saying that if we kept the low energy prices, the government would have to channel even more of the taxpayers' money into covering the losses of the utilities, which would eventually trigger even bigger hikes in the future? Or is he saying that if we kept the prices low, thereby encouraging waste, we would one day pay for our wasteful behavior in the form of severe pollution?

最近關於政府計畫提高油電價格的爭議，已經突顯了一件事實，就是我們的國家缺乏清楚的能源政策。總統已經爲了迅速的決策辯護。爲了要讓能源的價格「正常化」，以支付龐大的公用事業的虧損，他聲稱，如果我們現在不能承受短期的痛苦，我們最後將會受更多的苦。他這個聲明眞正的意思是什麼，或是在暗示什麼？他是說如果我們持續維持低能源費用，政府就必須轉移更多納稅者的錢來支付公用事業的損失，這最後會導致未來更大的漲幅？還是他是在說，如果我們保持低價，因而鼓勵浪費，我們會有一天將爲我們浪費的行爲所形成的嚴重污染而付出代價？

**

recent〔'risn̩t〕*adj.* 最近的　　controversy〔'kɑntrə,vɜsɪ〕*n.* 爭論
move〔muv〕*n.* 行動；步驟　　raise〔rez〕*v.* 提高
electricity〔ɪ,lɛk'trɪsətɪ〕*n.* 電　　gasoline〔'gæsəl̩,in〕*n.* 汽油
underscore〔,ʌndə'skɔr〕*v.* 強調；清楚地表示；突顯
fact〔fækt〕*n.* 事實　　lack〔læk〕*v.* 缺乏
energy〔'ɛnə-dʒɪ〕*n.* 能源　　policy〔'pɑləsɪ〕*n.* 政策
justify〔'dʒʌstə,faɪ〕*v.* 爲…辯護
swift〔swɪft〕*adj.* 快速的；立即的
normalize〔'nɔrml̩,aɪz〕*v.* 使正常化；使標準化

cover〔ˋkʌvɚ〕v. 支付　　huge〔hjudʒ〕adj. 巨大的
loss〔lɔs〕n. 損失
utilities〔juˋtɪlətɪz〕n. pl. 公共事業（水、電、瓦斯等）
claim〔klem〕v. 宣稱　　endure〔ɪnˋdjʊr〕v. 忍受
short-term〔͵ʃɔrtˋtɝm〕adj. 短期的　　pain〔pen〕n. 痛苦
suffer〔ˋsʌfɚ〕v. 受苦　　**in the long run** 最後
assertion〔əˋsɝʃən〕n. 主張　　imply〔ɪmˋplaɪ〕v. 暗示
government〔ˋgʌvɚnmənt〕n. 政府
channel〔ˋtʃænḷ〕v. 把…導向；將（資金等）用於…
taxpayer〔ˋtæks͵peɚ〕n. 納稅人

eventually〔ɪˋvɛntʃʊəlɪ〕adv. 最後
trigger〔ˋtrɪgɚ〕v. 引發；導致
hike〔haɪk〕n.（薪資、物價等的）提高；上漲
thereby〔͵ðɛrˋbaɪ〕adv. 從而；因此
encourage〔ɪnˋkɝɪdʒ〕v. 鼓勵；助長　　waste〔west〕n. 浪費
pay for 為…付出代價　　wasteful〔ˋwestfəl〕adj. 浪費的
behavior〔bɪˋhevjɚ〕n. 行為　　**in the form of** 以…的形式
severe〔səˋvɪr〕adj. 嚴重的　　pollution〔pəˋluʃən〕n. 污染

33. (**B**) What is this talk mainly about? 這段談話主要是關於什麼？

    A. Fighting pollution. 對抗污染。

    B. Rising energy costs. 上漲的能源價格。

    C. Enduring long-term pain. 忍受長期的痛苦。

    D. Raising taxes on utilities. 提高公用事業的稅。

    * fight〔faɪt〕v. 對抗　　rising〔ˋraɪzɪŋ〕adj. 上升的
    cost〔kɔst〕n. 費用；價格　　tax〔tæks〕n. 稅

34. (**A**) What is the author's attitude? 作者的態度是什麼？

    A. Concerned and confused. 擔心且困惑的。

    B. Outraged and defiant. 憤怒且反抗的。

    C. Dismissive and vain. 輕視且自負的。

    D. Arrogant and pushy. 自大且咄咄逼人的。

  * concerned〔 kən'sɜnd 〕*adj.* 擔心的
    confused〔 kən'fjuzd 〕*adj.* 困惑的
    outraged〔'aʊt,redʒd 〕*adj.* 憤怒的
    defiant〔 dɪ'faɪənt 〕*adj.* 反抗的；挑釁的
    dismissive〔 dɪs'mɪsɪv 〕*adj.* 輕視的
    vain〔 ven 〕*adj.* 自負的；虛榮心強的
    arrogant〔'ærəgənt 〕*adj.* 自大的
    pushy〔'pʊʃɪ 〕*adj.* 咄咄逼人的

Questions 35 and 36 are based on the following report.

Bullying can be prevented, especially when the power of a community is brought together. Community-wide strategies can help identify and support children who are bullied, redirect the behavior of children who bully, and change the attitudes of adults and youth who tolerate bullying behaviors in peer groups, schools, and communities.

Bullying doesn't happen only at school. Community members can use their unique strengths and skills to prevent bullying wherever it occurs. For example, youth sports groups may train coaches to prevent bullying. Local businesses may make T-shirts with bullying prevention slogans for an event. After-care staff may read books about bullying to kids and discuss them. Hearing anti-bullying messages from the different adults in their lives can reinforce the message for kids that bullying is unacceptable.

霸凌是可以預防的，特別是當一個社區的力量團結起來的時候。整個社區的策略可以幫助辨識並支持受到霸凌的孩童，輔導霸凌他人的孩童的行為，並改變在同儕、學校，和社區裡，忍受霸凌行為的大人和年輕人的態度。

　　霸凌不是只發生在學校裡。不管霸凌發生在哪裡，社區的成員都可以運用他們獨特的優勢和技巧來防止霸凌。例如，年輕人的運動團體可以訓練教練來預防霸凌。當地的企業可以為了大型活動，製作有預防霸凌口號的 T 恤。輔導人員可以讀關於霸凌的書籍給孩子聽，並加以討論。在生活中聽到關於來自不同成人的反霸凌訊息，可以加強傳遞給孩子的訊息，那就是霸凌不能接受的。

＊＊

bully〔ˋbʊlɪ〕*v.* 霸凌　　prevent〔prɪˋvɛnt〕*v.* 預防
especially〔əˋspɛʃəlɪ〕*adv.* 尤其；特別是
community〔kəˋmjunətɪ〕*n.* 社區；團體
bring together 使結合　　N-wide *adj.* 整個…的
strategy〔ˋstrætədʒɪ〕*n.* 策略
identify〔aɪˋdɛntə͵faɪ〕*v.* 辨認　　support〔səˋport〕*v.* 支持
redirect〔͵ridəˋrɛkt〕*v.* 使改變方向　　adult〔əˋdʌlt〕*n.* 成人
youth〔juθ〕*n.* 年輕人　　tolerate〔ˋtɑlə͵ret〕*v.* 忍受；容許
peer〔pɪr〕*n.* 同儕　　unique〔juˋnik〕*adj.* 獨特的；獨有的

strength〔strɛŋθ〕*n.* 力量；長處　　skill〔skɪl〕*n.* 技巧；技能
for example 舉例來說　　coach〔kotʃ〕*n.* 教練
local〔ˋlokḷ〕*adj.* 當地的；地方的
business〔ˋbɪznɪs〕*n.* 公司；企業
prevention〔prɪˋvɛnʃən〕*n.* 預防
slogan〔ˋslogən〕*n.* 口號；標語　　event〔ɪˋvɛnt〕*n.* 大型活動
after-care *adj.* 善後輔導的　　staff〔stæf〕*n.* 全體工作人員
message〔ˋmɛsɪdʒ〕*n.* 訊息　　reinforce〔͵riɪnˋfors〕*v.* 加強
unacceptable〔͵ʌnəkˋsɛptəbḷ〕*adj.* 不能接受的；不能允許的

35. (**B**) What is this talk mainly about?　這段談話主要是關於什麼？
    A. Encouraging bullying. 鼓勵霸凌。
    B. Preventing bullying. 預防霸凌。
    C. Identifying bullying. 辨識霸凌。
    D. Tolerating bullying. 忍受霸凌。

36. (**C**) Which of the following statements is true?
    下面哪個敘述是正確的？
    A. Bullying only happens in school.
       霸凌只發生在學校內。
    B. Most adults are taught to ignore bullying.
       大多的成人被教導要忽視霸凌。
    C. Bullying is unacceptable. 霸凌是不能接受的。
    D. The community is helpless to stop bullying.
       社區對於阻止霸凌是無能為力的。
    * ignore〔 ɪg'nɔr 〕v. 忽視　　helpless〔'hɛlplɪs 〕adj. 無能為力的

Questions 37 and 38 are based on the following report.

  With an estimated 12,500 plastic bottles being discarded every 8 seconds, environmentalists are trying to come up with creative new uses for this synthetic waste that is rapidly filling our landfills and harming our marine life. Now, some developing nations are finding a new use for these discarded bottles—building much-needed schools. A Central American organization called Pura Vida ("pure life" in Spanish) was the first to come up with this innovative idea. Instead of using cinder blocks, they stuffed plastic bottles with inorganic trash and built walls by stacking them between chicken wire. They then covered up the whole thing with a light coat of cement. The resulting structure was not only eco-friendly and cheap but also as strong as a structure built using normal materials.

　　據估計，每八秒就有 12,500 個塑膠瓶被丟棄，環境保護者正試著想出創新的用途來處理這合成的廢棄物，它們正快速地填滿我們的垃圾掩埋場並傷害我們海洋中的生物。現在，有些開發中國家正在為這些被丟棄的瓶子尋找一個新的用途──建造特別需要的學校。一個名叫 Pura Vida（西班牙文的「純粹生活」）的中美洲組織最先想出這個創新的點子。他們不使用煤渣磚，而是用無機的垃圾填滿塑膠瓶，並把它們疊放在細鐵絲網圍欄之間來建造牆。然後他們在上面覆蓋一層薄薄的水泥。這樣建造出來的建築物不僅環保、便宜，而且和使用一般建材的建造的一樣堅固。

** ────────────────

estimated〔ˈɛstəˌmetɪd〕*adj.* 估計的
plastic〔ˈplæstɪk〕*adj.* 塑膠的　　bottle〔ˈbatḷ〕*n.* 瓶子
discard〔dɪsˈkard〕*v.* 丟棄　　second〔ˈsɛkənd〕*n.* 秒
environmentalist〔ɪnˌvaɪrənˈmɛntḷɪst〕*n.* 環境保護者
come up with 想出　　creative〔krɪˈetɪv〕*adj.* 創新的
use〔jus〕*n.* 使用；用途　　synthetic〔sɪnˈθɛtɪk〕*adj.* 合成的
waste〔west〕*n.* 廢棄物　　rapidly〔ˈræpɪdlɪ〕*adv.* 快速地

fill〔fɪl〕*v.* 填滿；裝滿　　landfill〔ˈlændˌfɪl〕*n.* 垃圾掩埋場
harm〔harm〕*v.* 傷害；破壞　　marine〔məˈrin〕*adj.* 海洋的
life〔laɪf〕*n.* 生物
developing〔dɪˈvɛləpɪŋ〕*adj.* 發展中的；開發中的
much-needed *adj.* 急需的；特別是需要的
Central American 中美洲的

organization〔ˌɔrgənəˈzeʃən〕*n.* 組織
pure〔pjʊr〕*adj.* 純的　　Spanish〔ˈspænɪʃ〕*n.* 西班牙語
innovative〔ˈɪnoˌvetɪv〕*adj.* 創新的　***instead of*** 不…而~
cinder〔ˈsɪndɚ〕*n.* 煤渣　　block〔blɑk〕*n.* 一塊
cinder block 煤渣磚　　stuff〔stʌf〕*v.* 塞入；裝滿
inorganic〔ˌɪnɔrˈgænɪk〕*adj.* 無機的　　trash〔træʃ〕*n.* 垃圾
stack〔stæk〕*v.* 堆積；堆放　　***chicken wire*** 細鐵絲網圍欄
cover up 蓋住；掩蓋　　light〔laɪt〕*adj.* 輕的；薄的

coat〔kot〕*n.* 層　　cement〔səˈmɛnt〕*n.* 水泥
resulting〔rɪˈzʌltɪŋ〕*adj.* 因而發生的；從而產生的
structure〔ˈstrʌktʃɚ〕*n.* 結構；建築物
not only…but also ~　不僅…而且~
eco-friendly〔ˈikoˌfrɛndlɪ〕*adj.* 環保的
strong〔strɔŋ〕*adj.* 堅固的
normal〔ˈnɔrml̩〕*adj.* 一般的；普通的
material〔məˈtɪrɪəl〕*n.* 材料

37. (**A**) Why are discarded plastic bottles useful?
　　　　爲何被丟棄的塑膠瓶是有用的？

　　A. They are cheaper than normal building materials.
　　　　它們比一般的建材便宜。

　　B. They are harming the environment.
　　　　它們會傷害環境。

　　C. They are more effective than schools.
　　　　它們比學校還有效。

　　D. They are becoming eco-friendly.
　　　　它們漸漸變得環保。

　　building material 建築材料
　　　effective〔ɪˈfɛktɪv〕*adj.* 有效的

38. (**B**) What did Pura Vida do with the plastic bottles?

　　　純粹生活怎麼處理塑膠瓶？

　　　A. They built a road.　他們建造了一條道路。

　　　B. They built a school.　它們建造了一間學校。

　　　C. They built a landfill.

　　　　它們建造了一個垃圾掩埋場。

　　　D. They built a bottle factory.

　　　　它們建造了一個瓶子工廠。

　　　* *do with*　處理

Questions 39 and 40 are based on the following report.

People who are trying to lose weight often think that by cutting out sweets and high-calorie foods like French fries, they are eliminating their main sources of excess fat. Unfortunately, they fail to recognize that sugar is just as problematic as fat when it comes to losing weight. Furthermore, they might be surprised to learn that the majority of sugar in a normal diet comes from beverages. Carbonated soft drinks are the biggest culprits, for they contain great amounts of sugar and so-called empty calories. One serving of Coca-Cola contains as much sugar as three pieces of chocolate cake. Most people don't consider soft drinks to be dessert, but that's what they are. If you're serious about dropping some unwanted pounds, the first thing you should do is put down the sugar-laden beverages.

　　想要減重的人常常認為，藉由去除甜食和高熱量的食物，像是薯條，他們就能消除他們多餘脂肪的主要來源。不幸的是，他們並不知道，談到減重時，糖份跟脂肪的問題一樣嚴重。此外，他們可能會很驚訝地發現，在一般的飲食中，大多數的糖份來自於飲料。碳酸汽水是最大的罪魁禍首，因為它們包含大量的糖份，和所謂的空熱量。一份可口可樂包含的糖分，和三片巧克力蛋糕一樣多。大多數的人不認為汽水是甜點，但是它們就是甜點。如果你很認真想要減去一些多餘的體重，首先要做的，就是停止喝含糖的飲料。

**

lose weight 減重　　　***cut out*** 去掉；戒除
sweets〔swits〕*n. pl.* 甜食
high-calorie *adj.* 高卡路里的；高熱量的
French fries 薯條　　eliminate〔ɪ'lɪmə,net〕*v.* 除去
main〔men〕*adj.* 主要的　　source〔sors〕*n.* 來源
excess〔ɪk'sɛs〕*adj.* 多餘的　　fat〔fæt〕*n.* 脂肪
unfortunately〔ʌn'fɔrtʃənɪtlɪ〕*adv.* 不幸地；遺憾地
fail to V. 未能～　　recognize〔'rɛkəg,naɪz〕*v.* 認清
sugar〔'ʃʊgɚ〕*n.* 糖
problematic〔,prɑblə'mætɪk〕*adj.* 有問題的
when it comes to 一提到

furthermore〔'fɝðɚ,mor〕*adv.* 此外　　learn〔lɝn〕*v.* 知道
majority〔mə'dʒɔrətɪ〕*n.* 大多數；大部分
normal〔'nɔrml̩〕*adj.* 一般的；普通的
diet〔'daɪət〕*n.* 飲食　　beverage〔'bɛv(ə)rɪdʒ〕*n.* 飲料
carbonated〔'kɑrbə,netɪd〕*adj.* 含二氧化碳的
soft drink 汽水；不含酒精的飲料
culprit〔'kʌlprɪt〕*n.* 犯罪者；引起問題的事物
contain〔kən'ten〕*v.* 包含　　***great amounts of*** 大量的
so-called〔,so'kɔld〕*adj.* 所謂的
empty calorie 空熱量；無營養卡路里
serving〔'sɝvɪŋ〕*n.* 一份

Coca-Cola〔͵kokə'kolə〕n. 可口可樂
consider〔kən'sɪdɚ〕v. 認爲　　dessert〔dɪ'zɝt〕n. 甜點
serious〔'sɪrɪəs〕adj. 認眞的　　drop〔drɑp〕v. 去掉
unwanted〔ʌn'wɑntɪd〕adj. 不要的；多餘的
pound〔paʊnd〕n. 磅【重量單位，約等於 0.454 公斤】
put down 放下；停止
N-laden〔'ledn̩〕adj. 充滿…的【lade〔led〕v. 裝載】

39.（**D**）What is this talk mainly about?
本段談話主要是關於什麼？

A. Health. 健康。

B. Nutrition. 營養。

C. Exercise. 運動。

D. Weight loss. 減重。

* nutrition〔nju'trɪʃən〕n. 營養

40.（**C**）What is true about many carbonated soft drinks?
關於許多的碳酸汽水，何者爲眞？

A. They contain high amounts of fat.
它們包含大量的脂肪。

B. They are often treated as desserts.
它們常常被當作是甜點。

C. They contain a lot of sugar.
它們包含很多糖份。

D. They can help dieters lose weight faster.
它們可以幫助節食的人更快減重。

* ***be treated as*** 被視爲
dieter〔'daɪətɚ〕n. 節食者

高中英聽測驗模擬試題 ② 詳解

一、看圖辨義：第一部分

For question number 1, please look at the four pictures.

1. (**C**) It's seven o'clock in the morning. Dennis is having breakfast. 現在是早上七點，丹尼斯正在吃早餐。

 * have〔hæv〕v. 吃

For question number 2, please look at the four pictures.

2. (**D**) Stanley doesn't get along with his older sister. She's always scolding him.

 史丹利跟他的姐姐處得不好。她總是在罵他。

 * *get along with* 和…和睦相處　　scold〔skold〕v. 罵

For question number 3, please look at the four pictures.

3. (**B**) Bob joined the army after college. Now he's a soldier.
鮑伯大學畢業後從軍去了。他現在是一個軍人。

* join〔dʒɔɪn〕v. 加入　　***join the army*** 從軍
solider〔'soldʒə〕n. 軍人

For question number 4, please look at the four pictures.

4. (**C**) Pete is chatting with a friend on the Internet. His friend
just told a funny joke. 彼特正跟一個朋友在網路上聊天。
他的朋友剛剛說了一個很好笑的笑話。

* chat〔tʃæt〕v. 聊天
Internet〔'ɪntə‚nɛt〕n. 網際網路
funny〔'fʌnɪ〕adj. 好笑的　　joke〔dʒok〕n. 笑話

一、看圖辨義：第二部分

For question number 5, please look at picture 5.

5. (**B**、**D**) Which TWO of the following are true about the picture? 關於這張圖片，下列哪兩項為真？

    A. Laura just kissed Nancy on the lips.
       蘿拉剛剛親了南西的嘴唇。

    B. Fred just hit Norman in the head with a soda can.
       佛瑞德剛剛用一個汽水罐打到諾曼的頭。

    C. Laura is angry. 蘿拉很生氣。

    D. Fred is careless.
       佛瑞德很不小心。

    * kiss〔kɪs〕v. 親吻
      lip〔lɪp〕n. 嘴唇
      soda〔'sodə〕n. 蘇打；汽水   can〔kæn〕n. 罐子
      careless〔'kɛrlɪs〕adj. 不小心的；粗心的

For question number 6, please look at picture 6.

6. (**A**、**D**) Which TWO of the following are true about the picture? 關於這張圖片，下列哪兩項為真？

    A. They are not impressed with the sea lion.
       他們沒有被這隻海獅打動。

    B. They have caught a very big fish. 他們抓了一條非常大的魚。

    C. One girl is dressed as a mermaid.
       有個女孩打扮成美人魚。

    D. One boy is dressed as a pirate.
       有個男孩裝扮成一個海盜。

* impress〔ɪm'prɛs〕v. 使印象深刻；感動；打動
sea lion 海獅　　***be dressed as*** 裝扮成
mermaid〔'mɝ,med〕n. 美人魚　　pirate〔'paɪrət〕n. 海盜

For question number 7, please look at picture 7.

7. (**C、D**) Which TWO of the following are true about the picture? 關於這張圖片，下列哪兩項為真？

   A. It's Christmas.
      現在是聖誕節。

   B. The boy is not wearing a
      hat. 這個男孩沒有戴帽子。

   C. The old man is holding an envelope.
      這個老人正拿著一個紅包。

   D. It's Chinese New Year. 現在是農曆新年。

   * hold〔hold〕v. 拿著
   envelope〔'ɛnvə,lop〕n. 信封【在此指「紅包」(*red envelope*)】
   Chinese New Year 農曆新年

For question number 8, please look at picture 8.

8. (**A、C**) Which TWO of the following are true about the picture? 關於這張圖片，下列哪兩項為真？

   A. Lucy found a $1,000 bill on the sidewalk.
      露西在人行道上發現一張千元紙鈔。

   B. Fiona found a dog wandering the streets of Paris.
      費歐娜發現一隻狗在巴黎的街道上流浪。

   C. Lucy is in front of a 7-Eleven.
      露西在一家 7-Eleven 前面。

   D. Fiona is in her office.
      費歐娜在她的辦公室裡。

* bill〔bɪl〕*n.* 紙鈔　　sidewalk〔'saɪd,wɔk〕*n.* 人行道
wander〔'wɑndɚ〕*v.* 在⋯徘徊；在⋯流浪
Paris〔'pærɪs〕*n.* 巴黎【法國首都】
in front of 在⋯的前面

For question number 9, please look at picture 9.

9. (**B、C**) Which TWO of the following are true about the
picture? 關於這張圖片，下列哪兩項爲眞？

　　A. Steven is a careful driver.
　　　史蒂芬是一個很小心的駕駛人。
　　B. Rachel is a careless driver.
　　　瑞秋是一個很不小心的駕駛人。
　　C. There are four people in the picture.
　　　圖片裡有四個人。
　　D. There are three cats in the picture.
　　　圖片裡有三隻貓。
　　* careful〔'kɛrfəl〕*adj.* 小心的　　driver〔'draɪvɚ〕*n.* 駕駛

For question number 10, please look at picture 10.

10. (**A、C**) Which TWO of the following are true about the
picture? 關於這張圖片，下列哪兩項爲眞？

　　A. The post office is next to the
library.
　　　郵局在圖書館的旁邊。
　　B. The shoe store is next to
the bakery. 鞋店在麵包店的旁邊。
　　C. The bakery is next to the post office.
　　　麵包店在郵局的旁邊。

D. The courthouse is above the liquor store.
法院在賣酒的商店的上面。

* ***post office*** 郵局　　***next to*** 在…的旁邊
library〔ˈlaɪˌbrɛrɪ〕 *n.* 圖書館
bakery〔ˈkekərɪ〕 *n.* 麵包店
courthouse〔ˈkortˌhaʊs〕 *n.* 法院
liquor〔ˈlɪkɚ〕 *n.* (烈) 酒　　***liquor store*** 賣酒的商店

(二) 對答

11. (**C**) Mary is always running late. Let's get started without her. 瑪莉總是遲到。我們不等她，直接開始吧。

A. She must be in good shape. 她一定很健康。

B. Is she American or Canadian?
她是美國人還是加拿大人？

C. No, let's give her a few more minutes.
不，我們再給她幾分鐘時間。

D. You must be proud of her. 你一定非常以她爲榮。

* ***run late*** 晚到；遲到　　***get started*** 開始
be in a good shape 健康狀況良好
Canadian〔kəˈnedɪən〕 *adj.* 加拿大人的
be proud of 以…爲榮

12. (**D**) The special today is meat loaf with mashed potatoes and bacon gravy. 今日的特餐是肉餅加薯泥與培根肉汁。

A. Is it vegetarian? 是素食的嗎？

B. Will I have it iced? 會是冰的嗎？

C. Do you make it without salt?
你做的時候可以不加鹽嗎？

D. Can I get it with the gravy on the side?
可以幫我把肉汁淋在旁邊嗎？

* special〔'spεʃəl〕 *n.* 特餐　　meat〔mit〕 *n.* 肉
loaf〔lof〕 *n.* 一條（麵包）;【當作菜名時】大塊燒烤的食物
meat loaf 碎肉烤餅;肉餅
mash〔mæʃ〕 *v.* 把…搗碎;使成糊狀
mashed potatoes 馬鈴薯泥
bacon〔'bekən〕 *n.* 培根　　gravy〔'grevɪ〕 *n.* 肉汁
vegetarian〔ˌvεdʒə'tεrɪən〕 *adj.* 素食的
iced〔aɪst〕 *adj.* 冰過的　　salt〔sɔlt〕 *n.* 鹽

13. (**B**) Do any of your friends speak Japanese?
你有任何一位朋友會說日文嗎?

　　A. Tony is. 湯尼是。　　B. Tony does. 湯尼會。
　　C. It's Tony. 是湯尼。
　　D. Tony isn't Japanese. 湯尼不是日本人。
　　* Japanese〔ˌdʒæpə'niz〕 *n.* 日文;日本人　*adj.* 日本人的

14. (**C**) Are you leaving in the morning? 你要早上離開嗎?
　　A. Yes, three of them. 對,他們三個人。
　　B. Yes, quite easily. 是,相當容易。
　　C. No, I've decided to stay another day.
　　　　不,我已經決定再多留一天。
　　D. No, I'll see you in the morning. 不,我們早上見你。

15. (**A**) Hello, I'd like to speak with Mr. Evans.
喂,我想要跟伊凡斯先生說話。
　　A. May I tell him who is calling?
　　　　我可以告訴他是誰打過來的嗎?
　　B. For here or to go? 內用還是外帶?
　　C. Mr. Evans. 伊凡斯先生。
　　D. Just leave it on his desk. 就把它放在他的桌上。
　　* ***for here*** 內用　***to go*** 外帶

16. (**B**) I'm not accustomed to this humidity.

我對這裡的濕度很不習慣。

　　A. Be careful. It's wet. 小心。很潮濕。

　　B. Don't worry. You'll get used to it.

　　　　不用擔心。你會習慣的。

　　C. I see. Well, maybe you can bring it next time.

　　　　我知道。嗯，也許你下次可以帶它來。

　　D. You'll have to go through customs first.

　　　　你必須先通過海關。

　　* **be accustomed to** 習慣於 (= be used to)
　　　humidity〔hju'mɪdətɪ〕n. 潮濕；濕氣
　　　wet〔wɛt〕adj. 濕的　　**get used to** 習慣
　　　I see. 我知道了；我了解了。　　customs〔'kʌstəmz〕n. 海關

17. (**D**) Did you buy anything at the book fair?

在書展你有買任何書嗎？

　　A. I don't think it was fair. 我不覺得那樣是公平的。

　　B. I almost forgot about you. 我差點忘了你。

　　C. I saw it in a book. 我在一本書上看到的。

　　D. I didn't find anything I wanted.

　　　　我沒有找到任何我想要的。

　　* fair〔fɛr〕n. 博覽會；展示會　adj. 公平的　　**book fair** 書展

18. (**C**) What time does the game start? 這場比賽什麼時候開始？

　　A. I'll be at the game. 我會來這場比賽。

　　B. Whenever you're ready. 你準備好隨時可以。

　　C. Seven p.m. 下午七點。

　　D. April 4th. 四月四日。

　　* game〔gem〕n. 比賽　　**p.m.** 下午 (= post meridiem)

19. (**A**) You're going to join us at the picnic, aren't you?

　　你會來加入我們的野餐，對不對？

　　A. Yes, I will. 是的，我會。

　　B. Yes, time is running out. 是的，沒時間了。

　　C. Yes, you'd better hurry. 是的，你最好趕快。

　　D. Yes, I won't. 是的，我不會。

　　* ***run out*** 用完；耗盡　　***had better*** 最好

　　　hurry〔ˈhɝɪ〕v. 趕快

20. (**A**) That homeless man is dressed in rags.

　　那個無家可歸的男子穿著破舊的衣服。

　　A. And he smells bad, too. 而且他味道很臭。

　　B. I'll be at home. 我會在家。

　　C. Home is where the heart is. 家是心之所在。

　　D. She's had a rough life. 她一直過得很艱難。

　　* homeless〔ˈhomlɪs〕adj. 無家可歸的；流浪的

　　　be dressed in rags 衣衫藍縷；穿著破衣服

　　　Home is where the heart is.【諺】心有所屬的地方就是家。

　　　(= *People long to be at home = Your home is whatever place*

　　　you long to be.)　　rough〔rʌf〕adj. 簡陋的；不講究的

（三）簡短對話

For question 21, you will listen to a short conversation.

　　W : It was nice of the Petersons to invite us over for dinner.

　　　彼得生家邀請我們去吃晚餐，他們人真好。

　　M : Yes, it would be great to see them. But we need to find

　　　a sitter for the kids.

　　　是呀，能見到他們真好。但我們必須幫孩子們找臨時褓姆。

W : I'll ask my sister if she has plans this Saturday night.

我會問我的妹妹她禮拜六晚上是否有計畫。

M : If she can't do it, maybe my mother wouldn't mind watching them for a few hours.

如果她不能來，也許我媽媽不會介意來看孩子幾小時。

> * ***invite*** *sb.* ***over*** 邀請某人來家裡
>
> sitter (ˈsɪtɚ) *n.* 臨時褓姆 (= *baby-sitter*)
>
> mind (maɪnd) *v.* 介意　　watch (watʃ) *v.* 照顧；看護

21. (**C**) Q : Who are the speakers?　這些說話者是誰？

A. Brother and sister. 兄妹。

B. Father and daughter. 父女。

C. Husband and wife. 夫妻。

D. Mr. and Mrs. Peterson. 彼得生夫婦。

For question 22, you will listen to a short conversation.

M : Let's watch a movie tonight. What would you like to see? 我們今晚來看電影吧。你想看什麼？

W : Anything but a horror movie. 絕對不要看恐怖片。

M : What's wrong with horror movies? 恐怖片怎麼了嗎？

W : They're too violent. Let's watch a comedy instead.

它們太暴力了。我們改看一部喜劇片吧。

> * ***anything but*** 絕不　　***horror movie*** 恐怖片
>
> violent (ˈvaɪələnt) *adj.* 暴力的
>
> comedy (ˈkamədɪ) *n.* 喜劇
>
> instead (ɪnˈstɛd) *adv.* 作為代替

22. (**B**) Q : What does the woman think of horror movies?

這位女士覺得恐怖片如何？

A. They're too funny. 它們太有趣了。

B. They're too violent. 它們太暴力了。

C. They're too expensive. 它們太貴了。

D. They're too sad. 它們太難過了。

* ***think of*** 認為　　funny〔ˈfʌnɪ〕*adj.* 好笑的；有趣的

For question 23, you will listen to a short conversation.

M : What's the matter? You're walking with a limp.

怎麼了？你走路一跛一跛的。

W : I twisted my ankle during my workout this afternoon.

我今天下午運動時扭到我的腳踝。

M : Did you go see a doctor? 你有去看醫生嗎？

W : No, it's not that bad. I'll take a painkiller and see how

I feel tomorrow.

沒有，沒那麼嚴重。我會先服用止痛藥，然後再看明天感

覺怎樣。

M : Maybe you should stay off your feet for a while.

也許你應該一陣子不要站著。

* ***What's the matter?*** 怎麼了？　　limp〔lɪmp〕*n.* 跛腳

walk with a limp 跛行　　twist〔twɪst〕*v.* 扭曲；扭傷

ankle〔ˈæŋkl̩〕*n.* 腳踝　　workout〔ˈwɜk,aʊt〕*n.* 運動

go see a doctor 去看醫生（= *go to see a doctor*）

bad〔bæd〕*adj.* 嚴重的　　take〔tek〕*v.* 服用

painkiller〔ˈpen,kɪlɚ〕*n.* 止痛藥　　stay〔ste〕*v.* 保持

off *one's* ***feet*** 坐著；躺著；不要走路　　***for a while*** 一陣子

23. (**D**) Q : What does the man suggest? 這位男士建議什麼？

    A. That the woman work out tomorrow.

        建議那位女士明天運動。

    B. That the woman take some medicine.

        建議那位女士吃些藥。

    C. That the woman stop taking painkillers.

        建議那位女士停止吃止痛藥。

    D. That the woman get some rest.

        建議那位女士休息一下。

    * suggest〔sə(g)′dʒɛst〕v. 建議　　***work out*** 運動
    take medicine 吃藥　　***get some rest*** 休息一下

For question 24, you will listen to a short conversation.

    W : Are you really going to have another beer?

        你真的要再喝一杯啤酒嗎？

    M : Yes, why? I've only had two all night.

        對呀，怎麼了？我一整晚才喝兩杯。

    W : Didn't you drive here? 你不是開車來這的嗎？

    M : No, I took a taxi and I'll take one home, too.

        不，我搭計程車，我也會搭計程車回家。

    W : Oh, in that case, drink up! 噢，那樣的話，儘量喝吧。

    * have〔hæv〕v. 吃；喝　　case〔kes〕n. 情況
    drive〔draɪv〕v. 開車　　drive〔draɪv〕v. 開
    in that case 那樣的話　　***drink up*** 喝完；儘量喝吧！

24. (**C**) Q : Why was the woman concerned about the man's
            drinking? 這位女士為什麼擔心這位男士喝酒？

A. He had too much. 他喝太多了。

B. He can't afford a taxi. 他付不起計程車錢。

C. She thought he would be driving home.
她以為他會開車回家。

D. She thought he was going to give her a ride home.
她以為他要載她回家。

* concerned〔kən'sɜnd〕adj. 擔心的

afford〔ə'ford〕v. 負擔得起　　　*give sb. a ride* 讓某人搭便車

For questions 25 and 26, you will listen to a short conversation.

M：Grayson's Department Store. Lost and found. How can
I help you? 格雷森百貨公司失物招領處。需要我為您服務嗎？

W：Yes, I was wondering if anyone turned in a cell phone.
是的，我想知道是否有人有拿手機來招領。

M：I've got several cell phones here. Can you give me a
description? 我們這裡有幾支手機。您能描述一下嗎？

W：It's a black Nokia. I'm afraid I don't remember the
model. 是一支黑色的諾基亞。我恐怕不記得它的機型。

M：I've got one of those. Come down to the store and have
a look. If you have proof of ownership, that would
help, too.
我們有一支黑色的諾基亞。請到百貨公司這裡來看一下。如
果你能夠證明是你擁有的，那也會有幫助。

* *department store* 百貨公司　　　*lost and found* 失物招領處

wonder〔'wʌndɚ〕v. 想知道　　　*turn in* 提交

cell phone 手機　　　*have got* 有（＝ *have*）

description〔dɪ'skrɪpʃən〕*n.* 描述　*I am afraid⋯* 恐怕⋯
model〔'mɑdḷ〕*n.* 款式；型號　　down〔daʊn〕*adv.* 到附近
have a look 看一下　　proof〔pruf〕*n.* 證明
ownership〔'onɚˏʃɪp〕*n.* 物主身份；所有權

25. (**A**) Q：Where did the woman lose her cell phone?
　　　　　　這位女士在哪裡弄丟她的手機？

　　A. In a department store.　在百貨公司。
　　B. On a public bus.　在公車上。
　　C. At the zoo.　在動物園。
　　D. In a restaurant.　在餐廳裡。

　　* lose〔luz〕*v.* 遺失　　public〔'pʌblɪk〕*adj.* 公共的
　　　zoo〔zu〕*n.* 動物園

26. (**D**) Q：What does the man say?　這位男士說了什麼？

　　A. He doesn't have the woman's cell phone.
　　　他沒有這位女士的手機。
　　B. The store will close in half an hour.
　　　這家店半小時後關門。
　　C. The woman should never return to the store.
　　　這位女士應該永遠都不會回到這家店。
　　D. It's possible he has the woman's phone.
　　　他可能有這位女士的手機。

　　* close〔kloz〕*v.* 停止營業；打烊
　　　in〔ɪn〕*prep.* 再過⋯

For questions 27 and 28, you will listen to a short conversation.

　M：Have you seen the new Mission: Impossible movie yet?
　　　你看過新的「不可能的任務」了嗎？

W：No, and I'm not interested in seeing it with you, either.
還沒有，而且我也沒有興趣跟你一起看。

M：Who said anything about that? I was just making conversation. 誰說要跟妳一起看的？我只是聊聊而已。

W：I just assumed you were asking me out.
我剛剛以為你在約我出去。

M：You need to get over yourself. Just because a guy asks you a question, it doesn't mean he's interested in you.
妳別臭美了。只因為有個男生問妳一個問題，並不表示他對妳有興趣。

＊ *Mission*: *Impossible* 【電影名】不可能的任務
be interested in 對⋯有興趣
conversation〔͵kɑnvɚˋseʃən〕*n.* 對話；談話
make conversation 聊天；閒聊
assume〔əˋsjum〕*v.* 以為　　*ask sb. out* 邀請某人外出
guy〔gaɪ〕*n.* (男) 人；傢伙
get over yourself 別自以為是；少臭美 (= *don't flatter yourself*)

27. (**C**) Q：What did the man ask the woman?
　　　這位男士問了這位女士什麼？

　　A. If she wanted to see a movie. 她是否想看一部電影。
　　B. If she wanted to go on a date. 她是否想去約會。
　　C. If she had seen a particular movie.
　　　她是否看過某部特定的電影。
　　D. If she was interested in him. 她是否對他有興趣。

　　＊ *go on a date* 去約會
　　particular〔pɚˋtɪkjələ〕*adj.* 特定的

28. (**C**) Q : What does the man think about the woman?
　　　　　這位男士覺得這位女士怎麼樣？

　　　A. She is beautiful.　她很漂亮。

　　　B. She is boring.　她很無聊。

　　　C. She is vain.　她很自以為是。

　　　D. She is wealthy.　她很有錢。

　　　* boring〔'borɪŋ〕*adj.* 無聊的
　　　　vain〔ven〕*adj.* 自以為是的；自負的；虛榮心強的
　　　　wealthy〔'wɛlθɪ〕*adj.* 有錢的

For questions 29 and 30, you will listen to a short conversation.

W : Here are the files you asked for.　你要的檔案在這裡。

M : Thanks.　I've got another favor to ask, if you don't mind.
　　謝謝你。如果你不介意的話，我想請你再幫我另一個忙。

W : Not at all.　That's what I'm here for.　How can I help?
　　一點也不。這是我的職責。我可以怎麼樣幫助你？

M : These essays need to be corrected and the grades entered
　　to the computer.
　　這些文章需要批改，而且這些成績要輸入電腦。

　　* file〔faɪl〕*n.* 檔案　　*ask for* 要求
　　　favor〔'fevɚ〕*n.* 請求；幫忙　　*ask a favor* 請求幫忙
　　　mind〔maɪnd〕*v.* 介意　　*not at all* 一點也不
　　　be here for sth. 職責是做某事　　essay〔'ɛse〕*n.* 論說文；短文
　　　correct〔kə'rɛkt〕*v.* 訂正；批改　　grade〔gred〕*n.* 成績
　　　enter〔'ɛntɚ〕*v.* 輸入

29. (**B**) Q : What is the most probable relationship between the
　　　　　speakers?　說話者之間最有可能是什麼關係？

A. Supervisor and customer. 主管與顧客。

B. Teacher and assistant. 老師與助理。

C. Captain and lieutenant. 上尉與中尉。

D. Brother and sister. 兄妹。

* probable ('prɑbəbḷ) *adj.* 可能的
relationship (rɪ'leʃən͵ʃɪp) *n.* 關係
supervisor ('supə͵vaɪzə) *n.* 主管
customer ('kʌstəmə) *n.* 顧客
assistant (ə'sɪstənt) *n.* 助理
captain ('kæptən) *n.* 隊長；陸軍上尉
lieutenant (lu'tɛnənt) *n.* 小隊長；陸軍中尉

30. (**A**) Q : What will the man most likely do next?
這位男士下一步最有可能做什麼？

A. Look at the files he just received.
看他剛剛收到的檔案。

B. Grade the essays. 幫文章打分數。

C. Ask another favor of the woman.
請這位女士幫他另一個忙。

D. Surf the Internet. 上網。

* likely ('laɪklɪ) *adv.* 可能地　　grade (gred) *v.* 打…的分數
ask a favor of *sb.* 請求某人幫忙
surf (sɜf) *v.* 瀏覽；上 (網)　　***surf the Internet*** 上網

四、短文聽解

Questions 31 and 32 are based on the following report.

Research shows that insects are a good source of
protein and could meet the nutritional needs of a growing
global population, which is why Marcel Dicke, a professor

at a Dutch university specializing in food and food
production, has written a cookbook to promote the use of
bugs as a food source.　To mark the book's launch, an
insect chef will attempt to bake the world's largest
grasshopper pie.　Still, it will undoubtedly be difficult to
convince many people, particularly those in Western
cultures that typically shun eating insects, to trade their
beef and pork for mealworms and grasshoppers.

　　研究顯示，昆蟲是一個很好的蛋白質來源，可以符合全球人
口成長的需要，這就是爲什麼專門研究食物與食品生產的荷蘭大
學教授馬賽爾・迪克，會寫了一本食譜，來提倡用昆蟲作爲食物
來源的原因。爲了慶祝這本書的發行，有位昆蟲主廚將嘗試烤出
世上最大的蚱蜢派。儘管如此，要說服很多人把牛肉及豬肉換成
黃粉蟲與蚱蜢，毫無疑問是很困難的，特別是在向來避免吃昆蟲
的西方文化中。

**

research (ˈrisɝtʃ) n. 研究　　show (ʃo) v. 顯示
insect (ˈɪnsɛkt) n. 昆蟲　　source (sors) n. 來源
protein (ˈprotiɪn) n. 蛋白質　　meet (mit) v. 達到；符合
nutritional (njuˈtrɪʃənḷ) adj. 營養的
needs (nidz) n. pl. 需求
global (ˈglobḷ) adj. 全球的
population (ˌpɑpjəˈleʃən) n. 人口
professor (prəˈfɛsɚ) n. 教授　　Dutch (dʌtʃ) adj. 荷蘭的
specialize (ˈspɛʃəlˌaɪz) v. 專攻 < in >
production (prəˈdʌkʃən) n. 生產；製造
cookbook (ˈkʊkˌbʊk) n. 食譜
promote (prəˈmot) v. 推廣；提倡
use (jus) n. 使用　　bug (bʌg) n. 蟲

mark〔mɑrk〕*v.* 表示；慶祝　　launch〔lɔntʃ〕*n.* 發行

chef〔ʃɛf〕*n.* 主廚　　attempt〔ə'tɛmpt〕*v.* 嘗試

bake〔bek〕*v.* 烘烤　　grasshopper〔'græs,hɑpɚ〕*n.* 蚱蜢

still〔stɪl〕*adv.* 然而；儘管如此

undoubtedly〔ʌn'daʊtɪdlɪ〕*adv.* 無疑地

convince〔kən'vɪns〕*v.* 說服

particularly〔pɚ'tɪkjələlɪ〕*adv.* 尤其；特別

Western〔'wɛstɚn〕*adj.* 西方的　　culture〔'kʌltʃɚ〕*n.* 文化

typically〔'tɪpɪkḷɪ〕*adv.* 通常

shun〔ʃʌn〕*v.* 避免（= *avoid*）　　***trade*** A ***for*** B　用 A 換 B

beef〔bif〕*n.* 牛肉　　pork〔pork〕*n.* 豬肉

mealworm〔'mil,wɝm〕*n.* 黃粉蟲【生於穀類、麵粉中的甲蟲之幼蟲】

31. (**A**) What did Marcel Dicke do?

馬賽爾・迪克做了什麼？

A. He wrote a book. 他寫了一本書。

B. He made a film. 他拍了一部電影。

C. He taught a class. 他教了一堂課。

D. He gave a speech. 他發表了一場演講。

* film〔fɪlm〕*n.* 電影

give a speech 發表演講

32. (**C**) What does Marcel Dicke want to do?

馬賽爾・迪克想要做什麼？

A. Read his cookbook. 讀他的食譜。

B. Break a world record in competitive eating.

在大胃王比賽中打破世界紀錄。

C. Promote the use of bugs as a food source.

提倡用昆蟲作為一種食物來源。

D. Study population growth. 研究人口成長。

* competitive〔kəmˋpɛtətɪv〕*adj.* 競爭的；比賽的
　　study〔ˋstʌdɪ〕*v.* 研究　　growth〔groθ〕*n.* 成長

Questions 33 and 34 are based on the following report.

For the past two weeks it has been so cold and rainy that we have had to turn on the heat. We are lucky, because our heater works and we can pay our heating bills. Some people in Los Angeles were not so lucky. Unable to use their home heater, a family burned charcoal in a barbecue grill. The heat kept them warm, but the carbon monoxide killed them. Deaths from carbon monoxide poisoning happen every winter in Los Angeles. Everyone knows that smoke detectors are required in Los Angeles. But many people don't know about, or don't think they need, carbon monoxide detectors. They're not expensive. A \$25 investment can save a family from death. People always think that nothing bad will happen to them; it always happens to "the other guy." So they forget to put fresh batteries into their smoke detectors annually, and they don't bother to buy carbon monoxide detectors.

　　過去這兩個禮拜以來，天氣一直濕冷，所以我們必須打開暖氣。我們很幸運，因爲我們的暖氣很正常，我們也付得起暖氣的帳單。有些在洛杉磯的人可就沒這麼好運。因爲家用暖氣無法使用，所以全家人就用只能燒烤肉架裡的木炭。這個熱源讓他們能夠保暖，但一氧化碳卻讓他們喪命。每年冬天，在洛杉磯都會發生一氧化碳中毒死亡事件。每個人都知道，煙霧偵測器在洛杉磯是必要的。但很多人不知道，或是認爲他們不需要一氧化碳偵測

器。這種器材並不貴。一個 25 美元的的投資，可以拯救全家人免
於死亡。人總是認為不會有壞事會發生在自己身上；認為壞事一
定會發生在別人身上。所以他們會忘記每年將新的電池放入煙霧
偵側器裡，而且他們也懶得去買一氧化碳偵測器。

** ——————————————

rainy〔ˋrenɪ〕adj. 下雨的　　**turn on** 打開（電器）
the heat 暖氣；暖氣設備（= heater）
work〔wɝk〕v. 運作　　**heating bill** 暖氣費
Los Angeles〔lɔsˋændʒələs〕n. 洛杉磯（= L.A.）
unable〔ʌnˋebl̩〕adj. 不能…的　　burn〔bɝn〕v. 燃燒
charcoal〔ˋtʃɑr͵kol〕n. 木炭　　barbecue〔ˋbɑrbɪ͵kju〕n. 烤肉
grill〔grɪl〕n. 烤架　　keep〔kip〕v. 使…（處於某種狀態）
carbon monoxide〔ˋkɑrbən məˋnɑk͵saɪd〕n. 一氧化碳

poisoning〔ˋpɔɪzənɪŋ〕n. 中毒　　smoke〔smok〕n. 煙
detector〔dɪˋtɛktɚ〕n. 偵測器
required〔rɪˋkwaɪrd〕adj. 必須的；規定的
investment〔ɪnˋvɛstmənt〕n. 投資　　**save…from** 拯救…免於
happen to 發生於　　guy〔gaɪ〕n. 人；傢伙
fresh〔frɛʃ〕adj. 尚未使用的；新的
battery〔ˋbætərɪ〕n. 電池　　annually〔ˋænjʊəlɪ〕adv. 每年地
bother〔ˋbʌðɚ〕v. 費心；麻煩

33.（**B**）What often happens every winter in L.A.?
　　洛杉磯每年冬天常會發生什麼事？

　　A. Heating bills get too high for some people.
　　　　暖氣帳單對某些人來說太貴。

　　B. People die from carbon monoxide poisoning.
　　　　人們死於一氧化碳中毒。

　　C. Rainstorms knock out power to the city.
　　　　暴風雨使城市的電力癱瘓。

D. Families burn charcoal in a barbeque grill.
有些家庭會用燒烤肉架裡的木炭。

* ***die from*** 死於　　rainstorm〔'ren,stɔrm〕*n.* 暴風雨
　knock out 使癱瘓；摧毀　　power〔'pauɚ〕*n.* 電力

34. (**C**) What is required in L.A.?
在洛杉磯什麼是必要的？
A. Heat during the winter months. 冬季時的暖氣。
B. Barbeque grills. 烤肉架。
C. Smoke detectors. 煙霧偵測器。
D. Carbon monoxide detectors. 一氧化碳偵測器。

Questions 35 and 36 are based on the following report.

Milton Hershey, founder of the Hershey Chocolate Company, originally created Hershey Park for his employees. Situated along a creek, it was a good spot for boating, picnicking, and enjoying baseball, which is what visitors did on the park's first day in 1907. The next year, the park added its first ride, a carousel. Over the decades, as the park acquired more attractions, it grew from a regional amusement to a national attraction.

　　賀喜巧克力公司的創辦人米爾頓・賀喜，當初為了員工蓋了賀喜樂園。樂園座落在溪旁，很適合划船、野餐、打棒球，這是在 1907 年樂園的開園第一天遊客所做的事。隔年，樂園新增了它的第一項遊樂設施，旋轉木馬。經過數十年，這個樂園有了更多吸引人的事物，它已經從一個區域性的遊樂園，成長為全國性的旅遊勝地。

** ———————————————————

founder〔'faʊndɚ〕*n.* 創立者
chocolate〔'tʃɔk(ə)lɪt〕*n.* 巧克力
originally〔ə'rɪdʒənḷɪ〕*adv.* 原本；最初
create〔krɪ'et〕*v.* 創造　　employee〔͵ɛmplɔɪ'i〕*n.* 員工
situated〔'sɪtʃʊ͵etɪd〕*adj.* 位於…的
along〔ə'lɔŋ〕*prep.* 沿著　　creek〔krik〕*n.* 溪流
spot〔spɑt〕*n.* 地點　　boat〔bot〕*v.* 划船；乘船
picnic〔'pɪknɪk〕*v.* 野餐
visitor〔'vɪzətɚ〕*n.* 觀光客；遊客　　add〔æd〕*v.* 增加

ride〔raɪd〕*n.* 供乘騎的遊樂設施
carousel〔͵kærə'zɛl〕*n.* 旋轉木馬（＝ *merry-go-round*）
over〔'ovɚ〕*prep.* 在…期間　　decade〔'dɛked〕*n.* 十年
acquire〔ə'kwaɪr〕*v.* 獲得
attraction〔ə'trækʃən〕*n.* 吸引人的景點（或事物）；勝地
regional〔'ridʒənḷ〕*adj.* 區域的
amusement〔ə'mjuzmənt〕*n.* 消遣；娛樂
national〔'næʃənḷ〕*adj.* 全國的

35.（**C**）For whom did Hershey create Hershey Park?
　　賀喜為誰蓋了賀喜樂園？

　　A. His grandchildren. 他的孫子。
　　B. His business associates. 他的生意夥伴。
　　C. His employees. 他的員工。
　　D. His stockholders. 他的股東。

　　* associate〔ə'soʃɪɪt〕*n.* 同伴；夥伴
　　　stockholder〔'stɑk͵holdɚ〕*n.* 股東

36.（**A**）Which could the visitors NOT do in 1907?
　　在 1907 年，遊客不能做什麼？

A. Ride a carousel. 坐旋轉木馬。

B. Play baseball. 打棒球。

C. Have a picnic. 野餐。

D. Go for boat rides. 去坐船。

* ride〔raɪd〕*v. n.* 騎；乘坐　　***have a picnic*** 野餐

go for a ride 去乘坐（馬、火車等）

Questions 37 and 38 are based on the following report.

Scientists have captured the first images of an adult white orca—or killer whale—in the wild. Iceberg, as he has been affectionately named, was spotted swimming with his pod off the coast of eastern Russia. Orcas are typically black, with white on their undersides, above each eye, and on each flank. Until now, the only all-white orcas that had been observed were young, and none had ever been recorded surviving into adulthood. Researchers hope that future observation will help them determine whether Iceberg is a true albino or whether some other factor is responsible for his unique lack of color.

科學家已經首次捕捉到一隻野生成年的白色殺人鯨的影像。這隻殺人鯨與他的小鯨群在靠近東俄羅斯的沿海巡游時被發現，並且被親切地命名爲「冰山」。殺人鯨通常是黑色的，白色部分分佈在其下側、眼睛上方，及雙側。從以前到現在，唯一一隻被看到的全白殺人鯨年齡很輕，而且根據紀錄，沒有一隻能存活到成年期。研究人員希望未來的觀察能幫助他們確定冰山是得了白化病，或是有其他因子，造成牠獨特的缺色現象。

** ─────────────────

capture〔ˈkæptʃɚ〕v. 捕捉

image〔ˈɪmɪdʒ〕n. 影像　　adult〔əˈdʌlt〕adj. 成年的

whale〔hwel〕n. 鯨魚　　orca〔ˈɔrkə〕n. 殺人鯨

or〔ɔr〕conj. 也就是　　***killer whale*** 殺人鯨

in the wild 在野外　　iceberg〔ˈaɪsˌbɝg〕n. 冰山

affectionately〔əˈfɛkʃənɪtlɪ〕adv. 深情地

name〔nem〕v. 命名　　spot〔spɑt〕v. 發現；認出

pod〔pɑd〕n.（海豹、鯨等的）小群

off the coast of 在…的沿海

eastern〔ˈistɝn〕adj. 東方的　　Russia〔ˈrʌʃə〕n. 俄羅斯

typically〔ˈtɪpɪklɪ〕adv. 通常

underside〔ˈʌndɚˌsaɪd〕n. 下側；底面

flank〔flæŋk〕n. 側面　　observe〔əbˈzɝv〕v. 觀察；看到

record〔rɪˈkɔrd〕v. 記錄　　survive〔sɚˈvaɪv〕v. 存活

adulthood〔əˈdʌltˌhʊd〕n. 成年（期）

researcher〔rɪˈsɝtʃɚ〕n. 研究人員

observation〔ˌɑbzɝˈveʃən〕n. 觀察

determine〔dɪˈtɝmɪn〕v. 確定

albino〔ælˈbaɪno〕n. 白化病者；白子

some〔sʌm〕adj. 某個　　factor〔ˈfæktɚ〕n. 因素

be responsible for 導致；造成；是…的原因

unique〔juˈnik〕adj. 獨特的　　lack〔læk〕n. 缺乏；沒有

37.（ **B** ）What is Iceberg?　「冰山」是什麼？

　　A. A giant block of ice. 一塊巨大的冰。

　　B. A white killer whale. 一隻白色的殺人鯨。

　　C. A Russian research facility. 一個俄羅斯的研究設施。

　　D. A black dolphin. 一隻黑海豚。

* giant〔'dʒaɪənt〕adj. 巨大的　　block〔blɑk〕n. 一塊
  Russian〔'rʌʃən〕adj. 俄國的
  facility〔fə'sɪlətɪ〕n. 設施　　dolphin〔'dɑlfɪn〕n. 海豚

38. (**B**) What is special about Iceberg?

「冰山」有何特別之處？

A. It's the only whale found in eastern Russia.

它是唯一在東俄羅斯被發現的鯨魚。

B. It's the only full-grown, all-white orca ever recorded.

它是有史以來唯一一隻成年，而且全白的殺人鯨。

C. It's the first true albino orca seen in the wild.

它是第一隻在野外發現的真正白子殺人鯨。

D. It's the last black orca to survive in captivity.

它是最後一隻在被人工飼養而且存活的黑色殺人鯨。

* full-grown　adj. 發育完全的；成熟的
  captivity〔kæp'tɪvətɪ〕n. 囚禁
  in captivity 被囚禁；人工飼養的

Questions 39 and 40 are based on the following report.

　　Ladies and gentlemen, for your safety, federal guidelines prohibit the use of all electronic devices during takeoff and landing, as they can interfere with the aircraft flight instruments. All portable electronic devices such as personal stereos, laptop computers, and calculators, must be turned off at this time, and cell phones must not be used at any time. In a few minutes we'll be screening a safety video about this aircraft. You'll also find a safety briefing card in the seat pocket in front of you. We require that you give us your careful attention. Thank you.

　　各位先生，各位女士，爲了您的安全，聯邦政府飛行準則規定，禁止於起飛、降落時使用任何電子用品，因爲它們可能干擾飛機的飛行儀器。所有手提的電子用品，像是個人音響、筆電，以及計算機，這時務必關機，而且任何時候都禁止使用手機。幾分鐘後，我們將播放關於這架飛機的安全影片。你也可以在你座位前的袋子內找到安全須知卡。我們需要你的留心注意。謝謝！

**

federal ('fɛdərəl) adj. 聯邦的
guidelines ('gaɪd͵laɪnz) n. pl. 指導方針；準則
prohibit (pro'hɪbɪt) v. 禁止
electronic (ɪ͵lɛk'trɑnɪk) adj. 電子的
device (dɪ'vaɪs) n. 用具；裝置；設備
takeoff ('tek͵ɔf) n. 起飛　　landing ('lændɪŋ) n. 降落
interfere (͵ɪntə'fɪr) v. 妨礙 < with >
aircraft ('ɛr͵kræft) n. 飛機　　flight (flaɪt) n. 飛行
instrument ('ɪnstrəmənt) n. 儀器

portable ('portəbḷ) adj. 手提的
such as 像是　　personal ('pɝsn̩ḷ) adj. 個人的
stereo ('stɛrɪo) n. 立體音響　　laptop ('læp͵tɑp) n. 筆記型電腦
calculator ('kælkjə͵letə) n. 計算機　　*turn off* 關閉 (電器)
cell phone 手機　　screen (skrin) v. 放映
video ('vɪdɪ͵o) n. 影片　　*safety video* 飛安影片；航空安全影片
briefing ('brifɪŋ) n. 簡要提示
safety briefing card 安全須知卡　　*seat pocket* 座椅背後口袋
require (rɪ'kwaɪr) v. 要求；需要
give…careful attention 留心注意…

39. (**C**) Where is this announcement most likely made?

這項宣布最有可能在哪裡進行？

A. On a tour bus. 在遊覽車上。

B. On a ferry boat. 在渡輪上。

C. On an airplane. 在飛機上。

D. On a subway train. 在地鐵車廂內。

* announcement〔əˋnaʊnsmənt〕*n.* 宣布
tour bus 遊覽車
ferry〔ˋfɛrɪ〕*n.* 渡輪（= *ferry boat*）
subway〔ˋsʌb͵we〕*n.* 地下鐵
train〔tren〕*n.* 車廂

40. (**A**) What will most likely happen next?

接下來最有可能發生什麼事情？

A. A safety demonstration. 一段安全示範。

B. Food will be served. 將會供應餐點。

C. The captain will speak. 機長會說話。

D. A question and answer session. 現場問答。

* demonstration〔͵dɛmənˋstreʃən〕*n.* 示範
serve〔sɝv〕*v.* 供應；上（菜）
captain〔ˋkæptən〕*n.* 機長
session〔ˋsɛʃən〕*n.* 一段時間
question and answer session 問答時間；現場問答

高中英聽測驗模擬試題 ③ 詳解

一、看圖辨義：第一部分

For question number 1, please look at the four pictures.

1. (**B**) Tom is ill. He has a fever. 湯姆生病了。他發燒了。

        * ill〔ɪl〕*adj.* 生病的   fever〔'fivɚ〕*n.* 發燒

For question number 2, please look at the four pictures.

2. (**C**) George and Tina are having a disagreement. They aren't speaking to each other at this time.

       喬治與蒂娜意見不合。他們這時候彼此都不講話。

        * disagreement〔ˌdɪsə'grimənt〕*n.* 意見不合

For question number 3, please look at the four pictures.

3. (**A**) Tracy has been studying all night. But what she'd really
like is a slice of chocolate cake.　崔西整晚都在讀書。然而
她現在眞正想要的，是一片巧克力蛋糕。

　　＊ slice〔slaɪs〕*n.* 一片　　chocolate〔'tʃɔk(ə)lɪt〕*n.* 巧克力

For question number 4, please look at the four pictures.

4. (**C**) The teacher is explaining the concept of shapes. Her
students now understand the difference between circles,
squares, and triangles.　這位老師正在解釋形狀的概念。她的
學生現在知道圓形、正方形，以及三角形的不同了。

　　＊ explain〔ɪk'splen〕*v.* 解釋；說明
concept〔'kɑnsɛpt〕*n.* 概念　　shape〔ʃep〕*n.* 形狀
difference〔'dɪfərəns〕*n.* 不同　　circle〔'sɝkl〕*n.* 圓形
square〔skwɛr〕*n.* 正方形　　triangle〔'traɪ,æŋgl〕*n.* 三角形

一、看圖辨義：第二部分

For question number 5, please look at picture 5.

5.（**A**、**D**）Which TWO of the following are true about the
picture? 關於這張圖片，下列哪兩項為眞？

A. Ted is selling a bicycle.
泰德正在賣一台腳踏車。

B. Ted is selling a dresser.
泰德正在賣一個梳妝台。

C. Ted is selling a stereo system.
泰德正在賣一組立體音響。

D. Ted is selling a television. 泰德正在賣一台電視。

＊ dresser〔'drɛsɚ〕*n.* 梳妝台　　stereo〔'stɛrɪo〕*n.* 立體音響
system〔'sɪstəm〕*n.* 系統；機械裝置

For question number 6, please look at picture 6.

6.（**C**、**D**）Which TWO of the following are true about the
picture? 關於這張圖片，下列哪兩項為眞？

A. The girl is getting married.
這位女孩要結婚了。

B. The girl is driving the truck.
這位女孩正在開卡車。

C. The girl is sitting in the passenger seat of the
truck. 這位女孩正坐在卡車的乘客座位。

D. The man looks angry. 這位男士看起來很生氣。

＊ ***get married*** 結婚　　truck〔trʌk〕*n.* 卡車；貨車
passenger〔'pæsṇdʒɚ〕*n.* 乘客
passenger seat（汽車駕駛座邊的）乘客座；副駕駛座

For question number 7, please look at picture 7.

7. (**A、D**) Which TWO of the following are true about the picture? 關於這張圖片，下列哪兩項為眞？

    A. Jack is a student. 傑克是個學生。

    B. Jack is an adult.

       傑克是成年人。

    C. Jack isn't studying history.

       傑克現在沒有在讀歷史。

    D. Jack failed the history exam.

       傑克歷史考試不及格。

    * adult〔ə'dʌlt〕*n.* 成人　　history〔'hɪstrɪ〕*n.* 歷史
　　　fail〔fel〕*v.* 考（試）不及格

For question number 8, please look at picture 8.

8. (**A、B**) Which TWO of the following are true about the picture?

    關於這張圖片，下列哪兩項為眞？

    A. Vince is ordering fast food.

       文斯正在點速食。

    B. Vince is wearing sunglasses.

       文斯正戴著太陽眼鏡。

    C. Vince wants to go home. 文斯想要回家。

    D. Vince doesn't have a car. 文斯沒有車。

    * order〔'ɔrdɚ〕*v.* 點餐　　***fast food*** 速食
　　　wear〔wɛr〕*v.* 穿；戴
　　　sunglasses〔'sʌn,glæsɪz〕*n. pl.* 太陽眼鏡

For question number 9, please look at picture 9.

9. (**B** 、 **C**) Which TWO of the following are true about the picture?　關於這張圖片，下列哪兩項為眞？

A. The boy on the right has curly hair.
在右邊的男孩有一頭捲髮。

B. A wheel has come off of the toy truck.
一個輪子從這台玩具卡車掉了下來。

C. The boys are sorry for what they've done.
男孩們對他們所做的事感到抱歉。

D. The boy on the right is angry.
在右邊的男孩很生氣。

* curly〔'kɜlɪ〕*adj.* 捲曲的
　wheel〔hwil〕*n.* 輪子
　come off (*of*) 從…脫落　　toy〔tɔɪ〕*n.* 玩具

For question number 10, please look at picture 10.

10. (**A** 、 **B**) Which TWO of the following are true about the picture?　關於這張圖片，下列哪兩項為眞？

A. James appears to be happy with his test result.
詹姆士似乎對他的考試成績感到滿意。

B. Sally got an A on her test.
莎莉考試得到 A。

C. Only James did well on the test. 只有詹姆士考試考得好。

D. Neither James nor Sally did well on the test.
詹姆士與莎莉考試都沒有考好。

* appear〔ə'pɪr〕*v.* 看起來；似乎
　be happy with 對…感到滿意　　***test result*** 考試成績
　do well 表現好；考得好　　***neither…nor***〜 旣不…也不〜

二、對答

11. (**B**) What's wrong? You look awful.
   怎麼了?你看起來臉色很不好。

   A. Right. I saw it. 對。我看到它了。

   B. Oh, I didn't sleep well last night.
   喔,我昨晚沒睡好。

   C. That was awfully nice of her. 她人真的非常好。

   D. Three or four. I'm not sure. 三個或四個。我不確定。

   * look〔luk〕v. 看起來　　awful〔'ɔful〕adj. 很糟的
   awfully〔'ɔfulɪ〕adv. 非常地　　sure〔ʃur〕adj. 確定的

12. (**D**) How was your weekend? 你週末過得如何?

   A. This one looks a bit tight. 這一個看起來有點緊。

   B. Plump and juicy. 又大又圓,而且又多汁。

   C. Medium rare. 三分熟。

   D. Much too short. 太短了。

   * weekend〔'wik,ɛnd〕n. 週末　　*a bit* 一點點
   tight〔taɪt〕adj. 緊的
   plump〔plʌmp〕adj. 豐滿的;又大又圓的
   juicy〔'dʒusɪ〕adj. 多汁的
   medium rare 三分熟的　　*much too* 太;非常

13. (**A**) Did you back up the files on your hard drive?
   你有把檔案備份在硬碟嗎?

   A. Yes, I did. 是的,我有。

   B. Yes, I will. 是的,我會。

   C. No, I am. 不,我是。　　D. No, I won't. 不,我不會。

   * *back up* 備份(文件)　　file〔faɪl〕n. 檔案
   hard drive 硬碟

14. (**B**) Are you familiar with Microsoft Word?

你對微軟的文書處理軟體熟悉嗎？

A. Yes, I've met him before.

是的，我之前已經見過他了。

B. Yes, I use it frequently. 是的，我經常使用它。

C. Yes, you can have it. 是的，你可以拿走。

D. Yes, this one is good. 是的，這一個很好。

* *be familiar with* 熟悉

Microsoft〔'maɪkro,sɔft〕*n.*（美國）微軟公司

Microsoft Word 微軟文書處理軟體

frequently〔'frikwəntlɪ〕*adv.* 經常

15. (**C**) Is it safe to ride the subway at night? 晚上搭地鐵安全嗎？

A. Take the red line to Beitou. 搭紅線到北投。

B. The runner was safe. 這個賽跑者當時很安全。

C. Generally, yes. 一般來說，是安全的。

D. Two dollars for a round-trip ticket. 來回票要兩塊錢。

* ride〔raɪd〕*v.* 搭乘

subway〔'sʌb,we〕*n.* 地下鐵

line〔laɪn〕*n.*（鐵路、巴士等）路線

runner〔'rʌnɚ〕*n.* 賽跑者

generally〔'dʒɛnərəlɪ〕*adv.* 通常；一般地

round-trip *adj.* 來回的；雙程的

16. (**A**) Do you think your sister will win the contest?

你認為你妹妹會贏得這場比賽嗎？

A. I'm not sure, but I think she has a good chance.

我不確定，但我覺得她很有機會。

B. She entered the contest for the second time.

她已經是第二次參加比賽了。

C. This is the only way I know how to do it.
這是我所知道，做這件事唯一的方法。

D. Come with me on a journey. 跟我一起來旅行吧。

* contest〔ˋkɑntɛst〕n. 比賽
chance〔tʃæns〕n. 機會；勝算
enter〔ˋɛntɚ〕v. 參加　　journey〔ˋdʒɝnɪ〕n. 旅行

17. (**C**) How strict is your school's dress code?
你們學校的服裝規定有多嚴格？

A. It's wonderful. I can't wait to wear it.
太棒了。我等不及穿它了。

B. It's pretty liberal. We can talk whenever we want.
非常自由。我們隨時想說都可以說。

C. Not too bad. At least we don't have to wear
uniforms. 還不錯。至少我們不用穿制服。

D. One of the best. We're proud of the achievement.
最好的之一。我們以這項成就爲榮。

* strict〔strɪkt〕adj. 嚴格的　　code〔kod〕n. 準則；行爲規範
dress code 服裝規定　　wonderful〔ˋwʌnfɚfəl〕adj. 很棒的
can't wait to V. 等不及～　　pretty〔ˋprɪtɪ〕adv. 非常
liberal〔ˋlɪbərəl〕adj. 開放的；自由的　　**not too bad** 還不錯
at least 至少　　uniform〔ˋjunə͵fɔrm〕n. 制服
be proud of 以…爲榮　　achievement〔əˋtʃivmənt〕n. 成就

18. (**A**) Wow! Mike certainly has a quick temper!
哇！麥克一定脾氣很暴躁！

A. Yeah. You don't want to anger him.
是的。你不會想要去激怒他的。

B. I think I'm the fastest guy here.
我覺得我是這裡最快的人。

C. You're right.　He's always on time.

你說的對。他總是很準時。

D. He might not make it tonight.　他今晚可能沒辦法來。

* wow〔waʊ〕*interj.* （表示驚訝、喜悅）哇
certainly〔'sɝtṇlɪ〕*adv.* 一定　　temper〔'tɛmpɚ〕*n.* 脾氣
have a quick temper 脾氣暴躁　anger〔'æŋgɚ〕*n.* 激怒
guy〔gaɪ〕*n.* 人；傢伙　　**on time** 準時　　**make it** 能來

19. (**B**)　OK, let's start the meeting.　好，我們開始開會吧。

A. I'm sorry.　Traffic was bad.　我很抱歉。交通狀況很糟。

B. Great.　I'll begin with an outline of today's agenda.

很好。我從今日的議程大綱開始。

C. Put it over there.　I'll check it later.

把它放在那裡。我晚點會去檢查。

D. It was a pleasure to meet you.　很高興認識你。

* meeting〔'mitɪŋ〕*n.* 會議　　traffic〔'træfɪk〕*n.* 交通
begin with 從…開始　　outline〔'aʊt,laɪn〕*n.* 大綱
agenda〔ə'dʒɛndə〕*n.* 議程　　**over there** 在那裡
check〔tʃɛk〕*v.* 檢查；查看
pleasure〔'plɛʒɚ〕*n.* 樂趣；高興的事；榮幸
meet〔mit〕*v.* 認識

20. (**A**)　What's the weather supposed to be like tomorrow?

天氣明天應該會如何？

A. Cloudy and cold.　多雲而且寒冷。

B. Black and blue.　鼻青臉腫的。

C. In and out.　進進出出的。

D. Shiny and new.　又亮又新的。

* **be supposed to V.** 應該～　　cloudy〔'klaʊdɪ〕*adj.* 多雲的
black and blue 鼻青臉腫的；遍體鱗傷的
in and out 進進出出　　shiny〔'ʃaɪnɪ〕*adj.* 發亮的

三、簡短對話

For question 21, you will listen to a short conversation.

M：I hired Tommy to paint the garage this weekend.

這個週末我雇了湯米來油漆車庫。

W：Are you sure that's a good idea?　He's only 12.

你確定這是個好主意嗎？他才只有 12 歲。

M：Well, he's quite mature for his age and I trust him.

嗯，就他這年紀來看他相當成熟，我相信他。

W：I understand, but will he do a good job?

我了解，但他真的能把車庫漆好嗎？

＊hire〔haɪr〕v. 雇用　　paint〔pent〕v. 油漆
garage〔gəˈrɑdʒ〕n. 車庫　　quite〔kwaɪt〕adv. 相當
mature〔məˈtʃʊr〕adj. 成熟的　　trust〔trʌst〕v. 信任；相信
do a good job 把工作做好

21. (**D**)　Q：How does the woman feel about Tommy painting the garage?

這位女士對於讓湯米來油漆車庫覺得如何？

A. Complementary. 互補的。

B. Supportive. 支持的。

C. Outraged. 憤慨的。

D. Apprehensive. 擔心的。

＊complementary〔͵kɑmpləˈmɛntərɪ〕adj. 互補的
supportive〔səˈportɪv〕adj. 支持的
outraged〔ˈaʊt͵redʒd〕adj. 憤慨的；被激怒的
apprehensive〔͵æprɪˈhɛnsɪv〕adj. 擔心的；憂慮的

For question 22, you will listen to a short conversation.

W：I'm going to try out for the basketball team.

我要去參加籃球隊的選拔。

M：Really? Have you ever played before?

真的嗎？妳以前打過嗎？

W：No, never. But it looks like so much fun. I've always wanted to try.

不，從來沒有。但它看來很有趣。我一直很想要試試。

M：I hate to rain on your parade, but there are a lot of talented girls trying to make the team this year.

我不想潑妳冷水，但今年有很多很有天分的女生想要加入球隊。

W：I know. That's OK. I might as well give it a shot.

我知道。沒關係。我不妨試試看。

* *try out for* 參加…的選拔　　*look like* 看起來像
parade〔pə'red〕*n.* 樂趣；有趣；有趣的是
hate〔het〕*v.* 討厭；不願意　　parade〔pə'red〕*n.* 遊行
rain on one's *parade* 潑某人冷水；掃某人的興（= *spoil* one's
plans or pleasure）　　talented〔'tæləntɪd〕*adj.* 有天分的
make〔mek〕*v.* 加入；進入　　team〔tim〕*n.* 隊
might as well 最好；不妨　　*give it a shot* 試試看

22. (**A**) Q：What does the woman mean?　這位女士的意思是什麼？

　　A. It never hurts to try. 去試試看也無妨。

　　B. She has high expectations. 她有很高的期望。

　　C. The other girls are not as talented.

　　　　其他的女孩沒有那麼有天分。

　　D. She'll bring a gun. 她會帶一把槍。

    * ***it never hurts to V.*** 做…也無妨

    expectation 〔ˌɛkspɛkˈteʃən 〕 *n.* 期待；期望

    gun 〔 gʌn 〕 *n.* 手槍

For question 23, you will listen to a short conversation.

M : You're not eating your burger.　Is there something wrong with it?　你沒有在吃你的漢堡。那個漢堡怎麼了嗎？

W : No, it's fine.　I'm just waiting for it to cool down.　Then I'll eat it.

沒有啦，漢堡沒問題。我只是在等它變涼。然後我就會吃了。

M : Well, you're in for a treat.　This place has the best burgers in town.

嗯，你一定會喜歡的。這家餐廳有城裡最好的漢堡。

    * burger 〔 ˈbɝgɚ 〕 *n.* 漢堡

    cool down 變涼　　treat 〔 trit 〕 *n.* 樂事；樂趣

    be in for a treat 某人會喜歡的

    place 〔 ples 〕 *n.* 餐廳　　town 〔 taun 〕 *n.* 城鎮

23. (**B**)　Q : How does the woman feel about her burger?

　　　　　　　這位女士覺得她的漢堡如何？

    A. It's overcooked.　煮得太熟了。

    B. It's too hot.　太燙了。

    C. It's more than she bargained for.

       比她所預料的多。

    D. It's the best in town.　是城裡最好的。

    * overcooked 〔ˌovɚˈkukt 〕 *adj.* 煮得過熟的

    bargain for 預料；預期 (= *expect*)

For question 24, you will listen to a short conversation.

　W：This is a picture of my son.　這是我兒子的照片。

　M：My goodness, he's a handsome boy!

　　　天啊，他是個很帥的男孩！

　W：Thank you.　He's sharp as a tack, too.

　　　謝謝你。他也很聰明喔。

　　*　picture〔'pɪktʃɚ〕*n.* 照片
　　***My Goodness**.* 天啊。(= *My God.*)
　　sharp〔ʃɑrp〕*adj.* 銳利的；聰明的
　　tack〔tæk〕*n.* 大頭釘；平頭釘
　　(as) sharp as a tack 很聰明 (= *very intelligent*)

24. (**C**)　What does the woman say about her son?
　　　這位女士說了什麼關於他的兒子的事？
　　　A.　He's ill-mannered.　他很沒有禮貌。
　　　B.　He's intelligent but homely.　他很聰明但卻相貌平凡。
　　　C.　He's attractive and smart.　他很吸引人而且又聰明。
　　　D.　He's big for his age.　在他這個年紀他算長得很大的。

　　*　ill-mannered〔'ɪl'mænɚd〕*adj.* 無禮的
　　ɪntelligent〔ɪn'tɛlədʒənt〕*adj.* 聰明的
　　homely〔'homlɪ〕*adj.* 樸實的；相貌平凡的
　　attractive〔ə'træktɪv〕*adj.* 吸引人的
　　smart〔smɑrt〕*adj.* 聰明的

For questions 25 and 26, you will listen to a short conversation.

　W：Mr. Vickers, I've been with this company for five years,
　　　and I've never asked for anything.　維克斯先生，我已經在
　　　這間公司五年了，我從來沒有要求過什麼。

M : But you are about to now, aren't you, Janet? Let me
guess. You want a raise?
但妳現在就要提出要求了，對不對，珍妮特？讓我猜。妳是
想要加薪嗎？

W : I think I deserve it. 我認為那是我應得的。

M : I disagree. Despite being here five years, your work
habits and attendance record hardly merit an increase
in salary. 我不同意。雖然妳在這裡五年了，但是妳的工作
習慣及出席紀錄不太值得加薪。

* with〔wɪθ〕*prep.* 受雇於
  ask for 要求　　***be about to V.*** 即將～；正要～
  guess〔gɛs〕*v.* 猜　　raise〔rez〕*n.* 加薪
  deserve〔dɪˋzɝv〕*v.* 應得　　disagree〔͵dɪsəˋgri〕*v.* 不同意
  despite〔dɪˋspaɪt〕*prep.* 儘管　　habit〔ˋhæbɪt〕*n.* 習慣
  attendance〔əˋtɛndəns〕*n.* 出席　　hardly〔ˋhɑrdlɪ〕*adv.* 幾乎不
  merit〔ˋmɛrɪt〕*v.* 值得（= *deserve*）
  increase〔ˋɪnkris〕*n.* 增加　　salary〔ˋsæBlərɪ〕*n.* 薪水

25. (**D**) Q : What is the relationship between the speakers?
　　　　 說話者之間的關係是什麼？

　　A. Husband and wife. 夫妻。

　　B. Teammates. 隊友。

　　C. Business partners. 生意夥伴。

　　D. Employer and employee. 雇主與員工。

* relationship〔rɪˋleʃən͵ʃɪp〕*n.* 關係
  teammate〔ˋtim͵met〕*n.* 隊友　　business〔ˋbɪznɪs〕*n.* 生意
  partner〔ˋpɑrtnɚ〕*n.* 夥伴　　employer〔ɪmˋplɔɪɚ〕*n.* 雇主
  employee〔͵ɛmplɔɪˋi〕*n.* 員工

26. (**C**)　Q : Why did the man deny the woman's request?

　　　爲什麼這位男士拒絕了這位女士的請求？

　　A. Business has been suffering lately. 最近生意不好。

　　B. She hasn't worked there long enough.

　　　她在那裡工作的時間不夠久。

　　C. He isn't impressed with her work performance.

　　　他沒有對她的工作表現留下深刻印象。

　　D. To set an example for other students.

　　　要爲其他學生樹立榜樣。

　　* deny〔dɪ'naɪ〕*v.* 拒絕　　request〔rɪ'kwɛst〕*n.* 請求
　　suffer〔'sʌfɚ〕*v.* 受損失　　lately〔'letlɪ〕*adv.* 最近
　　impress〔ɪm'prɛs〕*v.* 使印象深刻；感動；打動
　　performance〔pɚ'fɔrməns〕*n.* 表現
　　set〔sɛt〕*v.* 樹立（榜樣）
　　example〔ɪg'zæmpl̩〕*n.* 例子；榜樣；模範

For questions 27 and 28, you will listen to a short conversation.

　W : Sir, this bill was due yesterday. I'm afraid there's a penalty for the late payment.

　　　先生，這個帳單昨天到期。恐怕會有逾期繳款的罰金。

　M : I understand, ma'am. But I was hoping you'd give me a break this time. I've never been late before.

　　　我了解，女士。但我希望妳這次能饒過我。我以前從來沒有遲交過。

　W : Unfortunately, I am not authorized to do that. Would you like to speak with my supervisor?

　　　很遺憾，我沒有權力這麼做。你要跟我的主管談談嗎？

* **sir** ﹝sɝ﹞ *n.* 先生   **bill** ﹝bɪl﹞ *n.* 帳單

due ﹝dju﹞ *adj.* 到期的   ***I'm afraid***… 恐怕…

penalty ﹝ˈpɛnḷtɪ﹞ *n.* 罰金；罰款   **late** ﹝let﹞ *adj.* 遲的

payment ﹝ˈpemənt﹞ *n.* 繳款   **ma'am** ﹝mæm﹞ *n.* 太太；小姐

give sb. a break 饒過某人；給某人一個機會

this time 這一次

unfortunately ﹝ʌnˈfɔrtʃənɪtlɪ﹞ *adv.* 不幸地；遺憾地

authorize ﹝ˈɔθəˌraɪz﹞ *v.* 授權；賦與權力

supervisor ﹝ˈsupəˌvaɪzə﹞ *n.* 主管

27. (**C**) Q：What is the man's problem? 這位男士的問題是什麼？

    A. He is late for an appointment. 他與別人有約卻遲到了。

    B. He is late for work. 他上班遲到了。

    C. He didn't pay his bill on time.

       他沒有準時付他的帳單。

    D. He doesn't have the money to pay the penalty.

       他沒有錢來付罰金。

    * **appointment** ﹝əˈpɔɪntmənt﹞ *n.* 約會   ***on time*** 準時

28. (**D**) Q：What will the man most likely do next?

       這位男士接下來最可能會做什麼？

    A. Pay his bill. 付他的帳單。

    B. Burst out crying. 突然大哭。

    C. Ask for directions. 問路。

    D. Speak with the woman's supervisor.

       與這位女士的主管說話。

    * **likely** ﹝ˈlaɪklɪ﹞ *adv.* 可能地

    burst out + ***V-ing*** 突然～起來

    direction ﹝dəˈrɛkʃən﹞ *n.* 方向

For questions 29 and 30, you will listen to a short conversation.

M : Who is handling the preparations for this year's science fair? 誰負責今年科展的準備工作？

W : Bill Ford and Julie Meyers are heading the committee. That's all I know.

比爾・福特及茱莉・梅耶斯負責委員會。我只知道這些。

M : There hasn't been much communication among the faculty, but it's safe to assume we'll be asked to pitch in at some point. 教職員之間還沒有做很多的溝通，但先假設我們某個時候會被要求來幫忙，這樣想比較保險。

* handle〔'hændl〕v. 處理
preparations〔,prɛpə'reʃənz〕n. pl. 準備
fair〔fɛr〕n. 博覽會；展示會　　*science fair* 科展
head〔hɛd〕v. 掌管；負責　　committee〔kə'mɪtɪ〕n. 委員會
communication〔kə,mjunə'keʃən〕n. 溝通
faculty〔'fækltɪ〕n. 全體教職員
assume〔ə'sjum〕v. 假定；認為　　*pitch in* 協力；做出貢獻
some〔sʌm〕adj. 某個　　point〔pɔɪnt〕n. 時刻

29. (**B**) Q : Who are the speakers? 說話者是誰？
   A. Classmates. 同學。　　B. Teachers. 老師。
   C. Husband and wife. 夫妻。
   D. Brother and sister. 兄妹。

30. (**B**) Q : What does the man imply? 這位男士暗示什麼？
   A. He is eager to participate in the science fair.
      他很想要去參加這場科展。
   B. He will probably help out at the science fair.
      他可能會幫忙這場科展。

C. He is disappointed with the science fair.
　　他這這場科展很失望。

D. He will not compete in the science fair.
　　他將不會參加這場科展的比賽。

　* imply〔ɪm'plaɪ〕v. 暗示　　eager〔'igɚ〕adj. 渴望的
　　participate〔par'ɪsə,pet〕v. 參與 < in >
　　probably〔'prɑbəblɪ〕adv. 可能　　**help out** 幫忙
　　disappointed〔,dɪsə'pɔɪntɪd〕adj. 失望的
　　compete〔kəm'pit〕v. 競爭；競賽

四、短文聽解

Questions 31 and 32 are based on the following report.

　　The Statue of Liberty is one of the most recognizable icons of the United States. In the old days, when immigrants came to America from Europe by boat, the Statue was one of the first things they saw. Standing on Liberty Island in New York Harbor, the statue was a gift from the people of France to the U.S. in 1886. Dubbed "Lady Liberty," the statue honors the centennial of the signing of the United States Declaration of Independence. The statue is of a robed woman holding a torch, and is made of pure copper and steel. The flame of the torch is coated in gold leaf. It stands atop a rectangular stonework pedestal with a foundation in the shape of an irregular eleven-pointed star. The statue is 151 feet tall, but with the pedestal and foundation, stands 305 feet tall, and on a clear day, it is visible from as far as New Jersey, some 12 miles away.

自由女神像是最容易識別的美國圖像之一。以前當移民搭船從歐洲來到美國時，這座雕像是他們最先看到的事物之一。矗立在紐約港的自由島上，這座雕像是法國人民在 1886 年所送給美國人的禮物。這座雕像被命名為自由女神，是為了紀念美國簽署獨立宣言一百週年。這座雕像是一個手拿火炬身穿長袍的女士，是用純銅與鋼鍛造而成。火炬的火焰用金箔包覆。它矗立在長方型的石製基座上，基底是個有 11 個星芒的不規則的星星。這座雕像 151 呎高，但如果加上底座及地基，則是 305 呎高，在晴朗的日子，在大約 12 哩外的紐澤西州都能看見它。

** ——————————————————

statue〔ˈstætʃʊ〕 *n.* 雕像　　liberty〔ˈlɪbətɪ〕 *n.* 自由
the Statue of Liberty 自由女神像
recognizable〔ˈrɛkəgˌnaɪzəbl〕 *adj.* 可辨別的；可以看得出的
icon〔ˈaɪkɑn〕 *n.* (繪畫、雕刻等) 像；圖像；偶像
the old days 以前　　immigrant〔ˈɪməgrənt〕 *n.* 移入者；移民
Europe〔ˈjʊrəp〕 *n.* 歐洲　　stand〔stænd〕 *v.* 矗立；位於
Liberty Island 自由島【舊稱 Bedloe's Island，是美國紐約港中的
　　一個無人居住的小島，因島上矗立自由女神像而聞名世界】

harbor〔ˈhɑrbɚ〕 *n.* 港口；海港
dub〔dʌb〕 *v.* 把⋯稱作；給⋯取綽號
honor〔ˈɑnɚ〕 *v.* 向⋯表示敬意
centennial〔sɛnˈtɛnɪəl〕 *n.* 一百年紀念
sign〔saɪn〕 *v.* 簽名；簽署　　declaration〔ˌdɛkləˈreʃən〕 *n.* 宣言
independence〔ˌɪndɪˈpɛndəns〕 *n.* 獨立
the United States Declaration of Independence 美國獨立宣言

robe〔rob〕 *v.* 給⋯穿上長袍　　hold〔hold〕 *v.* 拿著；握著
torch〔tɔrtʃ〕 *n.* 火炬；火把　　***be made of*** 由⋯做成
pure〔pjʊr〕 *adj.* 純的　　copper〔ˈkɑpɚ〕 *n.* 銅
steel〔stil〕 *n.* 鋼　　flame〔flem〕 *n.* 火焰
coat〔kot〕 *v.* 給⋯塗上一層；用⋯覆蓋
gold〔gold〕 *adj.* 金的　　leaf〔lif〕 *n.* 箔

atop〔ə'tɑp〕*prep.* 在…上面
rectangular〔rɛk'tæŋgjələ〕*adj.* 長方形的
stonework〔'ston,wɜk〕*n.* 石製品
pedestal〔'pɛdɪstḷ〕*n.*（柱子或雕像的）座；基座
foundation〔faʊn'deʃən〕*n.* 基礎；基座
in the shape of 以…的形狀
irregular〔ɪ'rɛgjələ〕*adj.* 不規則的

point〔pɔɪnt〕*n.* 尖端；呈尖型伸出的部位
stand〔stænd〕*v.* 高…　　clear〔klɪr〕*adj.* 晴朗的
visible〔'vɪzəbḷ〕*adj.* 看得見的
as far as 遠至
New Jersey〔nju'dʒɜzɪ〕*n.* 紐澤西州【美國東部大西洋岸的一州】
some〔sʌm〕*adv.*【用於數字前】大約（= *about*）

31.（ **C** ）What is the Statue of Liberty's nickname?
　　自由女神的暱稱是什麼？

　　A. Lassie Liberty. 自由萊茜。

　　B. Larry Liberty. 自由賴瑞。

　　C. Lady Liberty. 自由女神。

　　D. Laura Liberty. 自由蘿拉。

　　* nickname〔'nɪk,nem〕*n.* 綽號；暱稱

32.（ **C** ）Who gave the Statue of Liberty to the U.S.?
　　誰把自由女神送給美國？

　　A. The people of Europe. 歐洲人。

　　B. Immigrants from Europe. 來自歐洲的移民。

　　C. The people of France. 法國人民。

　　D. Immigrants from New Jersey.
　　　　來自紐澤西州的移民。

Questions 33 and 34 are based on the following report.

This is Rick Stevens with your Monday morning weather forecast. It's going to be a wet one out there today. Expect periods of thunderstorms and heavy precipitation, especially along the coast, where we'll see accumulations of 1 to 2 inches over the next 24 hours or so. Inland areas will get a little less rain, maybe half an inch, but watch out for flash flooding in the Sierras. Winds will be out of the southeast at 5-10 miles per hour with occasional gusts of up to 20. The cause of all this rain is a low pressure system that is expected to hang around the Reno area through the weekend, so if you have travel plans, make sure to call ahead for airport flight delays, and if you're driving, keep your radio tuned to AM 900 for frequent updates on road conditions. I'm Rick Stevens. Now over to Jane Jones with your traffic update.

我是里克‧史蒂文斯，歡迎收聽週一晨間氣象。今天外面將會是有雨的一天。預期將有數次大雷雨及大量的降雨，尤其是沿岸地區，接下來 24 小時左右，那裡的累積雨量將達一到二吋。內陸地區雨勢較小，可能達半英吋，但須注意內華達山區會山洪爆發。今日將有時速 5 到 10 哩的東南風，以及時速可達 20 哩的瞬間陣風。所有這些降雨是來自一個低壓系統，此低壓預期將逗留在雷諾地區一整個週末，所以如果你有旅遊計畫，務必事先電洽航班誤點狀況，如果你是開車，請將廣播調到調幅 900，再持續收聽最新路況。我是里克‧史蒂文斯。現在輪到珍‧瓊斯，提供您最新的交通概況。

＊＊

This is~ 我是~　　***weather forecast*** 氣象預報

wet〔wɛt〕*adj.* 濕的；下雨的　　***out there*** 外面

expect〔ɪk'spɛkt〕*v.* 期待；預期會有　　period〔'pɪrɪəd〕*n.* 期間

thunderstorm〔'θʌndə‚storm〕*n.* (夾著強風的) 雷雨

heavy〔'hɛvɪ〕*adj.* 大量的

precipitation〔prɪ‚sɪpə'teʃən〕*n.* 降雨

especially〔ə'spɛʃəlɪ〕*adv.* 尤其；特別是　　coast〔kost〕*n.* 海岸

accumulation〔ə‚kjumə'leʃən〕*n.* 累積 (物)

inch〔ɪntʃ〕*n.* 吋【一吋為 2.54 公分】　　***or so***【用於名詞後】大約

inland〔'ɪnlənd〕*adj.* 內陸的；內地的

watch out for 注意；提防　　flash〔flæʃ〕*adj.* 瞬間的

flooding〔'flʌdɪŋ〕*n.* 氾濫　　***flash flooding*** 山洪爆發

sierra〔sɪ'ɛrə〕*n.* 齒狀山脊

the Sierras 內華達山脈【原名為 The Sierra Nevada】

out of 來自於　　southeast〔‚sauθ'ist〕*n.* 東南方

per〔pə〕*prep.* 每⋯　　occasional〔ə'keʒənl〕*adj.* 偶爾的

gust〔gʌst〕*n.* 一陣強風　　cause〔kɔz〕*n.* 原因

up to 高達　　***low pressure*** 低氣壓

system〔'sɪstəm〕*n.* 系統　　***hang around*** 徘徊；逗留

Reno〔'rino〕*n.* 雷諾【美國內華達州西部的一個城市】

travel〔'trævl̩〕*n.* 旅行　　***make sure*** 確認；確定；一定要

ahead〔ə'hɛd〕*adv.* 預先　　airport〔'ɛr‚port〕*n.* 機場

flight〔flaɪt〕*n.* 班機　　delay〔dɪ'le〕*n.* 延誤

keep〔kip〕*v.* 使~ (處於某種狀態)

tune to 調整 (收音機等) 到 (某個頻率)

AM 調幅 (＝ *amplification modulation*)

frequent〔'frikwənt〕*adj.* 經常的

update〔'ʌpdet〕*n.* 最新的情況；最新的報導

on〔ɑn〕*prep.* 關於　　***road conditions*** 路況

over to sb. 輪到某人 (＝ *sb.'s turn*)

33. (**A**) Where was this announcement made?
這項宣布是在那裡進行的？
A. On the radio. 在廣播裡。
B. On a public bus. 在公車上。
C. On television. 在電視上。
D. On a ferry boat. 在渡船上。

* announcement〔əˈnaʊnsmənt〕*n.* 宣佈
ferry〔ˈfɛrɪ〕*n.* 渡船 (= *ferry boat*)

34. (**B**) What is causing the rain? 是什麼造成降雨？
A. Wind gusts up to 20 miles per hour.
風速高達每小時 20 英哩。
B. A low pressure system. 一個低壓系統。
C. Flash flooding. 山洪爆發。
D. Rick Stevens. 里克・史蒂文斯。

* cause〔kɔz〕*v.* 造成

Questions 35 and 36 are based on the following report.

Overall, travel in Thailand is relatively safe. Serious crime against foreigners is rare, but crime does occur in major cities like Bangkok and Chiang Mai. Of course, you must be alert and keep an eye on your valuables, especially your passport. In public, never let your belongings out of your sight, or you risk never seeing them again. You should be aware that the theft of foreign passports is on the increase. Major tourist sites attract thieves and pickpockets. Take extra care around street markets and transportation hubs. When traveling after dark, make sure you are not alone. If you resist a robbery attempt, it could lead to serious violence; the use of knives is fairly common. In addition, it's unwise to travel alone in isolated or sparsely populated areas, particularly in the northern countryside, where bandits control the roads. If you do so, you should leave your itinerary and expected time of return with a third party.

大致上來說，在泰國旅遊是相當安全的。儘管在邁谷、清邁等主要城市確實有犯罪發生，卻很少有對外國人的重大犯罪。當然，你必須提高警覺、看好財物，尤其是護照。在公共場所，絕不要讓你的財物離開視線，否則就有再也見不到它們的風險。你應該知道偷竊外國護照的案例正在增加。主要的旅遊景點會吸引小偷與扒手。請特別留意街頭市集及交通樞紐地區。晚上出遊時，請確定不是單獨一人。如果他人企圖強劫，而你反抗的話，可能導致嚴重的暴力事件；使用刀子的情況是很常見的。此外，在人口稀少的偏遠地區，獨自旅行是不智的，尤其是在受強盜控制的泰北鄉間道路。你如果這樣做的話，你應該留下你的路線圖，以及你預定要回來的時間讓其他第三人知道。

**

overall〔ˋovɚˏɔl〕adv. 整體來說　　Thailand〔ˋtaɪlənd〕n. 泰國

relatively〔ˋrɛlətɪvlɪ〕adv. 相對地；相當地

serious〔ˋsɪrɪəs〕adj. 嚴重的；重大的

crime〔kraɪm〕n. 罪；犯罪　　foreigner〔ˋfɔrɪnɚ〕n. 外國人

rare〔rɛr〕adj. 罕見的　　major〔ˋmedʒɚ〕adj. 主要的

Bangkok〔ˋbæŋkɑk〕n. 曼谷【泰國首都】

Chiang Mai〔ˋtʃɪɑŋ ˋmaɪ〕n. 清邁【泰國第二大都市】

alert〔əˋlɝt〕adj. 警覺的　　*keep an eye on* 注意；留心

valuables〔ˋvæljəblz〕n. pl. 貴重物品

passport〔ˋpæsˏport〕n. 護照　　*in public* 在公開場合

belongings〔bɪˋlɔŋɪŋz〕n. pl. 所有物

out of one's sight 離開某人的視線　　risk〔rɪsk〕v. 冒…的風險

aware〔ə'wɛr〕adj. 知道的；察覺到的；　　theft〔θɛft〕n. 竊盜

foreign〔'fɔrɪn〕adj. 外國的　　*on the increase* 增加中

tourist sites 旅遊景點　　attract〔ə'trækt〕v. 吸引

thieves〔θivz〕n. pl. 小偷【單數爲 thief】

pickpocket〔'pɪk,pɑkɪt〕n. 扒手　　*take extra care* 格外小心

street market 街市；集市

transportation〔,trænspə'teʃən〕n. 運輸；運送

hub〔hʌb〕n. 中心；中樞　　*after dark* 天黑之後

alone〔ə'lon〕adj. 獨自的；單獨的

resist〔rɪ'zɪst〕v. 反抗；抵抗　　robbery〔'rɑbərɪ〕n. 搶劫

attempt〔ə'tɛmpt〕n. 企圖；嘗試　　*lead to* 導致

violence〔'vaɪələns〕n. 暴力；暴行

knives〔naɪvz〕n. pl. 刀子【單數爲 knife】

fairly〔'fɛrlɪ〕adv. 相當地

common〔'kɑmən〕adj. 普遍的；常見的　　*in addition* 此外

unwise〔ʌn'waɪz〕adj. 不明智的

isolated〔'aɪsə,letɪd〕adj. 單獨的；偏遠的

sparsely〔'spɑrslɪ〕adv. 稀少地　　populate〔'pɑpjə,let〕v. 居住於

sparsely populated 人口稀少的

particularly〔pə'tɪkjələlɪ〕adv. 特別地；尤其

northern〔'nɔrðən〕adj. 北部的

countryside〔'kʌntrɪ,saɪd〕n. 鄉村地區

bandit〔'bændɪt〕n. 強盜　　leave〔liv〕v. 留下

itinerary〔aɪ'tɪnə,rɛrɪ〕n. 旅行計畫

expected〔ɪk'spɛktɪd〕adj. 預計的　　return〔rɪ'tɜn〕n. 回來

with〔wɪθ〕prep. 由…負責；由…看管；託付

a third party 第三者

35. (**B**) What is this talk mainly about? 這段談話的主旨爲何？

A. How to enjoy tourist sites in Chiang Mai.
　　如何享受清邁的旅遊景點。

B. How to protect yourself and belongings while traveling in Thailand.

在泰國旅遊時如何保護自己及財物。

C. How to resist robbery attempts in Bangkok.

在曼谷如何對抗他人對你的強盜企圖。

D. How to stay alert traveling in Thailand.

在泰國旅行時如何保持警覺。

* mainly〔'menlɪ〕 *adv.* 主要地　　protect〔prə'tɛkt〕 *v.* 保護
stay〔ste〕 *v.* 保持

36. (**C**) Why is it unwise to travel alone in the northern countryside? 為什麼在北部的鄉間獨自旅行是不明智的？

A. Tourist sites attract thieves. 旅遊景點會吸引小偷。

B. Crime against foreigners is common.

對外國人的犯罪很常見。

C. Bandits control the roads. 道路被強盜控制。

D. Hotels are hard to find. 旅館很難找。

* hard〔hɑrd〕 *adj.* 困難的

Questions 37 and 38 are based on the following report.

Why do you think our kids want to play sports? What is it that inspires them to sign up and play on a team? Well, after 30-some years of coaching youth sports programs, I think I can tell you. The number one reason? FUN! I hate to sound trite, but this is the main reason. Kids are kids, which means they want to have fun. Give them something fun and they will stay with it for a long time. It is really hard to stray from this No. 1 reason because it is true.

They will endure something that is not fun for a short time, but soon they will want out of it.　And, come on, can you blame them?　Aren't we as adults kind of the same?　If we do something in our spare time, it needs to be fun or we won't continue, right?

你覺得小孩為什麼會想要運動？什麼促使他們報名參加球隊？嗯，根據我指導三十多年少年運動課程的經驗，我想我可以告訴你。第一個原因是？好玩！我不想聽起來很老套，但這卻是主要原因。小孩子就是小孩子，也就是說他們想要玩得愉快。如果給他們有趣的東西，他們就會持續很久。如果沒有這個頭號理由是很困難的，因為這是事實。他們對於無聊的東西或許可以忍受一小段時間，但很快就會想要退出了。算了吧，你能怪他們嗎？身為大人的我們不也是這樣嗎？如果我們利用空閒時間做點事，那件事必須很有趣，否則我們也不會繼續下去，不是嗎？

**　━━━━━━━━━━━━━━

sport〔sport〕*n.* 運動；體育競技活動　*play sports* 做運動
what is it that… 到底是什麼…　inspire〔ɪn'spaɪr〕*v.* 激勵
sign up 報名　team〔tim〕*n.* (遊戲或體育運動的)隊
30-some *adj.* 三十幾的　coach〔kotʃ〕*v.* 指導；訓練
youth〔juθ〕*n.* 年輕；青年人　reason〔'rizn̩〕*n.* 理由；原因
fun〔fʌn〕*n.* 樂趣；有趣　*adj.* 有趣的
hate〔het〕*v.* 討厭；不願意

trite〔traɪt〕*adj.* 陳腐的；老調重彈的
main〔men〕*adj.* 主要的　mean〔min〕*v.* 意思是；表示
have fun 玩得愉快　*stay with* 繼續採用；把…維持下去
stray〔stre〕*v.* 背離；偏離＜*from*＞　endure〔ɪn'djʊr〕*v.* 忍受
out of 從…離開　*come on* 得了吧；算了吧
blame〔blem〕*v.* 責備；責怪　*kind of* 有點
spare〔spɛr〕*adj.* 多餘的　*spare time* 空閒時間 (＝*free time*)

37. (**D**) What does the speaker say about kids?

　　　這位說話者說了什麼關於孩子的事？

　　　A. They are easily bored. 他們很容易覺得無聊。

　　　B. They are not interested in sports. 他們對運動沒興趣。

　　　C. They are exactly like adults. 他們跟大人一模一樣。

　　　D. They want to have fun. 他們想要玩得很愉快。

　　　* bored〔bord〕*adj.* 無聊的　　*be interested in* 對…有興趣
　　　exactly〔ɪɡ'zæktlɪ〕*adv.* 完全地

38. (**C**) Why does he believe his opinion is justified?

　　　為什麼他相信自己的看法是正當合理的？

　　　A. Because kids are kids. 因為孩子就是孩子。

　　　B. Because adults get bored easily too.

　　　　　因為大人也很容易就會覺得無聊。

　　　C. Because he has coaching experience.

　　　　　因為他有當教練的經驗。

　　　D. Because it's true. 因為它是真的。

　　　* opinion〔ə'pɪnjən〕*n.* 意見；看法
　　　justify〔'dʒʌstə,faɪ〕*v.* 為…辯護；證明…為正當

Questions 39 and 40 are based on the following report.

　　　Have you noticed how some fast-food restaurants have parking lots designed like a maze at an amusement park? I recently drove over a 10-inch curb at a local Burger Clown restaurant, specifically the one at 100 Lincoln Avenue. The one and only exit out of this restaurant is straight ahead out of the drive-through and accommodates one car at a time. That's crazy! Especially during the busy lunch hour.

It takes longer to get out of the parking lot than it does to eat your lunch. When visiting on Jan. 18, I parked in the lot designed for eating in your car. There's no exit back onto the road, but the parking lot looks flush with Lincoln Avenue. When I attempted to leave the restaurant forward onto the road, I catapulted over the curb and my car got stuck. I was then forced to call a tow truck. I confronted the management at this Burger Clown. They had their insurance company write me a letter saying the parking lot wasn't their responsibility.

你是否有注意到，某些速食餐廳把停車場設計得像是遊樂場的迷宮一樣？我最近開車越過一個叫小丑漢堡的本地餐廳的路緣，精確地說，就是在林肯大道 100 號。唯一一個能離開這家餐廳的出口就是要開過得來速的前面，而那裡一次只能容納一台車。這超扯的！尤其是在最繁忙的中午用餐時間。把車開出停車場會比你吃午餐的時間還久。當我一月十八日去時候，我把車停在被設計成得在車內用餐的停車場。沒有回到馬路的出口，這個停車場看起來跟林肯大道高度一樣。當我試圖離開停車場上路時，我迅速駕車越過路緣，而我的車竟卡住了。然後我只好被迫打給拖吊車。我質問了這家小丑漢堡的管理階層。他們請保險公司寫了一封信給我，說這個停車場不在他們的責任範圍內。

** ————————————————————

notice (ˈnotɪs) v. 注意到
parking lot 停車場
design (dɪˈzaɪn) v. 設計
maze (mez) n. 迷宮
amusement park 遊樂園
recently (ˈrisṇtlɪ) adv. 最近
curb (kɝb) n. (人行道旁的) 邊石；路緣
local (ˈlokḷ) adj. 當地的
clown (klaʊn) n. 小丑
specifically (spɪˈsɪfɪkḷɪ) adv. 明確地；確切地說
avenue (ˈævəˌnju) n. 大道
exit (ˈɛgzɪt) n. 出口

straight〔stret〕*adv.* 直直地　　ahead〔ə'hɛd〕*adv.* 向前地
drive-through *n.* 得來速；免下車取餐服務口
accommodate〔ə'kɑmə,det〕*v.* 容納　***at a time*** 一次
crazy〔'krezɪ〕*adj.* 瘋狂的；不理智的
the lunch hour 午餐時間　　take〔tek〕*v.* 花（時間）
get out of 離開　　park〔pɑrk〕*v.* 停車
lot〔lɑt〕*n.* 一塊土地【這裡指 parking lot（停車場）】
flush〔flʌʃ〕*adj.* 同一平面的；同高的
be flush with 和…一樣高（＝ *be completely even with*）
attempt〔tə'tɛmpt〕*v.* 企圖；打算
forward〔'fɔrwəd〕*adv.* 向前地
catapult〔'kætə,pʌlt〕*v.* 快速移動；躍　***get stuck*** 被卡住
force〔fors〕*v.* 強迫；使不得不　***tow truck*** 拖車
confront〔kən'frʌnt〕*v.* 面對；當面對證
management〔'mænɪdʒmənt〕*n.* 管理；管理階層
insurance〔ɪn'ʃʊrəns〕*n.* 保險
responsibility〔rɪ,spɑnsə'bɪlətɪ〕*n.* 責任

39. (**B**) What is the speaker mainly talking about?
　　　這個說話者主要在談論什麼？
　　　A. The service at Burger Clown. 小丑漢堡的服務。
　　　B. The parking lot at Burger Clown. 小丑漢堡的停車場。
　　　C. The management at Burger Clown.
　　　　 小丑漢堡的管理階層。
　　　D. The food at Burger Clown. 小丑漢堡的食物。

40. (**B**) What does the speaker complain about exactly?
　　　這個說話者到底在抱怨什麼？
　　　A. The insurance company. 保險公司。
　　　B. The design of the parking lot. 停車場的設計。
　　　C. Eating in his car. 在他車內吃東西。
　　　D. Service time in the drive-through. 得來速的服務時間。

高中英聽測驗模擬試題 ④ 詳解

一、看圖辨義：第一部分

For question number 1, please look at the four pictures.

1. (**A**) Come to my house at noon. I'll meet you at the front
gate. 中午來我家吧。我會在前門迎接你。
    * meet〔mit〕*v.* 迎接　　***front gate*** 前門

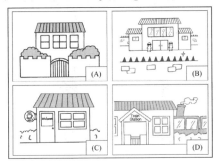

For question number 2, please look at the four pictures.

2. (**D**) Jack is at the post office. He's mailing a package to his
cousin in Brazil.
傑克在郵局裡。他正在郵寄包裹給他在巴西的表弟。
    * mail〔mel〕*v.* 郵寄　　package〔ˈpækɪdʒ〕*n.* 包裹
    cousin〔ˈkʌzn̩〕*n.* 表（堂）兄弟姊妹　　Brazil〔brəˈzɪl〕*n.* 巴西

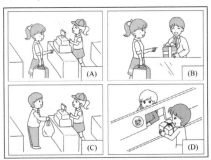

For question number 3, please look at the four pictures.

3. (**A**) Ken's just got dumped by his girlfriend. Maybe having a beer will help ease the pain of rejection.

    肯剛被他的女友甩了。也許喝杯啤酒能夠減輕被拒絕的痛苦。

    * dump〔dʌmp〕v. 抛棄   maybe〔'mebɪ〕adv. 或許
    have〔hæv〕v. 吃；喝   beer〔bɪr〕n. 啤酒
    ease〔iz〕v. 減輕；緩和   pain〔pen〕n. 痛苦
    rejection〔rɪ'dʒɛkʃən〕n. 拒絕

For question number 4, please look at the four pictures.

4. (**B**) Mom is cleaning the house. She's currently vacuuming the living room.

    媽媽正在打掃家裡。她現在正在用吸塵器打掃客廳。

    * clean〔klin〕v. 清理   currently〔'kɝəntlɪ〕adv. 目前；現在
    vacuum〔'vækjʊəm〕v. 用吸塵器打掃   *living room* 客廳

一、看圖辨義：第二部分

For question number 5, please look at picture 5.

5. (**A 、C**) Which TWO of the following are true about the
picture? 關於這張圖片，下列哪兩項為眞？

A. Jeff is building a model
airplane. 傑夫在組模型飛機。
B. Jeff is trying to solve a
puzzle. 傑夫在解一個難題。
C. Jeff is following the instructions listed on the
box. 傑夫正照著盒子上列出來的指示來做。
D. Jeff is putting the airplane together from
memory. 傑夫正在憑記憶組合這架飛機。

* build〔 bɪld 〕v. 組裝　　model〔'madl̩ 〕adj. 模型的
airplane〔'ɛrˏplen 〕n. 飛機　　solve〔 salv 〕v. 解決
puzzle〔'pʌzl̩ 〕n. 難題　　follow〔'falo 〕v. 遵循；依照
instructions〔 ɪn'strʌkʃənz 〕n. pl. 使用說明；操作指南
list〔 lɪst 〕v. 列出　　***put together*** 組合
from memory 憑記憶

For question number 6, please look at picture 6.

6. (**B 、D**) Which TWO of the following are true about the
picture? 關於這張圖片，下列哪兩項為眞？

A. Josh is sleeping in class.
賈許正在課堂上睡覺。
B. Josh is daydreaming.
賈許正在做白日夢。
C. Josh is talking to his buddy on the phone.
賈許正在跟他的好友講電話。

D. Josh is supposed to be studying.
   賈許現在應該要讀書。

* *in class* 課堂上；上課中
  daydream〔'de͵drim〕 *v.* 做白日夢
  talk to *sb.* ***on the phone*** 和某人講電話
  buddy〔'bʌdɪ〕 *n.* 好友；夥伴　　***be supposed to*** *V.* 應該

For question number 7, please look at picture 7.

7. (**A、B**) Which TWO of the following
   are true about the picture?
   關於這張圖片，下列哪兩項爲眞？

   A. Reggie got in trouble at
      school. 瑞吉在學校惹上麻煩。

   B. Reggie's parents are talking to the principal.
      瑞吉的父母正在跟校長講話。

   C. Reggie won an award at school.
      瑞吉在學校贏得了一個獎項。

   D. Reggie's teacher is pleased with his progress.
      瑞吉的老師對他的進步很滿意。

   * ***get in trouble*** 惹上麻煩　　principal〔'prɪnsəpl̩〕 *n.* 校長
     win〔wɪn〕 *v.* 贏得　　award〔ə'wɔrd〕 *n.* 獎
     be pleased with 對～很滿意
     progress〔'prɑgrɛs〕 *n.* 進步

For question number 8, please look at picture 8.

8. (**A、D**) Which TWO of the following
   are true about the picture?
   關於這張圖片，下列哪兩項爲眞？

   A. They are moving to a new
      house. 他們正在搬入新家。

B. They are going on vacation. 他們正要去度假。

C. The children are happy. 孩子們很高興。

D. The children are upset. 孩子們很不高興。

* move〔muv〕v. 搬家　***go on vacation*** 去度假
upset〔ʌpˈsɛt〕adj. 不高興的

For question number 9, please look at picture 9.

9. (**C**、**D**) Which TWO of the following are true about the picture? 關於這張圖片，下列哪兩項為真？

A. Mr. Reed is on a stage.
理德先生在舞台上。

B. Mr. Reed is dancing.
理德先生正在跳舞。

C. Mr. Reed is fishing. 理德先生正在釣魚。

D. Mr. Reed is in a boat. 理德先生在船上。

* stage〔stedʒ〕n. 舞台　dance〔dæns〕v. 跳舞
fish〔fɪʃ〕v. 釣魚　boat〔bot〕n. 船

For question number 10, please look at picture 10.

10. (**B**、**C**) Which TWO of the following are true about the picture? 關於這張圖片，下列哪兩項為真？

A. Two students are talking to a teacher. 兩個學生在跟老師說話。

B. Three students are talking to a teacher. 三個學生在跟老師說話。

C. Everybody is smiling. 每個人都在微笑。

D. Nobody is smiling. 沒有人在微笑。

* smile〔smaɪl〕v. 微笑

二、對答

11. (**A**) Please come in. Can I get you something to drink?

    請進。要喝點什麼嗎？

    A. A glass of water would be nice. 我想要一杯水。

    B. We've been drinking all night.

       我們已經喝了一整晚了。

    C. If it's not one thing, it's another.

       真是一波未平，一波又起。

    D. They won't come unless you drink.

       除非你喝酒，不然他們不會來。

    * get〔gɛt〕v. (去) 拿來
      If it's not one thing, it's another.【諺】一波未平，一波又起；
      禍不單行。
      unless〔ʌnˈlɛs〕conj. 除非

12. (**C**) Where did Kenneth go? 肯尼斯去哪裡了？

    A. Have you met Kenneth? 你有見到肯尼斯嗎？

    B. I'm in the bathroom. 我在廁所裡。

    C. He left for work. 他去工作了。

    D. The show starts at noon. 表演是中午開始。

    * bathroom〔ˈbæθˌrum〕n. 浴室；廁所 *leave for* 前往
      show〔ʃo〕n. 表演

13. (**D**) When did you return from your vacation?

    你什麼時候度完假回來？

    A. It was very relaxing. 真是令人放鬆。

    B. We went to Hawaii. 我們去了夏威夷。

    C. Just the two of us. 只有我們兩個。

    D. Last night. 昨天晚上。

* return〔rɪ'tɜn〕v. 回來　　vacation〔ve'keʃən〕n. 假期
relaxing〔rɪ'læksɪŋ〕adj. 令人放鬆的
Hawaii〔hə'waɪjə〕n. 夏威夷

14. (**C**) Do you enjoy visiting museums? 你喜歡參觀博物館嗎？

　　A. Art and science. 藝術與科學。

　　B. It was sold out. 它已經賣完了。

　　C. Sometimes. 有時候。

　　D. That's where I saw it. 那是我看到它的地方。

　　* visit〔'vɪzɪt〕v. 參觀　　museum〔mju'ziəm〕n. 博物館
　　art〔ɑrt〕n. 藝術　　science〔'saɪəns〕n. 科學
　　sell out 賣完

15. (**B**) The doctor says I'll need to have my tonsils removed.
　　醫生說必須要割除我的扁桃腺。

　　A. I didn't touch it. 我沒有碰。

　　B. Is that a dangerous procedure? 那是個危險的手術嗎？

　　C. Every six weeks. 每六周一次。

　　D. You had better see a doctor. 你最好看個醫生。

　　* tonsil〔'tɑnsḷ , 'tɑnsɪl〕n. 扁桃腺
　　remove〔rɪ'muv〕v. 除去
　　dangerous〔'dendʒərəs〕adj. 危險的
　　procedure〔prə'sidʒɚ〕n. 手續；手術
　　had better + ***V.*** 最好～

16. (**C**) Do you prefer traveling by train or bus?
　　你比較喜歡坐火車還是巴士去旅行？

　　A. Maybe tomorrow. 也許明天。

　　B. I took the bus. 我搭巴士。

　　C. The train is much more convenient and reliable.
　　　　火車方便可靠多了。

D. An hour by train, two hours on the bus.

一小時搭火車，兩小時搭巴士。

* prefer〔prɪˋfɝ〕v. 比較喜歡
　convenient〔kənˋvinjənt〕adj. 方便的
　reliable〔rɪˋlaɪəbl̩〕adj. 可靠的

17. (**D**)　Did Ricky change his phone number?

瑞奇換了他的電話號碼了嗎？

A. 999-0987. 999-0987。

B. It's ringing. 手機在響。

C. Hello, may I help you? 喂，需要我為您服務嗎？

D. Not that I am aware of. 據我所知沒有。

* change〔tʃendʒ〕v. 改變
　phone number 電話號碼　　**be aware of** 知道
　Not that I am aware of. 據我所知沒有。(= **Not that I know of.**)

18. (**B**)　Have you ever had lunch in the company cafeteria?

你有在公司的自助餐廳吃過午餐嗎？

A. Where do you want to eat? I'm starving.

你想在哪吃？我好餓。

B. No, never. Is it any good?

不，從來沒有。有什麼好吃的嗎？

C. Funny you should say that. Try this.

你會這樣說，有些奇怪。試試這個。

D. Gentlemen prefer the company of blondes.

男士們比較喜歡金髮美女的陪伴。

* company〔ˋkʌmpənɪ〕n. 公司；陪伴
　cafeteria〔͵kæfəˋtɪrɪə〕n. 自助餐廳　　　starve〔starv〕v. 飢餓
　funny〔ˋfʌnɪ〕adj. 怪的；奇特的　　should〔ʃʊd〕aux. 竟然
　gentleman〔ˋdʒɛntl̩mən〕n. 紳士【亦為一般男士的尊稱】
　blonde〔bland〕n. 金髮女子

19. (**C**) Mom! Where's my baseball uniform?
媽！我的棒球制服呢？

    A. Finish your homework. 要把你的功課做完。

    B. No one can deny that. 沒有人可以否認。

    C. It's in the dryer. 在烘乾機裡。

    D. Come sit here. 來坐這裡。

    * baseball〔'bes,bɔl〕*n.* 棒球　　uniform〔'junə,fɔrm〕*n.* 制服
homework〔'hom,wɜk〕*n.* 功課　　deny〔dɪ'naɪ〕*v.* 否認
dryer〔'draɪə〕*n.* 烘乾機（= *drier*）
come sit 過來坐（= *come to sit*）

20. (**C**) What's the best pizza place in town?
城裡最好的披薩店是哪一家？

    A. Kleenex. 可麗舒。　　　　B. Sony. 索尼。

    C. Angelo's. 安杰洛披薩。　　D. Apple. 蘋果公司。

    * pizza〔'pitsə〕*n.* 披薩　　***pizza place*** 披薩店
Kleenex〔'klinɛks〕*n.* 可麗舒【紙巾品牌】
Sony〔'sonɪ〕*n.* 索尼公司【日本電器品牌】
Apple〔'æpl̩〕*n.* 蘋果公司【美國手機、電腦品牌】

三、簡短對話

For question 21, you will listen to a short conversation.

    M : Are you busy? 你在忙嗎？

    W : Not really. 還好。

    M : I mean, " Is this a good time for you? "
我的意思「你現在方便嗎？」

    W : A good time for what? 方便幹麻？

M : Would you mind if I asked you a few questions?
你介意我問你幾個問題嗎？

W : No, go ahead. 不介意，說吧。

* busy〔'bɪzɪ〕adj. 忙碌的　　**not really** 不完全是
mean〔min〕v. 意思是　　**a good time** 適當時機
mind〔maɪnd〕v. 介意　　**go ahead** 請吧；說吧

21. (**D**) Q : What will the man probably do next?
這位男士接下來可能會做什麼？

A. Give a speech. 發表演說。
B. Take a nap. 小睡一下。
C. Lose his temper. 發脾氣。
D. Ask a question. 問一個問題。

* probably〔'prɑbəblɪ〕adv. 可能　　**give a speech** 發表演說
take a nap 小睡片刻　　**lose** one's **temper** 發脾氣

For question 22, you will listen to a short conversation.

W : Last night I had the best pizza I have ever eaten in my
life. It was incredible!
昨晚我吃到我這輩子吃過最好吃的披薩。它真是不可思議的
好吃！

M : Really? Where? 真的嗎？在哪裡？

W : Dino's Pizzeria in Belmont. 在貝爾蒙特的迪諾披薩店。

M : You're kidding, right? You must not know anything
about pizza, because Dino's is awful. I wouldn't even
call it pizza. 妳在開玩笑，是吧？妳一定一點也不懂披薩，
因為迪諾披薩店很糟。他們店的東西根本不叫披薩。

　* pizza〔'pitsə〕*n.* 披薩
　incredible〔ɪn'krɛdəbl̩〕*adj.* 不可思議的
　pizzeria〔ˌpitsə'riə〕*n.* 披薩店
　Belmont〔'bɛlmɔnt〕*n.* 貝爾蒙特【位於美國加州】
　be kidding 在開玩笑　　awful〔'ɔfʊl〕*adj.* 很糟的

22.(**B**) Q：What does the man think about Dino's pizza?
　　　　　這位男士覺得迪諾披薩店如何？

　　　　A. It's the best he's ever tasted. 是他品嚐過最好吃的。
　　　　B. It's not very good. 不是很好吃。
　　　　C. It's real pizza. 它是眞正的披薩。
　　　　D. It's fine if you like pizza.
　　　　　　如果你喜歡披薩的話，是還不錯。

　　　* taste〔test〕*v.* 品嚐

For question 23, you will listen to a short conversation.

　M：Excuse me, miss, but, we've been waiting a long time.
　　　Aren't there any tables available? 小姐，不好意思，但是
　　　我們已經等很久了。還沒有空桌的嗎？

　W：I'm very sorry, sir. We'll have you seated in just a few
　　　moments. 我很抱歉，先生。我們很快就會安排你們就座。

　M：OK. Do me a favor and bring us another round of
　　　cocktails. 好的。請再幫忙拿給我們雞尾酒。

　W：No problem. And those will be on the house—it's our
　　　way of saying "Thank you" for being so patient.
　　　沒問題。那些酒是免費的——這是我們感謝您耐心等候的方式。

　　　* miss〔mɪs〕*n.* 小姐　　***a long time*** 很久
　　　available〔ə'veləbl̩〕*adj.* 可獲得的

sir〔sɝ〕*n.* 先生　　seat〔sit〕*v.* 使入座；使就座

in a few moments 再過一會兒　　***do sb. a favor*** 幫某人忙

round〔raʊnd〕*n.*（酒等）一巡

cocktail〔'kɑk,tel〕*n.* 雞尾酒

be on the house 由店家請客；免費招待（= *free*）

patient〔'peʃənt〕*adj.* 有耐心的

23.（**B**）Q：Where are the speakers?　這些說話者在哪裡？

　　　A. In a supermarket.　在超市裡。
　　　B. In a restaurant.　在餐廳裡。
　　　C. In a bakery.　在麵包店裡。
　　　D. In a fast-food shop.　在速食店裡。

　　　* supermarket〔'supɚ,mɑrkɪt〕*n.* 超級市場
　　　　restaurant〔'rɛstərənt〕*n.* 餐廳　　bakery〔'bekərɪ〕*n.* 麵包店
　　　　fast-food shop 速食餐廳（= *fast-food restaurant*）

For question 24, you will listen to a short conversation.

　　W：What in God's name is that sound and where is it coming
　　　　from?　那究竟是什麼聲音，是從哪傳來的？

　　M：It's the kid upstairs.　Apparently, he now plays electric
　　　　guitar.　是樓上的小孩。他現似乎是在彈電吉他。

　　W：I'm calling the landlord.　This has got to stop.
　　　　我要打電話給房東。這必須停止。

　　M：Oh, come on now.　It's not that bad.
　　　　喔，算了啦。其實沒有那麼糟。

　　　* ***in God's name***【表示生氣、驚訝】究竟；到底
　　　　upstairs〔'ʌp'stɛrz〕*adv.* 在樓上
　　　　apparently〔ə'pærəntlɪ〕*adv.* 似乎

electric〔ɪˋlɛktrɪk〕*adj.* 電的；電動的

electric guitar 電吉他　　landlord〔ˋlænd͵lɔrd〕*n.* 房東

have got to 必須（= *have to*）　　***come on*** 得了吧；算了吧

24.（ **C** ）Q：What does the woman threaten to do?

　　　　　　這位女士揚言要做什麼？

　　A. Go upstairs and talk to the boy's parents.

　　　　上樓與那男孩的父母談談。

　　B. File a report with the authorities. 對當局提出報告。

　　C. Complain to the building owner about the noise.

　　　　向大樓房東抱怨這個噪音。

　　D. Physically prevent the boy from playing the guitar.

　　　　動手阻止男孩彈吉他。

　　* threaten〔ˋθrɛtn̩〕*v.* 威脅說（要做）　　file〔faɪl〕*v.* 提出
　　　report〔rɪˋport〕*n.* 報告
　　　authorities〔əˋθɔrətɪz〕*n. pl.* 官方；當局
　　　complain〔kəmˋplen〕*v.* 抱怨
　　　building〔ˋbɪldɪŋ〕*n.* 建築物；大樓
　　　owner〔ˋonɚ〕*n.* 所有者　　noise〔nɔɪz〕*n.* 噪音
　　　physically〔ˋfɪzɪklɪ〕*adv.* 身體上（= *bodily*）；實際上；
　　　　眞正地（= *actually*）　　***prevent…from~*** 阻止…做~

For questions 25 and 26, you will listen to a short conversation.

　　W：There's a free concert in the park tonight. Would you

　　　　like to go? 今天晚上公園有一場免費的音樂會。你想要去嗎？

　　M：Sure. Who will be performing? 當然想。誰會來表演？

　　W：Two jazz bands from Germany and a famous pianist

　　　　from Taiwan.

　　　　兩個從德國來的爵士樂團，以及一個來自台灣有名的鋼琴家。

M : Count me in. What time does it start?

把我算進去。什麼時候開始？

* free〔 fri 〕*adj.* 免費的　　concert〔ˈkɑnsɚt 〕*n.* 音樂會
would like to V. 想要~　　perform〔 pɚˈfɔrm 〕*v.* 表演
jazz〔 dʒæz 〕*n.* 爵士樂　　band〔 bænd 〕*n.* 樂團
Germany〔ˈdʒɝˈmənɪ 〕*n.* 德國　　famous〔ˈfeməs 〕*adj.* 有名的
pianist〔 pɪˈænɪst 〕*n.* 鋼琴家　　***count sb. in*** 把某人算進去

25. (**C**) Q : What are the speakers discussing?　說話者在討論什麼？

　　A. Their tastes in music.　他們對音樂的品味。

　　B. Their travel experiences.　他們的旅行經驗。

　　C. Their plans for the evening.　他們今晚的計畫。

　　D. Their career aspirations.　他們的職涯抱負。

* discuss〔 dɪˈskʌs 〕*v.* 討論　　taste〔 test 〕*n.* 品味
travel〔ˈtrævl̩ 〕*n.* 旅行　　plan〔 plæn 〕*n.* 計畫
career〔 kəˈrɪr 〕*n.* 職業；生涯
aspiration〔ˌæspəˈreʃən 〕*n.* 渴望；抱負

26. (**A**) Q : What will take place in the park?

　　公園裡會舉辦什麼活動？

　　A. A musical performance.　一場音樂表演。

　　B. A theatrical production.　一場戲劇表演。

　　C. A sporting event.　一場運動比賽。

　　D. A cultural exchange.　一場文化交流。

* ***take place*** 發生；舉行　　musical〔ˈmjuzɪkl̩ 〕*adj.* 音樂的
performance〔 pɚˈfɔrməns 〕*n.* 表演
theatrical〔 θɪˈætrɪkl̩ 〕*adj.* 戲劇的
production〔 prəˈdʌkʃən 〕*n.* (電影的) 製作；演出
sporting event 運動比賽　　cultural〔ˈkʌltʃərəl 〕*adj.* 文化的
exchange〔 ɪksˈtʃendʒ 〕*n.* 交換；交流

For questions 27 and 28, you will listen to a short conversation.

W : My company is sponsoring a trip to Disneyland this summer. 我們公司今年夏天會贊助一趟迪士尼樂園之旅。

M : Are you going? 你要去嗎？

W : No. My schedule this summer is crazy. I've got so much going on.

不要。我今年夏天的行程很瘋狂，我有超多事情要做。

M : That's too bad. Have you ever been to Disneyland?

很可惜。你去過迪士尼樂園嗎？

W : Yes. That's why I'm not very disappointed about skipping the trip.

有，這也就是為什麼我不去這個旅行卻沒有很失望的原因。

* company (ˈkʌmpənɪ) *n.* 公司
sponsor (ˈspɑnsɚ) *v.* 贊助
Disneyland (ˈdɪznɪˌlænd) *n.* 迪士尼樂園
schedule (ˈskɛdʒul) *n.* 行程；時間表
crazy (ˈkrezɪ) *adj.* 瘋狂的；荒唐的　　***go on*** 發生；進行
That's too bad. 太遺憾了。
disappointed (ˌdɪsəˈpɔɪntɪd) *adj.* 失望的
skip (skɪp) *v.* 跳過；略過；不出席

27. (**D**) Q : How does the woman feel about the trip to Disneyland?

這位女士對於這個迪士尼樂園之旅覺得如何？

A. Excited. 很興奮。　　　　B. Awkward. 很尷尬。
C. Disappointed. 很失望。
D. Indifferent. 漠不關心。

　　　* excited〔ɪk'saɪtɪd〕*adj.* 興奮的
　　　awkward〔'ɔkwəd〕*adj.* 笨拙的；尷尬的
　　　indifferent〔ɪn'dɪf(ə)rənt〕*adj.* 漠不關心的

28. (**A**)　Q : What does the woman imply?　這位女士暗示什麼？

　　　A. She is too busy to go on the trip.

　　　　　她忙到沒時間去旅行。

　　　B. She can't afford to take the trip.　她負擔不起旅費。

　　　C. She hates amusement parks.　她不喜歡遊樂園。

　　　D. She has a fear of heights.　她有懼高症。

　　　* imply〔ɪm'plaɪ〕*v.* 暗示　　***too…to~***　太…以致於不~
　　　go on a trip 去旅行（= *take a trip*）
　　　afford〔ə'fɔrd〕*v.* 負擔得起　　　hate〔het〕*v.* 討厭
　　　amusement park 遊樂園
　　　fear〔fɪr〕*n.* 恐懼　　　heights〔haɪts〕*n. pl.* 高處；高地

For questions 29 and 30, you will listen to a short conversation.

　M : Did you hear the news?　My sister got accepted to

　　　Harvard!　你聽到消息了嗎？我妹被哈佛錄取了！

　W : Wow!　That's awesome.　What's her major?

　　　哇！太棒了。她主修什麼？

　M : She hasn't declared yet, but she's leaning toward

　　　international law.

　　　她還沒有宣布，但她比較想修國際法。

　W : I wish her all the best.　我祝她一切順利。

　　　* news〔njuz〕*n.* 消息　　accept〔ək'sɛpt〕*v.* 接受
　　　Harvard〔'hɑrvəd〕*n.* 哈佛大學　　wow〔wau〕*interj.* 哇
　　　awesome〔'ɔsəm〕*adj.* 極好的　　major〔'medʒə〕*n.* 主修科目

declare〔dɪ'klɛr〕*v.* 宣布；公布　　***lean toward*** 傾向於
international〔ˌɪntə'næʃənḷ〕*adj.* 國際的
law〔lɔ〕*n.* 法律　　***wish sb. all the best*** 祝某人一切順利

29. (**B**) Q: What happened to the man's sister?
　　　　這位男士的妹妹怎麼了？
　　　　A. She was promoted at work. 她工作獲得升遷。
　　　　B. She was accepted to a university. 她被一所大學錄取。
　　　　C. She got a job in international law.
　　　　　　她得到一份國際法領域的工作。
　　　　D. She graduated from college. 她大學畢業了。

　　* promote〔prə'mot〕*v.* 使升遷
　　university〔ˌjunə'vɝsətɪ〕*n.* 大學
　　graduate〔'grædʒʊˌet〕*v.* 畢業

30. (**A**) Q: What is the woman's reaction to the news?
　　　　那位女士對這個消息的反應是什麼？
　　　　A. She is happy. 她很開心。
　　　　B. She is angry. 她很生氣。
　　　　C. She is confused. 她很困惑。
　　　　D. She is fearful. 她很害怕。

　　* reaction〔rɪ'ækʃən〕*n.* 反應 < *to* >
　　confused〔kən'fjuzd〕*adj.* 困惑的
　　fearful〔'fɪrfəl〕*adj.* 害怕的

四、短文聽解

Questions 31 and 32 are based on the following report.

　　Recycling electronics still isn't as easy as it should be,
but with the amount of heavy metals and other hazardous

components in TV sets, computers, cell phones, monitors
and other electronic devices, it's important to get the facts
on recycling electronics.　Americans now own about 24
electronic devices per household, according to the EPA,
and many of these get replaced regularly.　The average cell
phone user, for example, gets a new cell phone every 18
months.　Fortunately, recycling electronics is becoming
more popular, and about 100 million pounds of material is
recovered from electronics recycling plants each year.

　　電子產品回收應該是一件容易的事，但現在做起來仍然沒那
麼容易，然而因為電視、電腦、手機、螢幕及其他電子產品有大
量的重金屬及其他的有害零件，所以了解回收電子產品的相關資
訊是很重要的。依據美國環保署的說法，美國人每戶人家現在大
約擁有 24 個電子產品，並且很會定時更換。舉例來說，手機使用
者平均每十八個月就會買一支新手機。幸運的是，回收電子產品
變得越來越普及。每年有大約一億磅的材料被電子產品回收工廠
回收。

**————————————————————

recycle〔rɪˈsaɪkḷ〕v. 回收
electronics〔ɪˌlɛkˈtrɑnɪks〕n. pl. 電子設備
amount〔əˈmaʊnt〕n. 數量　　*heavy metal* 重金屬
hazardous〔ˈhæzɚdəs〕adj. 危險的（= *dangerous*）
component〔kəmˈponənt〕n. 零件　　*TV set* 電視機
computer〔kəmˈpjutɚ〕n. 電腦　　*cell phone* 手機
monitor〔ˈmɑnətɚ〕n. 顯示器；螢幕
electronic〔ɪˌlɛkˈtrɑnɪk〕adj. 電子的
device〔dɪˈvaɪs〕n. 裝置；設備　　*get the facts* 了解事實
on〔ɑn〕prep. 關於（= *about*）　　own〔on〕v. 擁有

per〔pɚ〕*prep.* 每…　　household〔'haʊs,hold〕*n.* 家庭；戶

EPA 美國環保署（ = *Environmental Protection Agency*）

replace〔rɪ'ples〕*v.* 更換；取代

regularly〔'rɛgjələlɪ〕*adv.* 定期地

average〔'ævərɪdʒ〕*adj.* 平均的　　user〔'juzɚ〕*n.* 使用者

for example 舉例來說　　get〔gɛt〕*v.* 買

fortunately〔'fɔrtʃənɪtlɪ〕*adv.* 幸運的是

popular〔'pɑpjəlɚ〕*adj.* 受歡迎的；流行的

pound〔paʊnd〕*n.* 磅　　material〔mə'tɪrɪəl〕*n.* 材料

recover〔rɪ'kʌvɚ〕*v.* 回收；重新利用　　plant〔plænt〕*n.* 工廠

31. (**C**) What is the speaker mainly talking about?

說話者主要在談論什麼？

A. Pollution. 污染。　　　B. The environment. 環境。

C. Recycling. 回收。　　　D. Cell phones. 手機。

* mainly〔'menlɪ〕*adv.* 主要地

pollution〔pə'luʃən〕*n.* 污染

environment〔ɪn'vaɪrənmənt〕*n.* 環境

32. (**B**) According to the article, how often does the average cell phone user get a new phone?

依據本文，一般手機使用者平均多久買一支新手機？

A. Once a year. 每年一次。

B. Once every 18 months. 每十八個月一次。

C. Once every 24 months. 每二十四個月一次。

D. Once every 100 years. 每一百年一次。

* article〔'ɑrtɪkl̩〕*n.* 文章　　***how often*** 多久一次

Questions 33 and 34 are based on the following report.

A Jersey County Board committee is considering a request to name U.S. Route 67 through Jersey County in memory of World War II hero Russell Dunham. Dunham, a Jersey County resident for 30 years, was a Medal of Honor recipient and also was awarded the Silver Star, Bronze Star and Purple Heart. He is the most decorated veteran ever from this area. In some ways, we are surprised this request hasn't come up before now, but we think among all the veterans in our region, Dunham deserves the salute because he is the only one ever to receive the Medal of Honor. We don't think highways or streets typically should be named after people, unless there is some special reason, but in this case, we can't see how Jersey County can go wrong doing this for Dunham and his family.

澤西郡郡務委員會正在考慮是否將通過澤西郡的 67 號公路，以二次世界大戰的英雄羅素‧鄧漢為其路名。鄧漢居住在澤西郡三十年。他是榮譽勳章的獲獎人，也曾獲銀星、銅心及紫心勳章。他是本地獲得最多勳章的退伍軍人。我們對於這個請求現在才出現，某種程度上是很驚訝的，不過我們認為，鄧漢因為是我們郡上所有的退伍軍人中唯一被授與榮譽勳章的，所以值得我們向他致敬。除非有特殊原因，否則我們覺得公路或街道通常是不應該以人名命名，但就這一個個案，我們看不出澤西郡為了鄧漢及他的家庭而這麼做，會有什麼問題。

** ────────────────

Jersey〔ˋdʒɝzɪ〕*n.* 澤西【位於美國伊利諾州】
county〔ˋkaʊntɪ〕*n.*（美國）郡
board〔bord〕*n.* 理事會；董事會
committee〔kəˋmɪtɪ〕*n.* 委員會　　consider〔kənˋsɪdɚ〕*v.* 考慮
request〔rɪˋkwɛst〕*n.* 請求；要求　　name〔nem〕*v.* 命名

in memory of 紀念　　*World War II* 第二次世界大戰

hero〔ˈhɪro〕*n.* 英雄　　*Russell Dunham* 羅素·鄧漢

resident〔ˈrɛzədənt〕*n.* 居民　　medal〔ˈmɛdl̩〕*n.* 獎章；獎牌

honor〔ˈɑnɚ〕*n.* 名譽；榮譽

Medal of Honor 榮譽勳章【由美國政府頒發的美國最高軍事榮銜，授

　予那些「在戰鬥中冒生命危險，在義務之外表現出英勇無畏」的軍人】

recipient〔rɪˈsɪpɪənt〕*n.* 接受者；領受人

award〔əˈwɔrd〕*v.* 頒發

Silver Star 銀星勳章【一項美軍跨軍種通用勳獎，它是美國聯邦軍事

　勳獎中等級最高的軍事獎章】　　bronze〔branz〕*n.* 青銅

Bronze Star 銅星勳章【是授予美國國軍中個人的美軍跨軍種通用勳

　獎，用於表彰「英勇或富有功績的成績或服務」】

Purple Heart 紫心勳章【是美國軍方的榮譽獎章，從 1932 年 2 月 22 日

　開始贈與，一般贈與於對戰事有貢獻，或於參戰時負傷的人員】

decorate〔ˈdɛkəˌret〕*v.* 授予勳章

veteran〔ˈvɛtərən〕*n.* 老兵；退役軍人　　area〔ˈɛrɪə〕*n.* 地區

in some ways 在某些方面；某種程度上

come up 被提到；被討論　　region〔ˈriʒən〕*n.* 地區

deserve〔dɪˈzɜv〕*v.* 應得　　salute〔səˈlut〕*n.* 致敬；致意

ever〔ˈɛvɚ〕*adv.* 有史以來；至今

typically〔ˈtɪpɪkl̩〕*adv.* 通常　　*be named after* 以…的名字命名

some〔sʌm〕*adj.* 某個　　*in this case* 在這個情況下

see〔si〕*v.* 認為　　*go wrong* 出錯；有問題

33. (**D**) What is this talk mainly about? 這段談話的主旨是什麼？

　　A. World War II. 第二次世界大戰。

　　B. The Medal of Honor. 榮譽勳章。

　　C. Russell Dunham's military career.

　　　羅素·鄧漢的軍旅生涯。

　　D. Naming a road after Russell Dunham.

　　　以羅素·鄧漢的名字為道路命名。

* military〔'mɪlə,tɛrɪ〕*adj.* 軍事的；軍人的
  career〔kə'rɪr〕*n.* 職業；生涯

34. (**B**)　What does the speaker think about the request?
    說話者認為這個請求如何？

    A.　He thinks more research needs to be done.
    　　他認為還要再多研究。

    B.　He thinks it's the right thing to do.
    　　他認為這是正確應做的事。

    C.　He thinks it's a disgrace to the community.
    　　他認為這是社區的恥辱。

    D.　He thinks the committee ought to reject it.
    　　他認為委員會應該拒絕。

    * research〔'risɝtʃ〕*n.* 研究
      disgrace〔dɪs'gres〕*n.* 丟臉；恥辱
      community〔kə'mjunətɪ〕*n.* 社區
      ought to 應該（= *should*）　　reject〔rɪ'dʒɛkt〕*v.* 拒絕

Questions 35 and 36 are based on the following report.

　　Taiwan tends to have a consistently pleasant
year-round climate.　There are no extremes of winter and
summer, only two seasons: wet and dry.　Because Taiwan
straddles the Tropic of Cancer, sunburn can occur rapidly,
even on a cloudy day.　Always use a strong sunscreen (at
least factor 30), making sure to reapply after swimming,
and always wear a wide-brimmed hat and sunglasses
outdoors.　Avoid lying in the sun during the hottest part of
the day (10 am to 2 pm).　If you become sunburned, stay out
of the sun until you have recovered, making sure to

drink plenty of liquids. Take frequent cold showers and painkillers for the discomfort. Pure aloe vera lotion is also helpful in alleviating the sting of sunburn. If blistering occurs, seek professional medical care immediately.

台灣氣候通常全年都一直是舒適宜人的。沒有極端的冬日及夏日氣候，而只有兩個季節：乾季與雨季。由於台灣橫跨了北迴歸線，因此可能很快就會曬傷，即使在陰天也一樣。一定要使用有效的防曬乳（防曬係數至少要 30），游泳後務必要再塗一次，而且在戶外一定要戴上寬邊的帽子及太陽眼鏡。要避免於一日中最熱的時候（早上 10 點到下午 2 點）躺在陽光下。如果你曬傷了，要遠離陽光直到復原為止，務必大量補充水分。要多用冷水淋浴，並服用止痛藥減緩不適。純蘆薈乳液也能有效舒緩曬傷的刺痛感。如果有出水泡，要立即尋求專業的醫療處理。

**

tend to V. 傾向～；通常～
consistently〔kən'sɪstəntlɪ〕*adv.* 經常；一直
pleasant〔'plɛznt〕*adj.* 令人愉快的　　year-round *adj.* 整年的
climate〔'klaɪmɪt〕*n.* 氣候　　extremes〔ɪk'strimz〕*n. pl.* 極端
dry〔draɪ〕*adj.* 乾的　　straddle〔'strædl〕*v.* 橫跨；跨越
the Tropic of Cancer 北迴歸線【因為黃道與赤道傾斜 23.5 度，大約在 2,000 年以前的夏至時間，太陽直射北迴歸線，太陽剛好處在這個星座位置，因此以巨蟹的地方（Tropic of Cancer）代表北迴歸線】
sunburn〔'sʌn,bɝn〕*n. v.* 曬傷　　occur〔ə'kɝ〕*v.* 發生

rapidly〔'ræpɪdlɪ〕*adv.* 迅速地
cloudy〔'klaʊdɪ〕*adj.* 多雲的
sunscreen〔'sʌn,skrin〕*n.* 防曬油　　*at least* 至少
factor〔'fæktɚ〕*n.* 係數　　*make sure* 確定
reapply〔,riə'plaɪ〕*v.* 再塗；重塗　　brim〔brɪm〕*n.* 帽緣
wide-brimmed *adj.* 寬邊的
sunglasses〔'sʌn,glæsɪz〕*n. pl.* 太陽眼鏡

outdoors (ˋaʊtˋdorz) adv. 在戶外　　avoid (əˋvɔɪd) v. 避免
lie (laɪ) v. 躺　　***in the sun*** 在陽光下　　***stay out of*** 遠離
recover (rɪˋkʌvə) v. 恢復　　***plenty of*** 許多的
liquid (ˋlɪkwɪd) n. 液體　　***take a shower*** 淋浴
frequent (ˋfrikwənt) adj. 頻繁的
painkiller (ˋpenͺkɪlə) n. 止痛藥
discomfort (dɪsˋkʌmfət) n. 不舒服　　pure (pjʊr) adj. 純的

aloe vera (ͺælo ˋvɪrə) n. 蘆薈　　lotion (ˋloʃən) n. (液狀) 乳液
helpful (ˋhɛlpfəl) adj. 有幫助的；有用的
alleviate (əˋlivɪͺet) v. 減輕；緩和　　sting (stɪŋ) n. 刺痛
blister (ˋblɪstə) v. 冒水泡　　seek (sik) v. 尋求
professional (prəˋfɛʃənl) adj. 專業的
medical care 醫療照顧；醫療處理
immediately (ɪˋmidɪɪtlɪ) adv. 立刻

35. (**A**) What is this talk mainly about? 這段談話的主旨是什麼？

　　A. Taiwan's weather. 台灣的天氣。

　　B. Taiwan's economy. 台灣的經濟。

　　C. Taiwan's location. 台灣的地點。

　　D. Taiwan's culture. 台灣的文化。

　　* economy (ɪˋkɑnəmɪ) n. 經濟　　location (loˋkeʃən) n. 地點
　　culture (ˋkʌltʃə) n. 文化

36. (**D**) What does the speaker specifically recommend?
　　這個說話者特別建議什麼？

　　A. Take frequent hot showers. 要經常洗熱水澡。

　　B. Avoid liquids. 要避免液體。

　　C. Visit Taiwan in the wet season. 要在雨季時造訪台灣。

　　D. Use plenty of sunscreen. 要多用防曬乳。

　　* specifically (spɪˋsɪfɪklͺɪ) adv. 明確地；特別地
　　recommend (ͺrɛkəˋmɛnd) v. 推薦；建議

Questions 37 and 38 are based on the following report.

The political season is upon us and that means that you and your friend are probably discussing the issues and candidates. Chances are, you'll end up disagreeing with at least some of what your friend believes politically. Without proper perspective, political disagreements can end a friendship, so it's important to get a handle on things before an argument goes so far that it gets out of hand. Most of the blow-ups that happen between friends occur because each is trying to change the other's mind. The discussion goes from a calm place to a major argument, perhaps even with yelling and personal attacks. It can be maddening to some people when a friend doesn't believe the same thing they do.

現在是選舉季，而這也意味著，你和你的朋友可能會討論候選人與政治議題。很有可能，你朋友的政治信念至少某一些是你所不認同的。如果沒有正確的眼光，政治意見不合可能會導致友誼的結束，因此在爭論越演越烈到不可收拾之前，充分了解情況是很重要的。大多數朋友間會突然劇烈爭吵都是因為想改變對方的想法。這樣的討論會從平和的討論變成重大的爭吵，甚至可能伴隨著大吼大叫及人身攻擊。對某些人而言，當朋友不相信他們所相信的事，可能是很令人抓狂的。

**

political〔pə'lɪtɪkḷ〕*adj.* 政治的
season〔'sizn〕*n.* 季節；活動時期
upon〔ə'pɑn〕*prep.* 將要發生；即將來臨
issue〔'ɪʃu〕*n.* 議題　　candidate〔'kændə,det〕*n.* 候選人
chances are (that) 很可能　　***end up*** + ***V-ing*** 結果~；最後~
disagree〔,dɪsə'gri〕*v.* 不同意；不一致 < *with* >
politically〔pə'lɪtɪkḷ〕*adv.* 在政治上

proper〔ˋprɑpɚ〕adj. 適當的；正確的
perspective〔pɚˋspɛktɪv〕n. 正確的眼光；洞察力；合理判斷
disagreement〔͵dɪsəˋgrimənt〕n. 意見不合
get a handle on 掌握；了解　　things〔ˋθɪŋz〕n. pl. 情況
argument〔ˋɑrgjəmənt〕n. 爭論　　far〔fɑr〕adv. 過份地
get out of hand 失去控制；不可收拾
blow-up〔ˋbloˏʌp〕n. 突然而激烈的爭吵

change one's ***mind*** 改變某人的想法
discussion〔dɪˋskʌʃən〕n. 討論　　calm〔kɑm〕adj. 平靜的
place〔ples〕n. 處境；立場
major〔ˋmedʒɚ〕adj. 重大的；嚴重的
perhaps〔pɚˋhæps〕adv. 或許　　yelling〔ˋjɛlɪŋ〕n. 大叫
personal〔ˋpɝsṇḷ〕adj. 個人的；人身的　　attack〔əˋtæk〕n. 攻擊
maddening〔ˋmædṇɪŋ〕adj. 使人生氣的；使人發狂的

37. (**C**) According to the speaker, what causes the most arguments between friends?

依據說話者的說法，最容易造成朋友間爭執的是什麼？

A. Political opinions. 政治意見。

B. The political season. 選舉季。

C. Each is trying to change the other's mind.
雙方都試著要改變對方的想法。

D. Support for different candidates. 支持不同的候選人。

* support〔səˋport〕n. 支持

38. (**A**) What does the speaker say can end a friendship?

說話者認為什麼可能會結束一段友誼？

A. A lack of perspective. 缺乏正確的眼光。

B. A change of season. 季節的變換。

C. Changing one's mind. 改變心意。

D. Going to a calm place. 到一個寧靜的地方。

* lack〔læk〕n. 缺乏

Questions 39 and 40 are based on the following report.

Crime rates are declining at Rock Spring Park in Alton, and that is a positive thing for the city's image. Previously, it was common to see vandalism and other crimes occurring at the park—especially thefts of wire being used for the annual Christmas Wonderland light display and burglaries at the Rock Springs Golf Course clubhouse— but efforts to curb those problems seem to be working. A summary provided by the Alton Police Department said that from 2007 through April, 2012, there were 113 incidents at the park, and most of the calls were minor. The Alton Parks and Recreation Department has used security guards to patrol Rock Spring for the past three years, and that also is making a difference.

奧爾頓的石泉公園的犯罪率正在下降，這對城市的形象是很正面的。之前公園內常常可看到破壞公物及其他犯罪行為——尤其是每年度聖誕樂園燈光表演的電纜線失竊，以及在石泉高爾夫球場俱樂部會館的偷竊——然而抑制這些問題的種種努力似乎起了作用。一份由奧爾頓警局提供的概要報告指出，從 2007 年到 2012 年四月，公園內共發生 113 個案件，其中多數報案都是較不嚴重的案件。奧爾頓公園與娛樂管理局請保全人員巡邏石泉公園已經三年了，這一點應該也發揮了影響力。

** ——————————————

crime〔kraɪm〕*n.* 罪；犯罪　　rate〔ret〕*n.* 比率
decline〔dɪ'klaɪn〕*v.* 下降　　spring〔sprɪŋ〕*n.* 泉水
Alton〔'ɔltən〕*n.* 奧爾頓【位於美國伊利諾州】
positive〔'pɑzətɪv〕*adj.* 正面的　　image〔'ɪmɪdʒ〕*n.* 形象
previously〔'privɪəslɪ〕*adv.* 以前
common〔'kɑmən〕*adj.* 普遍的；常見的

vandalism〔'vændḷ͵ɪzəm〕 *n.* 破壞公物
theft〔θɛft〕 *n.* 竊盜　　wire〔waɪr〕 *n.* 電線；電纜
annual〔'ænjʊəl〕 *adj.* 每年的；一年一度的
wonderland〔'wʌndɚ͵lænd〕 *n.* 仙境；美好的地方
display〔dɪ'sple〕 *n.* 展示；表演　***light display*** 燈光表演
burglary〔'bɝglərɪ〕 *n.*（入室）竊盜　***golf course*** 高爾夫球場
clubhouse〔'klʌb͵haʊs〕 *n.* 俱樂部會館　　effort〔'ɛfɚt〕 *n.* 努力
curb〔kɝb〕 *v.* 抑制　　work〔wɝk〕 *v.* 有效；起作用
summary〔'sʌmərɪ〕 *n.* 概要；摘要；總結

provide〔prə'vaɪd〕 *v.* 提供　***police department*** 警察局
incident〔'ɪnsədənt〕 *n.* 事件　　call〔kɔl〕 *n.* 電話；報案
minor〔'maɪnɚ〕 *adj.* 較小的；較不重要的
recreation〔͵rɛkrɪ'eʃṇ〕 *n.* 娛樂
department〔dɪ'partmənt〕 *n.* 部門；局
Parks and Recreation Department 公園與娛樂管理局
security〔sɪ'kjʊrətɪ〕 *n.* 安全；防衛；戒備　　guard〔gard〕 *n.* 警衛
security guard 保安人員；警衛　　patrol〔pə'trol〕 *v.* 巡邏
past〔pæst〕 *adj.* 過去的　　***make a difference*** 有差別；有影響

39.（**C**）What is declining at Rock Spring Park?
石泉公園中的什麼正在減少？

　　A. Police presence. 駐守的警察。
　　B. Visitors. 遊客。　　　　C. Crime. 犯罪。
　　D. Golfers. 打高爾夫球的人。

　　* presence〔'prɛzṇs〕 *n.* 存在；駐守；派遣
　　　golfer〔'galfɚ〕 *n.* 打高爾夫球的人

40.（**C**）What is the main reason for the decline?
減少的主要原因為何？

　　A. Fewer visitors. 遊客較少。
　　B. Vandalism. 破壞公物。
　　C. Increased security. 安全戒備的加強。
　　D. Community protests. 社區抗議。

　　* protest〔'protɛst〕 *n.* 抗議

高中英聽測驗模擬試題 ⑤ 詳解

一、看圖辨義：第一部分

For question number 1, please look at picture 1.

1. (**D**) Jenny fell down. Her friend Steve is helping her get up.
　　珍妮跌倒了。她的朋友史蒂夫正在扶她起來。

　　　　 * *fall down* 跌倒　　 *get up* 站起來

For question number 2, please look at picture 2.

2. (**C**) Polly is a cheerleader. But she doesn't jump or kick.
　　波麗是個啦啦隊隊員。但她不會跳躍或踢腿。

　　　　 * cheerleader〔'tʃɪr,lidɚ〕 *n.* 啦啦隊隊長
　　　　 jump〔dʒʌmp〕 *v.* 跳　　 kick〔kɪk〕 *v.* 踢

For question number 3, please look at picture 3.

3. (**A**) Jane has insomnia. It's way past her bedtime and she can't fall asleep.

　　珍患有失眠症。已經超過她就寢時間很久了，她仍無法入睡。

　　　* insomnia〔ɪnˋsɑmnɪə〕n. 失眠　　way〔we〕adv. 非常
　　　bedtime〔ˋbɛd͵taɪm〕n. 就寢時間　　**fall asleep** 睡著

For question number 4, please look at picture 4.

4. (**C**) Bobby plays the guitar. Sometimes he plays in public and passersby give him spare change.

　　鮑比會彈吉他。有時候他會公開彈奏，而路人就會給他零錢。

　　　* **play the guitar** 彈吉他　　**in public** 公開地；在公共場合
　　　passerby〔ˋpæsɚ͵baɪ〕n. 路人【複數形為 passersby】
　　　spare〔spɛr〕adj. 多餘的　　change〔tʃendʒ〕n. 零錢

一、看圖辨義：第二部分

For question number 5, please look at picture 5.

5. (**B**、**D**) Which TWO of the following are true about the
picture? 關於這張圖片，下列哪兩項為眞？

 A. Lisa usually gets a ride from her neighbor.
  麗莎通常搭她鄰居的車。

 B. Paul usually takes the bus
  home from school.
  保羅通常從學校搭公車回家。

 C. Everyone on the bus is well-behaved.
  在公車上所有的人都很守規矩。

 D. There's always a lot of fighting on the bus.
  公車上總是有很多打打鬧鬧的事。

 * ride〔raɪd〕*n.* 搭乘；便車　　neighbor〔'nebɚ〕*n.* 鄰居
 well-behaved〔'wɛlbɪ'hevd〕*adj.* 行為端正的；守規矩的
 fighting〔'faɪtɪŋ〕*n.* 打架；吵架

For question number 6, please look at picture 6.

6. (**A**、**C**) Which TWO of the following are true about the
picture? 關於這張圖片，下列哪兩項為眞？

 A. Nancy just got a new bike.
  南西剛買了一台新腳踏車。

 B. Nancy's new bike was stolen.
  南西的新腳踏車被偷了。

 C. Nancy has long hair. 南西留一頭長髮。

 D. Nancy has short hair. 南西留短髮。

 * get〔gɛt〕*v.* 買　　bike〔baɪk〕*n.* 腳踏車
 stolen〔'stolən〕*v.* 偷【steal 的過去分詞】

For question number 7, please look at picture 7.

7. （ **A、B** ） Which TWO of the following are true about the
picture? 關於這張圖片，下列哪兩項爲眞？

　　A. Both boys are wearing pants.
　　　　兩個男孩都穿著褲子。
　　B. Both boys are wearing
　　　　helmets.
　　　　兩個男孩都戴著安全帽。
　　C. One boy is not wearing pants.
　　　　有一個男孩沒有穿褲子。
　　D. One boy is not wearing a helmet.
　　　　有一個男孩沒有戴安全帽。

　　* pants〔pænts〕*n. pl.* 褲子　　helmet〔'hɛlmɪt〕*n.* 安全帽

For question number 8, please look at picture 8.

8. （ **B、C** ） Which TWO of the following are true about the
picture? 關於這張圖片，下列哪兩項爲眞？

　　A. They are waiting for a bus.
　　　　他們在等公車。
　　B. They are riding a train.
　　　　他們在搭火車。
　　C. The woman is pregnant. 那位女士懷孕了。
　　D. The man is carrying groceries.
　　　　那位男士提著許多食品雜貨。

　　* ride〔raɪd〕*v.* 搭乘
　　　pregnant〔'prɛgnənt〕*adj.* 懷孕的
　　　carry〔'kærɪ〕*v.* 攜帶；提著
　　　groceries〔'grosərɪz〕*n. pl.* 食品雜貨

For question number 9, please look at picture 9.

9. (**A、C**) Which TWO of the following are true about the picture? 關於這張圖片，下列哪兩項爲眞？

    A. Oscar likes to play with toys.
奧斯卡喜歡玩玩具。

    B. Oscar doesn't have any toys.
奧斯卡沒有任何玩具。

    C. Oscar is playing with his favorite toy.
奧斯卡在玩他最喜歡的玩具。

    D. Oscar is looking for his favorite toy.
奧斯卡在找他最喜歡的玩具。

    * toy (tɔɪ) *n.* 玩具　　favorite ('fev(ə)rɪt) *adj.* 最喜愛的
look for 尋找

For question number 10, please look at picture 10.

10. (**A、D**) Which TWO of the following are true about the picture? 關於這張圖片，下列哪兩項爲眞？

    A. The older boy has taken the car from the younger boy.
這個大男孩已經拿走小男孩的汽車。

    B. The older boy has given the car to the younger boy. 這個大男孩已經把汽車給了這個小男孩。

    C. The younger boy has his hand on the older boy's head. 這個小男孩把手放在大男孩的頭上。

    D. The younger boy has a look of surprise on his face. 這個小男孩臉上有驚訝的表情。

    * look (lʊk) *n.* 表情　　surprise (sə'praɪz) *n.* 驚訝

二、對答

11. (**D**) Did you finish your homework? 你功課做完了嗎？

    A. They give us too much homework.

       他給我太多功課了。

    B. No, I'll be home after work. 不，我下班後會回家。

    C. You started it. 是你先開始的。

    D. Yes, I'm finished. 是的，我已經做完了。

    * homework〔'hom,wɝk〕*n.* 功課；家庭作業

     after work 下班後　　finished〔'fɪnɪʃt〕*adj.* 完成的

12. (**B**) Your brothers seem to get along very well.

    你的兄弟們似乎相處得很好。

    A. I can't stand my brother, either.

       我也不能忍受我的兄弟。

    B. They are like two peas in a pod. 他們感情相當好。

    C. Of course, she's my sister. 當然，她是我妹妹。

    D. He is very handsome. 他非常帥。

    * seem〔sim〕*v.* 似乎　　***get along*** 相處

     stand〔stænd〕*v.* 忍受　　either〔'iðɚ〕*adv.* 也（不）

     pea〔pi〕*n.* 豌豆　　pod〔pɑd〕*n.* 豆莢

     like two peas in a pod 非常相似（= *very similar*）；非常親密

      （= *very close*）　　handsome〔'hænsəm〕*adj.* 英俊的

13. (**A**) How come your hair always looks perfect?

    為什麼你的頭髮總是看起來這麼完美？

    A. Actually, this is a wig. 其實這是假髮。

    B. I spend a lot of time there. 我花了很多時間在那裡。

    C. Yes, it's naturally blonde. 是啊，我天生就是金髮。

    D. Thanks. I just made it. 謝謝，我剛剛才做好。

* ***How come*** + ***S*** + ***V***. 為什麼～　　look〔luk〕v. 看起來
perfect〔ˈpɝfɪkt〕adj. 完美的
actually〔ˈæktʃʊəlɪ〕adv. 事實上　　wig〔wɪg〕n. 假髮
naturally〔ˈnætʃərəlɪ〕adv. 自然地；天生地
blonde〔blɑnd〕adj.（頭髮）金色的

14. (**B**) What did you wear to the party? 你穿了什麼去參加派對？

  A. It was great. 它很棒。

  B. My black Vera Wang dress. 我的王薇薇黑色禮服。

  C. He was smiling at me. 他當時正對我微笑。

  D. By taxi. 搭計程車。

  * ***Vera Wang*** 王薇薇【美國紐約州時裝設計師，以設計結婚禮服而
  著稱】　dress〔drɛs〕n. 洋裝

15. (**C**) Was Jack late for school this morning?
  今天早上傑克上學遲到了嗎？

  A. You're right. I'll wake up earlier.
   你說得對。我會更早起床的。

  B. All right. That makes sense. 好的。那樣很合理。

  C. No, he was right on time. 沒有，他剛好準時。

  D. Once or twice. 一兩次。

  * late〔let〕adj. 遲到的　　***wake up*** 起床
  all right 好的；對　　***make sense*** 有道理
  right〔raɪt〕adv. 正好；剛好　　***on time*** 準時的

16. (**B**) Do you have your driver's license? 你有駕照嗎？

  A. Yes. I've been eating there since I was a kid.
   是的，我從小就去那邊吃。

  B. Yes. I've been driving for five years now.
   有。我現在已經開車開五年了。

C. No. It's none of my business. 不。這不關我的事。

D. No. I wear contact lenses. 不是。我戴的是隱形眼鏡。

* *driver's license* 駕照

none of one's business 不關某人的事

contact lenses 隱形眼鏡

17. (**A**) I thought the movie was boring. 我覺得這部電影很無聊。

A. I agree. The ending was so predictable.

我同意。它的結局很好猜。

B. Let's sit in the back row. 我們坐後排吧。

C. That's when we left. 那是我們離開的時候。

D. I'm confused. We watched a movie.

我現在很困惑。我們看了一部電影。

* boring〔'borɪŋ〕*adj.* 無聊的　　agree〔ə'gri〕*v.* 同意

ending〔'ɛndɪŋ〕*n.* 結局

predictable〔prɪ'dɪktəbḷ〕*adj.* 可以預料的

back row 後排　　confused〔kən'fjuzd〕*adj.* 困惑的

18. (**C**) That was one of the best concerts I've seen in ages.

那是我長久以來所看過最好的演唱會之一。

A. Yes, it was really cold. 是的，它真的很冷。

B. Thankfully the tickets were free.

幸運的是，票是免費的。

C. Really? I wasn't impressed at all.

真的嗎？我根本沒有被感動到。

D. It certainly was tasty. 它的確很好吃。

* concert〔'kɑnsɝt〕*n.* 音樂會；演唱會　　*in ages* 很久

thankfully〔'θæŋkfəlɪ〕*adv.* 幸虧；幸運的是

ticket〔'tɪkɪt〕*n.* 票；入場券　　free〔fri〕*adj.* 免費的

impressed〔ɪm'prɛst〕*adj.* 印象深刻的；感動的

certainly〔'sɝtṇlɪ〕*adv.* 的確　　tasty〔'testɪ〕*adj.* 好吃的

19. (**A**) Why is your arm in a cast? 為什麼你的手臂上了石膏？

A. I broke it playing basketball. 我打籃球時折斷了。

B. I missed the auditions. 我錯過了試鏡。

C. I found it in the dumpster. 我在垃圾箱裡找到它。

D. I put it on a pedestal. 我把它放在雕像的基座上。

* cast〔kæst〕*n.* 石膏繃紮　　miss〔mɪs〕*v.* 錯過
audition〔ɔ'dɪʃən〕*n.* 試鏡；試演
dumpster〔'dʌmpstɚ〕*n.* 垃圾箱
pedestal〔'pɛdɪstl̩〕*n.* (圓柱、半身像等) 台；基座

20. (**B**) Was anyone hurt in the car accident?
有人在車禍中受傷嗎？

A. It wasn't my fault. 那不是我的錯。

B. The driver of the truck suffered a neck injury.
卡車駕駛頸部受傷。

C. I've never had an accident. 我從來沒有發生過意外。

D. On Route 44. 在 44 號公路上。

* *car accident* 車禍　　fault〔fɔlt〕*n.* 過錯
truck〔trʌk〕*n.* 卡車　　suffer〔'sʌfɚ〕*v.* 遭受
neck〔nɛk〕*n.* 脖子　　injury〔'ɪndʒərɪ〕*n.* 受傷
route〔rut〕*n.* 路；公路【和數字連用，在美國表示幹道的編號】

三、簡短對話

For question 21, you will listen to a short conversation.

M：Inflation is getting worse. The prices of everything are
going up. 通貨膨脹變得更糟了。所有的物價都在上漲。

W：The government needs to step in and do something about
it. 政府需要介入做點事情。

M : It's because of their policies that we're in this mess to
　　begin with. 一開始就是因爲他們的政策才會導致現在的困境。

　　* inflation〔ɪnˈfleʃən〕 *n.* 通貨膨脹
　　get worse 變更糟　　***go up*** 上升；上漲
　　government〔ˈgʌvənmənt〕 *n.* 政府　　***step in*** 介入
　　do something about it 採取行動；想想辦法；做點什麼
　　because of 因爲　　policy〔ˈpɑləsɪ〕 *n.* 政策
　　mess〔mɛs〕 *n.* 混亂；困境　　***to begin with*** 首先；一開始

21. (**B**) Q : What are the speakers mainly discussing?
　　　　　　說話者主要在討論什麼？
　　　　　　A. The weather. 天氣。
　　　　　　B. The economy. 經濟。
　　　　　　C. The military. 軍事。
　　　　　　D. The environment. 環境。

　　* mainly〔ˈmenlɪ〕 *adv.* 主要地
　　discuss〔dɪˈskʌs〕 *v.* 討論　　economy〔ɪˈkɑnəmɪ〕 *n.* 經濟
　　military〔ˈmɪləˌtɛrɪ〕 *adj.* 軍事的　　***the military*** 軍隊；軍方
　　environment〔ɪnˈvaɪrənmənt〕 *n.* 環境

For question 22, you will listen to a short conversation.

M : The light in the bathroom is out again. 廁所的燈又壞了。

W : Didn't you just replace that bulb last week? There must
　　be a problem with the wires.
　　你上禮拜不是才剛換過燈泡？線路一定有問題。

M : I'll call an electrician in the morning. 我早上會打給電工。

　　* out〔aʊt〕 *adj.* 熄滅的　　replace〔rɪˈples〕 *v.* 更換
　　bulb〔bʌlb〕 *n.* 燈泡　　wire〔waɪr〕 *n.* 電線
　　electrician〔ɪˌlɛkˈtrɪʃən〕 *n.* 電工

22. (**D**) Q : What will the man do tomorrow?
　　　　這位男士明天會做什麼？

　　　　A. Go to work. 去上班。
　　　　B. Change the light bulb. 換燈泡。
　　　　C. Fix the wires. 修理電線。
　　　　D. Call an electrician. 打電話給電工。

　　　　* ***light bulb*** 燈泡　　　fix〔fɪks〕*v.* 修理

For question 23, you will listen to a short conversation.

　　M : How's your essay coming along? 你的論文進展得如何？

　　W : Pretty good. My teacher was very pleased with the
　　　　revisions I made. 還不錯。我的老師很滿意我所作的修正。

　　M : So is it finished now? 所以現在已經完成了嗎？

　　W : Not quite. I've still got to type up a final draft and then
　　　　I'll turn it in.
　　　　還沒完全好。我仍然要把最終版本打出來，然後再交。

　　　　* essay〔'ɛse〕*n.* 文章；論文　　***come along*** 進展
　　　　be pleased with 對⋯滿意
　　　　revision〔rɪ'vɪʒən〕*n.* 校訂；修改　　***not quite*** 不完全地
　　　　have got to V. 必須~ (= *have to V.*)　　type〔taɪp〕*v.* 打字
　　　　type up 把⋯打字成文　　draft〔dræft〕*n.* 草稿
　　　　turn in 繳交 (= *hand in*)

23. (**C**) Q : What did the woman do? 這位女士做了什麼？

　　　　A. She typed her essay. 她打了她的論文。
　　　　B. She turned in her essay. 她交了她的論文。
　　　　C. She made changes to her essay. 她修改了她的論文。

D. She asked the man to edit her essay.

      她要求那位男士來校訂改她的論文。

    * ***make changes to*** 修改　　edit〔ˈɛdɪt〕v. 編輯；校訂

For question 24, you will listen to a short conversation.

W : Are they ever going to finish construction on that office
building?　他們那棟辦公大樓到底要不要完工？

M : I don't know.　It's been like that for almost a year.
我不知道。這樣的情況已經快一年了。

W : It looks like they gave up on it.
看起來好像他們已經放棄了。

M : What an awful waste of resources!　真是太浪費資源了！

    * ever〔ˈɛvɚ〕adv. 在任何時候
    construction〔kənˈstrʌkʃən〕n. 建築；施工
    office building 辦公大樓
    it looks like 看起來好像（= *it seems*）
    give up on 放棄　　awful〔ˈɔfʊl〕adj. 很糟的；非常的
    waste〔west〕n. 浪費　　resource〔rɪˈsors〕n. 資源

24. (**C**) Q : What are they talking about?　他們在討論什麼？

    A. The lack of natural resources. 天然資源的匱乏。

    B. Whether or not to rent an office.
      是否要租間辦公室。

    C. An abandoned construction project.
      一個被放棄的建設計畫。

    D. A business transaction. 一個商業交易。

    * lack〔læk〕n. 缺乏　　natural〔ˈnætʃərəl〕adj. 天然的
    rent〔rɛnt〕v. 租

abandoned〔ə'bændənd〕*adj.* 被放棄的
project〔'prɑdʒɪkt〕*n.* 計畫
transaction〔træns'ækʃən〕*n.* 交易；買賣

For questions 25 and 26, you will listen to a short conversation.

M：Do you have an e-mail address?

你有電子郵件地址嗎？

W：You bet. Which would you prefer? GSN, Yeehaw! or

BOL？ 當然。你喜歡那一個？GSN，Yeehaw! 還是 BOL？

M：Geez, why so many? 哇，為什麼那麼多？

W：Well, I use GSN for my friends, Yeehaw! for my family,

and BOL for work.

這個嘛，我用 GSN 聯絡朋友，家人用 Yeehaw!，工作用 BOL。

M：Then I guess I fall in the GSN category, don't I?

那麼我想我是屬於 GSN 這個類別，不是嗎。

* e-mail〔'i,mel〕*n.* 電子郵件
address〔'ædrɛs〕*n.* 地址　　prefer〔prɪ'fɝ〕*v.* 比較喜歡
geez〔dʒiz〕*interj.*【表示驚奇、憤怒等】唉呀
guess〔gɛs〕*v.* 猜；認為　***fall in*** 屬於（= *fall into*）
category〔'kætə,gorɪ〕*n.* 類別

25. (**C**) Q：How many different e-mail addresses does the
woman have? 那位女士有多少不同的電郵地址？

　　A. One. 一個。

　　B. Two. 二個。

　　C. Three. 三個。

　　D. Four. 四個。

26. (**D**) Q : Which of the following does the woman NOT have
a separate e-mail for?

那位女士並沒有在下列哪一個類別使用獨立的電郵帳號？

A. Friends. 朋友。　　　　　B. Family. 家庭。

C. Work. 工作。　　　　　　D. School. 學校。

* separate (ˈsɛpərɪt) *adj.* 不同的；個別的

For questions 27 and 28, you will listen to a short conversation.

W : Oh, no! It looks like it's going to rain again. Don't you
just hate rainy days?

喔，不！看來又要下雨了。你不是很討厭下雨天嗎？

M : Actually, I don't mind the rain at all. It's kind of
soothing. Like a warm shower.　其實我一點也不在意
下雨。雨能使人平靜。就像來個溫暖的淋浴一樣。

W : I think it's depressing. The sky is gray and everything
is all wet.

我覺得雨天令人沮喪。天空灰濛濛的，所有東西都濕濕的。

M : You should try looking at it from a different perspective.

你應該試試從不同的角度來看它。

* hate (het) *v.* 討厭　　rainy (ˈrenɪ) *adj.* 下雨的
actually (ˈæktʃuəlɪ) *adv.* 事實上
mind (maɪnd) *v.* 介意　　*not…at all* 一點也不…
kind of 有一點　　soothing (ˈsuðɪŋ) *adj.* 使人鎮靜的；撫慰的
shower (ˈʃauɚ) *n.* 淋浴
depressing (dɪˈprɛsɪŋ) *adj.* 令人沮喪的
gray (gre) *adj.* 灰色的　　wet (wɛt) *adj.* 濕的
try + *V-ing* 試看看~　　perspective (pɚˈspɛktɪv) *n.* 觀點

27. (**B**) Q : What is the woman's attitude toward rain?

　　　　這位女士對下雨有何看法？

　　　　A. She likes it. 她喜歡下雨。

　　　　B. She hates it. 她討厭下雨。

　　　　C. She doesn't mind it. 她不介意下雨。

　　　　D. She has no opinion. 她沒有意見。

　　　　* attitude ('ætə,tjud) *n.* 態度；看法；感覺
　　　　　opinion (ə'pɪnjən) *n.* 意見

28. (**C**) Q : What is the man's attitude toward rain?

　　　　這位男士對下雨有何看法？

　　　　A. He loves it. 他喜歡下雨。

　　　　B. He hates it. 他討厭下雨。

　　　　C. He doesn't mind it. 他不介意下雨。

　　　　D. He can't live without it. 他不能沒有雨。

For questions 29 and 30, you will listen to a short conversation.

　M : Where's Miranda? 米蘭達在哪裡？

　W : Um…I thought you were going to pick her up on your
　　　way home from work.

　　　嗯…我以為你在下班回家的路上會去接她。

　M : No. You were supposed to pick her up on your way
　　　home from yoga class.

　　　不是。妳應該在上完瑜珈課後回家路上去接她的。

　W : I don't have yoga on Wednesdays, remember?

　　　我禮拜三沒有瑜珈課，你記得嗎？

M：Oh, my gosh, you're right. What time is it? She's probably furious by now.

噢，天啊，妳說得對。現在幾點了？她現在可能很生氣。

pick sb. up 接某人　　um〔ʌm〕*interj.*【表示遲疑】嗯
be supposed to V. 應該～　　yoga〔'jogə〕*n.* 瑜珈
probably〔'prɑbəblɪ〕*adv.* 可能
furious〔'fjʊrɪəs〕*adj.* 狂怒的　　*by now* 現在

29. (**A**) Q：Why isn't Miranda at home? 爲什麼米蘭達不在家？

　　A. The man forgot to pick her up. 這位男士忘了去接她。

　　B. The man didn't want to pick her up.
　　　　這位男士不想去接她。

　　C. The woman forgot to call her. 這位女士忘了打給她。

　　D. The woman didn't pick her up.
　　　　這位女士沒有去接她。

30. (**D**) Q：What does the man imply about Miranda?

　　　　關於米蘭達的情況，這位男士暗示什麼？

　　A. She is probably unconcerned about the situation.
　　　　她可能不關心這個情況。

　　B. She is probably confused by her parents.
　　　　她可能被父母弄糊塗了。

　　C. She is probably walking home. 她可能正走路回家。

　　D. She is probably angry for having to wait.
　　　　她可能因爲必須等待而生氣。

imply〔ɪm'plaɪ〕*v.* 暗示
unconcerned〔͵ʌnkən'sɝnd〕*adj.* 不關心的
situation〔͵sɪtʃu'eʃən〕*n.* 情況
confuse〔kən'fjuz〕*v.* 使混亂；使糊塗

四、短文聽解

Questions 31 and 32 are based on the following report.

　　Shopping at farmers' markets is the easiest way to eat locally. You know where the food comes from. After all, the growers are right there and you can ask them. More than one shopper, however, has come home with bags of produce that went uneaten. And many others have left after a morning's tour around the stalls only to go home with a bunch of carrots and a dazed expression. A bit of planning can keep weekly shopping for produce at a farmer's market fun and make cooking a snap all week long.

　　在農夫市集買東西是吃當地食材最簡單的方式。你知道食物是從哪裡來的。畢竟種的人就在那裡,你可以問他們。不過,有不少購物的顧客都會大包小包的帶著未食用的農產品回家。也有很多人會逛一個早上後,帶著一大堆紅蘿蔔及茫然的表情回家。稍微計畫一下就可以使每週在農夫市場買菜變得有趣,而且可以把一整週的料理輕鬆搞定。

** ────────────

shop〔ʃɑp〕v. 購物
farmers' market 農夫市集【直接與農夫買,與一般傳統市場不同,市集大多由農夫現場介紹自家種植的蔬果,稱斤稱兩地聊天,藉由直接的交易,讓農夫獲得最多的利潤,讓民眾以第一手的價格買到好物】
locally〔'lokəlɪ〕adv. 在本地　　　*after all* 畢竟
grower〔'groɚ〕n. 栽培者;種植商
produce〔'prɑdjus〕n. 農產品　　shopper〔'ʃɑpɚ〕n. 購物的顧客
go〔go〕v. 處於…狀態　　uneaten〔ʌn'itn̩〕adj. 未吃的
tour〔tur〕n. 遊覽;參觀　　stall〔stɔl〕n. 攤位
only to V. 結果卻~　　bunch〔bʌntʃ〕n. 一串;大量
carrot〔'kærət〕n. 紅蘿蔔　　dazed〔dezd〕adj. 暈眩的;茫然的

expression〔ɪkˋsprɛʃən〕*n.* 表情　　*a bit of* 一點點的
planning〔ˋplænɪŋ〕*n.* 計畫；規劃
weekly〔ˋwiklɪ〕*adj.* 每週的　　fun〔fʌn〕*adj.* 有趣的
snap〔snæp〕*n.* 輕而易舉的事　　*all week long* 整個禮拜

31. (**A**) What can you buy at a farmers' market?

你在農夫市集裡可以買什麼？

　A. Food. 食物。　　　　B. Office supplies. 辦公用品。
　C. Farming equipment. 農耕設備。
　D. Cookware. 烹飪用具。

* supplies〔səˋplaɪz〕*n. pl.* 供應品；物資
office supplies 辦公用品；文具用品
farming〔ˋfɑrmɪŋ〕*n.* 耕種；農業
equipment〔ɪˋkwɪpmənt〕*n.* 設備
cookware〔ˋkʊkˌwɛr〕*n.* 烹飪用具；炊具

32. (**B**) What is implied about farmers' markets?

關於農夫市集，本文暗示什麼？

　A. They can save consumers a lot of money.
　　農夫市集可以讓消費者省很多錢。
　B. They can be an overwhelming experience.
　　農夫市集可能是個令人不知措的消費經驗。
　C. They can help the national economy.
　　農夫市集可以幫助全國的經濟。
　D. They can reduce food waste.
　　農夫市集可以減少食物浪費。

* imply〔ɪmˋplaɪ〕*v.* 暗示　　consumer〔kənˋsumɚ〕*n.* 消費者
overwhelming〔ˌovɚˋhwɛlmɪŋ〕*adj.* 壓倒性的；令人不知所措的
national〔ˋnæʃənḷ〕*adj.* 全國的
economy〔ɪˋkɑnəmɪ〕*n.* 經濟
reduce〔rɪˋdjus〕*v.* 降低；減少　　waste〔west〕*n.* 浪費

Questions 33 and 34 are based on the following report.

If you suffer with a health issue or simply want to improve an area of your health, there are probably behaviors that you are doing that are standing in your way. We talk a lot about those things that we should be doing for optimum health and well-being, but we don't talk as much about the things we need to stop doing. Sometimes these behaviors are simply things that you do that get in the way of success, like eating the wrong things or succumbing to addictions. Other times you might find yourself engaging in self-blame, isolating yourself, or being afraid to ask for help. No matter what the behavior, it is important to recognize the things that you are doing that are hampering your health and well-being.

如果你有健康問題，或只是想改善你某個部份的健康，可能你在做的某些行為會妨礙你。我們討論了很多我們為了最佳的健康與幸福所該做的事，但我們較少談到應該停止不做的事。有時候這些行為其實就只是會妨礙你成功的事，像是吃錯東西、或無法擺脫上癮的事物。有時你可能會發現你苛責自己、孤立自己，或害怕尋求幫助。無論是哪種行為，認清那些你所正在做、會妨礙你健康幸福的事情，是很重要的。

** ——————————————

suffer with 因⋯而感到不適　　health〔hɛlθ〕*n.* 健康
issue〔'ɪʃu〕*n.* 議題；問題　　probably〔'prɑbəblɪ〕*adv.* 可能
behavior〔bɪ'hevjɚ〕*n.* 行為
stand in one's **way** 擋住某人的路；妨礙某人
optimum〔'ɑptəməm〕*adj.* 最佳的

well-being〔'wɛl'biɪŋ〕n. 幸福
simply〔'sɪmplɪ〕adv. 僅僅；只
get in the way of 阻擋；妨礙　　success〔sək'sɛs〕n. 成功
succumb〔sə'kʌm〕v. 屈服　　**succumb to** 向…屈服
addiction〔ə'dɪkʃən〕n. 上癮
engage〔ɪn'gedʒ〕v. 從事；忙於 < in >
self-blame〔'sɛlf'blem〕n. 自責　　isolate〔'aɪsḷ,et〕v. 使孤立
afraid〔ə'fred〕adj. 害怕的　　**ask for** 請求
recognize〔'rɛkəg,naɪz〕v. 辨識　　hamper〔'hæmpɚ〕v. 妨礙

33. (**B**) What is the speaker mainly discussing?

這位說話者主要是在討論什麼？

A. Academic achievement. 學術成就。

B. Health and well-being. 健康與幸福。

C. The keys to success. 成功的關鍵。

D. Motivational weight-loss techniques.

激勵減重的技巧。

* mainly〔'menlɪ〕adv. 主要地
　 discuss〔dɪ'skʌs〕v. 討論
　 academic〔,ækə'dɛmɪk〕adj. 學術的
　 achievement〔ə'tʃivmənt〕n. 成就
　 key〔ki〕n. 關鍵 < to >
　 motivational〔,motə'veʃənḷ〕adj. 激發性的；誘導的
　 weight-loss adj. 減重的
　 technique〔tɛk'nik〕n. 技巧；方法

34. (**A**) What is suggested by the speaker? 說話者暗示什麼？

A. Behavior is related to well-being.

行為和幸福有關。

B. Addiction is the cause of most health issues.

上癮是大多數的健康問題的原因。

C. Talking about health will increase your well-being.
　　討論健康會增進幸福。

D. Most people are afraid to ask for help.
　　大多數的人害怕尋求協助。

* suggest〔sə(g)ˈdʒɛst〕v. 建議；暗示；表示
  be related to 和…有關　　cause〔kɔz〕n. 原因
  increase〔ɪnˈkris〕v. 增加

Questions 35 and 36 are based on the following report.

Good afternoon, ladies and gentlemen, and welcome aboard the Victoria Marie. This is your captain speaking. In just a few minutes we'll depart for our cruise of the San Francisco Bay and we certainly have a nice day for it, especially compared to yesterday. As a reminder, please remain seated with your safety belts fastened until we have cleared the harbor, at which point a ship steward will indicate when it is safe to move about the cabin and the stern deck. It's also my duty to tell you that federal and state regulations prohibit smoking anywhere on board the vessel and violators are subject to fines.

各位先生，各位女士午安，歡迎搭乘維多莉亞‧瑪莉號。我是船長。再過幾分鐘我們就要出發，在舊金山灣航行，我們肯定會有個晴朗的一天，尤其是與昨天相比的話。提醒您，請勿離開座位。並繫上安全帶直到我們離開港口，到時船上服務員會說明何時可以安全地在船艙內及船尾甲板上走動。同時我也有責任提醒您，聯邦政府與州政府的規定都禁止在船上任何一個地方抽煙，違規者將被處以罰款。

** ─────────────

aboard〔ə'bord〕*prep.* 在（車、船、飛機）上
captain〔'kæptən〕*n.* 船長　　depart〔dɪ'pɑrt〕*v.* 出發
depart for 前往（= *leave for* ）　　cruise〔kruz〕*n.* 巡航
San Francisco 舊金山【美國加利福尼亞州（California）北部】
bay〔be〕*n.* 灣；海灣　　certainly〔'sɜtṇlɪ〕*adv.* 一定
especially〔ə'spɛʃəlɪ〕*adv.* 特別地；尤其
compared to 和⋯相比（= *compared with* ）

reminder〔rɪ'maɪndɚ〕*n.* 提醒物　　remain〔rɪ'men〕*v.* 保持
seated〔'sitɪd〕*adj.* 就座的　　**safety belt** 安全帶
fasten〔'fæsṇ〕*v.* 綁緊；繫上　　clear〔klɪr〕*v.* （船）離（港）
harbor〔'hɑrbɚ〕*n.* 海港；港口
point〔pɔɪnt〕*n.* 時間點；時刻
steward〔'stuwɚd〕*n.* （飛機、輪船等）服務人員
indicate〔'ɪndə,ket〕*v.* 指出；表示
move about 在⋯到處走動（= *move around* ）

cabin〔'kæbɪn〕*n.* 船艙　　stern〔stɜn〕*n.* 船尾
deck〔dɛk〕*n.* 甲板　　duty〔'djutɪ〕*n.* 責任；義務
federal〔'dɛdərəl〕*adj.* 聯邦的　　state〔stet〕*adj.* 州的；州立的
regulation〔,rɛgjə'leʃən〕*n.* 規定；法規
prohibit〔pro'hɪbɪt〕*v.* 禁止　　vessel〔'vɛsḷ〕*n.* 船
on board the vessel 在船上　　violator〔'vaɪə,letɚ〕*n.* 違反者
be subject to 受⋯支配的；遭受　　fine〔faɪn〕*n.* 罰款

35.（**C**）Where is this announcement taking place?
　　這個公告是在哪裡發布的？

　　A. On an airplane. 在飛機上。
　　B. On a bus. 在公車上。
　　C. On a boat. 在船上。
　　D. On a train. 在火車上。

　　* announcement〔ə'naʊnsmənt〕*n.* 公告；宣布事項
　　take place 發生　　airplane〔'ɛr,plen〕*n.* 飛機

36. (**B**)　What does the speaker say about smoking?
　　　說話者說了什麼關於抽煙的事？

　　A.　It's only allowed on the stern deck.
　　　只能在船尾甲板上抽煙。

　　B.　It's not allowed anywhere on the boat.
　　　船上任何地方都禁止抽煙。

　　C.　It's allowed once the boat has cleared the harbor.
　　　只要船一離港就容許抽煙。

　　D.　It's bad for your health.　抽煙對你的健康不好。

　　* allow〔ə'laʊ〕v. 允許　　health〔hɛlθ〕n. 健康

Questions 37 and 38 are based on the following report.

　　A commercial airplane crashed yesterday in Bartonville, about five aeronautical miles from the Dallas-Fort Worth airport, where it was trying to land in bad weather. There is little hope that any of the 127 people on board survived, and though the plane went down in a wheat field, it is possible that there were some casualties on the ground. Investigators are trying to determine the cause of the crash and believe that severe weather—thunderstorms, high winds, and limited visibility—may have played a role. In 2010, another plane flying from Denver to Dallas-Fort Worth crashed during landing, killing 152.

　　一架商用飛機昨天在巴頓維爾墜毀，大約是在距離達拉斯–沃斯機場五個航空英里遠的地方，當時飛機在惡劣的氣候下試圖在那裡降落。機上127人能夠生還的機會很渺茫，儘管飛機在小麥田

裡墜毀，還是有可能造成地面上的一些傷亡。調查人員試圖確定墜
機的原因，認為極端的氣候——雷雨、強風，與受限的能見度——
可能對飛機造成影響。在 2010 年，另一架從丹佛往達拉斯–沃斯堡
的飛機於降落時墜毀，造成 152 人死亡。

**──────────

commercial〔kə'mɝʃəl〕adj. 商業的　　crash〔kræʃ〕v. 墜毀
Bartonville〔'bɑrtənvɪl〕n. 巴頓維爾【位於美國德州】
aeronautical〔ˌɛrə'nɔtɪkḷ〕adj. 航空的　　mile〔maɪl〕n. 英里
Dallas-Fort Worth 達拉斯–沃斯堡【達拉斯（Dallas）位於美國
　　德州（Texas）東北部，和位於西部的沃斯堡（Fort Worth）是一
　　個面積與台北市相當的都會區。達拉斯–沃斯堡的民用機場，是德州
　　最大、最繁忙的機場】
airport〔'ɛr,port〕n. 機場　　land〔lænd〕v. 降落
on board 在飛機上　　survive〔sə'vaɪv〕v. 存活；生還
go down 墜落　　wheat〔hwit〕n. 小麥
field〔fild〕n. 田野　　casualties〔'kæʒʊəltɪ〕n. pl. 死傷人數
investigator〔ɪn'vɛstgə,getə〕n. 調查人員
determine〔dɪ'tɝmɪn〕v. 決定；確定　　cause〔kɔz〕n. 原因
severe〔sə'vɪr〕adj. 惡劣的
thunderstorm〔'θʌndə,stɔrm〕n. 雷雨
high wind 疾風；大風（= *strong wind*）
limited〔'lɪmɪtɪd〕adj. 有限的
visibility〔ˌvɪzə'bɪlətɪ〕n. 能見度　　***play a role*** 起作用
Denver〔'dɛnvə〕n. 丹佛【美國科羅拉多州（Colorado）的首都】
kill〔kɪl〕v. 使喪生

37. (**C**) What is this report about? 這份報告是關於什麼？

    A. Bad weather. 壞天氣。

    B. A natural disaster. 天災。

    C. A plane crash. 墜機。

    D. Dallas-Fort Worth. 達拉斯–沃斯堡。

    * natural〔'nætʃərəl〕adj. 天然的　　disaster〔dɪz'æstə〕n. 災難

38. (**B**) What are investigators trying to determine?

調查員試著確定什麼？

A. The number of casualties on the ground.

地面上的傷亡人數。

B. The cause of the crash. 墜機的原因。

C. Where the crash occurred. 墜機發生的地點。

D. How many passengers were on the plane.

有多少乘客在飛機上。

* occur〔ə'kɝ〕v. 發生　　passenger〔'pæsn̩dʒɚ〕n. 乘客

Questions 39 and 40 are based on the following report.

Here's a tip that will change your relationships with people forever: Let them be who they want to be. Don't try to change them or what they believe. Understand that everyone has an opinion based on the unique things that have gone on in their life. Change your focus from "Why doesn't my friend vote like I do" to "I want to understand my friend's views about politics and life." Just try and understand, even if you don't agree. It's a challenge, but it can be done.

這裡有個可以永遠改變你人際關係的建議：讓他們隨心所欲地做自己。不要試圖改變他們或他們所相信的事。要了解每個人都有自己的見解，那是基於他生命中所發生的獨特事件而來的。請你把焦點從「為什麼我朋友不跟我投票給一樣的人」轉變成「我想了解我朋友對於政治及生活的看法」。要試著去了解，即使你不同意。這雖然是個挑戰，但卻是可以做得到的。

**

tip〔tɪp〕*n.* 建議　　relationship〔rɪ'leʃənˌʃɪp〕*n.* 關係
forever〔fə'ɛvɚ〕*adv.* 永遠
opinion〔ə'pɪnjən〕*n.* 意見；看法
based on 基於；根據　　unique〔ju'nik〕*adj.* 獨特的
go on 進行；發生　　focus〔'fokəs〕*n.* 關注；焦點
vote〔vot〕*v.* 投票　　view〔vju〕*n.* 觀點
politics〔'pɑləˌtɪks〕*n.* 政治　　agree〔ə'gri〕*v.* 同意
challenge〔'tʃælɪndʒ〕*n.* 挑戰

39. (**C**) What is this talk mainly about? 這段談話的主旨爲何？

A. Personal hygiene. 個人衛生。
B. Personal finance. 個人財務。
C. Personal relationships. 人際關係。
D. Personal aspirations. 個人的抱負。

* mainly〔'menlɪ〕*adv.* 主要地
personal〔'pɝsn̩l〕*adj.* 個人的
hygiene〔'haɪdʒin〕*n.* 衛生
finance〔fə'næns〕*n.* 財務
aspiration〔ˌæspə'reʃən〕*n.* 渴望；抱負

40. (**A**) What does the speaker advise? 說話者建議什麼？

A. Keep an open mind. 保持開闊的心胸。
B. Don't show emotion. 不要展現情緒。
C. Choose friends wisely. 明智地選擇朋友。
D. Challenge your beliefs. 質疑你朋友的信念。

* advise〔əd'vaɪz〕*v.* 建議　　***open mind*** 開闊的心胸
emotion〔ɪ'moʃən〕*n.* 情感；情緒
wisely〔'waɪzlɪ〕*adv.* 明智地　　belief〔bɪ'lif〕*n.* 信念
challenge〔'eʃælɪnd〕*v.* 向…挑戰；質疑

高中英聽測驗模擬試題 ⑥ 詳解

一、看圖辨義：第一部分

For question number 1, please look at the four pictures.

1. (**D**) Larry enjoys fried chicken. He can eat a whole bucket
in one sitting. 賴瑞喜歡吃炸雞。他一次可以吃一整桶。

　　　* enjoy〔ɪnˋdʒɔɪ〕v. 喜歡　　　*fried chicken* 炸雞
　　　whole〔hol〕adj. 整個的　　　bucket〔ˋbʌkɪt〕n. 桶
　　　sitting〔ˋsɪtɪŋ〕n. 一次（坐著活動的時間）

For question number 2, please look at the four pictures.

2. (**B**) Tim plays baseball. He is waiting for the next pitch.
提姆會打棒球。他正在等待下一個投過來的球。

　　　* pitch〔pɪtʃ〕n. 投球

For question number 3, please look at the four pictures.

3. (**B**) Larry is listening to loud music in his bedroom. His mother is angry because she is trying to use the telephone. 賴瑞正在臥室裡大聲地聽音樂。他媽媽因為要講電話所以很生氣。

For question number 4, please look at the four pictures.

4. (**A**) The man was pulled over for drinking. The policeman is on a motorcycle.

這男士因為酒駕被要求停車。警察坐在摩托車上。

* ***pull over*** 令…停靠路邊
motorcycle〔ˈmotəˌsaɪkl̩〕 *n.* 摩托車

一、看圖辨義：第二部分

For question number 5, please look at picture 5.

5. (**B、D**) Which TWO of the following are true about the
picture? 關於這張圖片，下列哪兩項為真？

    A. They are standing.
      他們正站著。
    B. They are seated.
      他們坐著。
    C. They are wearing glasses. 他們戴著眼鏡。
    D. They are studying. 他們正在讀書。

For question number 6, please look at picture 6.

6. (**A、C**) Which TWO of the following are true about the
picture? 關於這張圖片，下列哪兩項為真？

    A. There is a book on the table.
      桌上有一本書。
    B. There are two people at the
      table. 有兩個人在桌子旁邊。
    C. The man on the left has just told a joke.
      在左邊的這位男士剛剛說了一個笑話。
    D. The woman in the middle has just gotten some
      bad news.
      中間這位女士剛才得知了某個壞消息。

For question number 7, please look at picture 7.

7. (**B、D**) Which TWO of the following are true about the
picture? 關於這張圖片，下列哪兩項為真？

A. They are waiting to board a ferry.

他們正等著上渡輪。

B. They will now board the bus.

他們現在將要上公車。

C. A man is exiting the train.

一位男士正在下火車。

D. The woman is second in line.

這位女士排在隊伍第二個位置。

* board〔bord〕v. 上（車、船、飛機）

ferry〔'fɛrɪ〕n. 渡輪 exit〔'ɛgzɪt〕v. 離開；退出

line〔laɪn〕n. 隊伍

For question number 8, please look at picture 8.

8. (**C**、**D**) Which TWO of the following are true about the picture? 關於這張圖片，下列哪兩項為真？

A. The students are in the cafeteria.

這群學生在自助餐廳裡。

B. The students are watching a film. 這群學生正在看電影。

C. The students are in a computer lab.

這群學生在電腦教室裡。

D. The students are working together on a project.

這群學生正在一起做專題報告。

* cafeteria〔ˌkæfə'tɪrɪə〕n. 自助餐廳

film〔fɪlm〕n. 電影 lab〔læb〕n. 實驗室

computer lab 電腦教室

project〔'prɑdʒɛkt〕n. 專題研究；計劃

For question number 9, please look at picture 9.

9. (**A、B**) Which TWO of the following are true about the
picture? 關於這張圖片，下列哪兩項爲眞？

A. Irene feels lonely.
艾琳覺得寂寞。

B. Irene is sitting by herself
on the curb.
艾琳正獨自坐在人行道旁。

C. Ashley and Andy are walking their dogs.
艾胥黎和安迪正在遛狗。

D. Ashley and Andy are holding hands.
艾胥黎和安迪正手牽著手。

* lonely (ˈlonlɪ) *adj.* 寂寞的　　***by oneself*** 獨自
curb (kɝb) *n.* 人行道的邊石　　***walk a dog*** 遛狗
hold hands 手挽著手；手牽著手

For question number 10, please look at picture 10.

10. (**A、C**) Which TWO of the following are true about the
picture? 關於這張圖片，下列哪兩項爲眞？

A. They are in an airport.
他們在機場裡。

B. They are in a jewelry store.
他們在珠寶店裡。

C. There is a man behind the counter.
有個男士在櫃台後面。

D. There is a woman behind the counter.
有個女士在櫃台後面。

* airport (ˈɛrˌport) *n.* 機場　　jewelry (ˈdʒuəlrɪ) *n.* 珠寶
counter (ˈkaʊntɚ) *n.* 櫃台

二、對答

11. (**B**) Is that your phone ringing? 是你的手機在響嗎？
      A. No, I didn't call you. 不是，我沒有打給你。
      B. No. Mine is on "vibrate." 不是，我的是轉震動模式。
      C. Yes, I'll ring it. 是的，我會響鈴。
      D. Yes. I can't help it. 是的，我忍不住。
      * ring〔rɪŋ〕v.（鈴）響；使鳴響　　*on vibrate* 轉震動模式
      can't help it 忍不住

12. (**A**) Were you surprised by the announcement?
      你對這項宣布很驚訝嗎？
      A. Shocked is more like it. 還不如說是很震驚。
      B. One at a time. 一次一個。
      C. Work hard, play hard. 努力工作，盡情玩樂。
      D. Turn it down. It's too loud. 關小聲一點，太大聲了。
      * announcement〔ə'naʊnsmənt〕n. 宣布
      shocked〔ʃɑkt〕adj. 震驚的　　*more like it* 還差不多
      at a time 一次　　*turn down* 關小聲

13. (**B**) What did you have for lunch? 你午餐吃了什麼？
      A. Twelve. 十二點。　　　　B. Pizza. 披薩。
      C. Numerous. 數不清。　　D. Cold. 很冷。
      * numerous〔'njumərəs〕adj. 許多的

14. (**D**) How was baseball practice? 棒球練習得如何？
      A. We lost. 我們輸了。
      B. Nine players on each team. 每隊九名選手。
      C. I'm a shortstop. 我是游擊手。
      D. It was a lot of fun. 很好玩。
      * player〔'pleə〕n. 選手　　team〔tim〕n. 隊
      shortstop〔'ʃɔrt,stɑp〕n. 游擊手　　fun〔fʌn〕n. 樂趣；有趣

15. (**B**) You've been to Taipei before, haven't you?
　　你以前去過台北，不是嗎？
　　A. Sometimes. 有時候。　B. Yes, I have. 是的，我去過。
　　C. Unless we go to Taipei. 除非我們去台北。
　　D. No, I won't. 不，我不會去。
　　* ***have been to*** 曾經去過　　unless〔ʌnˈlɛs〕 *n.* 除非

16. (**C**) Don't you think Julie is pretty? 你不覺得茉莉很漂亮嗎？
　　A. They sure will. I can't put my finger on it.
　　　他們一定會。我還不能確定。
　　B. He certainly is. I can't make head or tail of it.
　　　他的確是。我根本不了解這件事。
　　C. I sure do. I can't take my eyes off her.
　　　我當然覺得。我的視線無法離開她。
　　D. Just kidding. I can't keep a secret.
　　　開玩笑的。我不能保守秘密。
　　* ***put*** one's ***finger on*** 明確地指出；親自動手做
　　　cannot make head or tail of 根本不了解
　　　take one's ***eyes off*** 使眼睛離開；不看
　　　kid〔kɪd〕 *v.* 開玩笑　　***keep a secret*** 保守秘密

17. (**A**) Is this software free? 這軟體是免費的嗎？
　　A. No, this is a demo version. You have to pay for the
　　　real thing. 不是，這是試用版。你必須付費買正版的。
　　B. No, there are hidden messages. You have to pay
　　　attention. 不是，有隱藏訊息。你必須專心。
　　C. Yes, he guards the house. We've never had a
　　　problem. 是的，他會看家。我們從沒發生過問題。
　　D. Yes, it requires a fee. We've used it before.
　　　是的，它要收費。我們以前用過它。

* software (ˈsɔftˌwɛr) n. 軟體
　　demo (ˈdɛmo) n. 【電腦】試用軟體
　　version (ˈvɝʒən) n. 版本　　**demo version** 試用版
　　hidden (ˈhɪdn̩) adj. 隱藏的　　guard (gɑrd) v. 看守
　　require (rɪˈkwaɪr) v. 需要　　fee (fi) n. 費用

18. (**A**) Is the Internet working or not? 網路是否正常運作？

　　A. They're trying to fix it right now. 他們正在努力修復。

　　B. I saw it on the Internet. 我在網路上看到它。

　　C. Check my web page when you have time.
　　　　你有時間的時候上我的網頁看看。

　　D. Your inbox is full already. 你的收件匣已經滿了。

　　* **web page** 網頁　　inbox (ˈɪnˌbɑks) n. 收件匣；信箱

19. (**C**) You're late again. 你又遲到了。

　　A. They ordered the fish. 他們點了魚。

　　B. The water was cold, so I went home.
　　　　那水很冷，所以我就回家了。

　　C. My alarm didn't go off this morning.
　　　　我的鬧鐘今天早上沒有響。

　　D. I'm going to be late. 我要遲到了。

　　* order (ˈɔrdɚ) v. 點（餐）
　　alarm (əˈlɑrm) n. 鬧鐘（ = alarm clock ）
　　go off （警報、鬧鐘）響

20. (**B**) What happened to the ice cream?
　　那個冰淇淋發生了什麼事？

　　A. Jimmy drank it all. 吉米把它喝光了。

　　B. Jimmy ate it all. 吉米把它吃光了。

　　C. Jimmy cooked it all. 吉米把它全部都煮了。

　　D. Jimmy read it all. 吉米把它讀完了。

三、簡短對話

For question 21, you will listen to a short conversation.

M：How is school going? 學校課業還好吧？

W：Great but…I'm having a difficult time in English.
很好，但是…我有英文學習困難。

M：Why don't you hire a tutor? 妳何不請個家教？

W：Um…because I can't afford one. I'm just a poor college
student. 嗯…因爲我負擔不起。我只是個窮大學生。

　* school〔skul〕*n.* 學業；功課　　hire〔haɪr〕*v.* 雇用
　tutor〔'tjutɚ〕*n.* 家教　　afford〔ə'fɔrd〕*v.* 負擔得起
　poor〔pur〕*adj.* 窮的；可憐的

21.（**B**）Q：Why doesn't the woman hire a tutor?
爲什麼這位女士沒有請家教？
A. She's afraid of speaking. 她很怕說話。
B. She can't afford it. 她負擔不起。
C. She is thinking of dropping out. 她在考慮休學。
D. She works odd hours. 她的工作時間沒有規律。

　* ***drop out*** 輟學　　odd〔ɑd〕*adj.* 奇怪的；零星的；臨時的
　work odd hours 工作時間沒有規律

For question 22, you will listen to a short conversation.

M：Are you an animal lover? 妳是動物愛好者嗎？

W：Sure! I wish I could have a pet but we can't have them.
My sister has really bad allergies. 當然！我希望能養一隻
寵物，但是我們不能養。我妹妹有嚴重過敏。

M：That's too bad. Do you prefer dogs or cats?
太可惜了。妳比較喜歡狗還是貓？

W : If I had a choice, I'd have a dog.
嗯，如果讓我來選，我會選狗。

M : Me too. They're so lovable. 我也是，牠們好可愛。

* pet〔pɛt〕n. 寵物　　**have a pet** 養寵物（= keep a pet）
bad〔bæd〕adj. 嚴重的　　allergy〔'ælərdʒɪ〕n. 過敏症
prefer〔prɪ'fɝ〕v. 比較喜歡　　lovable〔'lʌvəbḷ〕adj. 可愛的

22. (**D**) Q : What does the woman imply? 這位女士暗示什麼？

A. Pets aren't allowed in her apartment building.
她的公寓不允許養寵物。

B. Dogs are very lovable. 狗非常可愛。

C. She wishes she didn't have so many pets.
她希望她沒有這麼多寵物。

D. Her sister can't be around pets.
她的妹妹不能跟寵物處在一塊。

* imply〔ɪm'plaɪ〕v. 暗示　　allow〔ə'laʊ〕v. 允許
around〔ə'raʊnd〕prep. 在…附近

For question 23, you will listen to a short conversation.

M : Did you hear about John? 妳有聽過約翰的事嗎？

W : Yes, he had a terrible accident. Do you know if he's
going to be OK?
有，他發生嚴重的意外。你知道他的情況會是否會好轉嗎？

M : He's in intensive care right now, but they expect him to
make it. 他現在在加護病房，但他們希望他能撐過去。

* terrible〔'tɛrəbḷ〕adj. 可怕的；非常嚴重的
intensive〔ɪn'tɛnsɪv〕adj. 密集的　　care〔kɛr〕n. 照顧
intensive care 加護病房（= intensive care unit）
make it 成功；辦到；（病痛等）好轉；得救

23. (**B**) Q : What does the man imply?　這位男士暗示什麼？

    A. John had it coming.　約翰自作自受。

    B. John will probably survive.　約翰可能活得下來。

    C. John is a poor driver.　約翰是一個差勁的駕駛人。

    D. John won't live another day.　約翰活不過今天。

    * ***have it coming*** 應得報應；活該

    survive〔sər'vaɪv〕*v.* 存活；生還

For question 24, you will listen to a short conversation.

W : Do you frequently use e-mail?　你經常使用電子郵件嗎？

M : No, I seldom use it.　不，我很少用。

W : How do you communicate with people?
　　你都怎樣跟人溝通聯絡？

M : By talking to them.　用說的。

    * frequently〔'frikwəntlɪ〕*adv.* 時常
    e-mail〔'i,mel〕*n.* 電子郵件
    communicate〔kə'mjunə,ket〕*v.* 溝通；聯繫；通信

24. (**A**) Q : What does the woman imply?　這位女士暗示什麼？

    A. She relies on e-mail to communicate with people.
       她靠電子郵件跟人聯絡。

    B. She thinks the Internet is a waste of time.
       她認為網路很浪費時間。

    C. She doesn't have time to use e-mail.
       她沒有時間用電子郵件。

    D. She wants the man to open up about his feelings.
       她想要這位男士毫無保留地說出他的感受。

    * ***rely on*** 依靠　　waste〔west〕*n.* 浪費
    open up 自由自在地談；沒有拘束地談；暢談

For questions 25 and 26, you will listen to a short conversation.

> W : You're home early. What's going on?
>
> 你提早到家了。怎麼了？
>
> M : I'm not feeling very well.　我覺得不太舒服。
>
> W : Do you need to see a doctor?　你需要看醫生嗎？
>
> M : No, I don't think so. I just need to get some rest. The last few weeks have been a killer. 不，我想不用。我只需要休息一下。過去這幾個禮拜快把我累死了。

> * rest〔rɛst〕n. 休息
>
> killer〔ˈkɪlə〕n. 殺手；導致死亡的人、動物或事物

25. (**D**) Q : Why is the man home early?

　　　 為什麼這位男士提早回家？

A. The boss sent everyone home.　老闆送每個人回家。

B. He has a doctor's appointment.　他與醫生有約。

C. The alarm went off.　鬧鐘響了。

D. He doesn't feel well.　他覺得不太舒服。

> * appointment〔əˈpɔɪntmənt〕n. 約會；約診
>
> alarm〔əˈlɑrm〕n. 鬧鐘（= *alarm clock*）　　*go off*（鬧鐘）響

26. (**A**) Q : What does the man imply?　這個男士暗示什麼？

A. He is tired rather than seriously ill.

　　他只是累了，不是病得很嚴重。

B. He is angry with his co-workers.　他很氣他的同事。

C. He is capable of murder.　他有能力殺人。

D. He is afraid of doctors.　他怕醫生。

> * *rather than* 而不是　　　*be seriously ill* 病得很嚴重
>
> co-worker〔koˈwɜkə〕n. 同事
>
> capable〔ˈkepəbəl〕adj. 有能力的
>
> *be capable of* 能夠　　murder〔ˈmɜdə〕n. 謀殺

For questions 27 and 28, you will listen to a short conversation.

W：I don't mean to be rude but, how old are you?
　　我無意對你無禮，但請問你幾歲？

M：I'll be fifty-four in August.　我八月就滿五十四歲了。

W：Wow! You don't look a day over thirty-five. How do
　　you do it?　哇啊！你看起來不超過三十五歲。你怎麼辦到的？

M：I really don't know. Positive thinking, I guess. You're
　　only as young as you feel, right?　我真的不知道。我想是
　　正面思考吧。妳感覺有多年輕自己就多年輕，不是嗎？

　　* *mean to V.* 故意　　　rude〔rud〕*adj.* 無禮的
　　positive〔'pɑzətɪv〕*adj.* 正面的

27. (**A**) Q：What does the woman imply?　這位女士暗示什麼？

　　A. It may be considered rude to ask someone's age.
　　　　問別人年紀可能被認為是很沒禮貌的。

　　B. The man is overweight.　這個男士體重超重。

　　C. She prefers dating older men.
　　　　她比較喜歡跟年紀較大的男性約會。

　　D. Positive thinking is superstition.　正面思考是迷信。

　　* consider〔kən'sɪdɚ〕*v.* 認為
　　overweight〔'ovɚ'wet〕*adj.* 體重過重的
　　date〔det〕*v.* 和…約會　　superstition〔ˌsupɚ'stɪʃən〕*n.* 迷信

28. (**B**) Q：How old is the man right now?　這位男士現在幾歲？

　　A. He turned fifty-four in August.
　　　　他八月的時候就五十四歲了。【過去式 turned 應改為未來
　　　　式 will turn】

　　B. Fifty-three.　五十三歲。

C. Only as old as he feels. 只要他覺得年紀有多大就多大。

D. Thirty-five and a day. 三十五歲又多一天。

    * turn〔tɝn〕v. 變成

For questions 29 and 30, you will listen to a short conversation.

W : How was your date with Kim last night?
　　你昨晚與金的約會怎麼樣?

M : It wasn't a date. We're just friends.
　　那不是約會。我們只是朋友。

W : Since when do you take your "friends" to dinner and a
　　movie? 什麼時候開始你會帶你的「朋友們」去吃晚餐和看電影?

M : Look, it's not what you think. We went Dutch on
　　everything. 哎,不是妳所想的那樣。我們都各付各的。

    * date〔det〕n. 約會　　look〔lʊk〕interj. 哎;喂;注意
　　go Dutch 各付各的

29. (**B**) Q: What did the man do last night?
　　　　　　　這位男士昨晚做了什麼事?

    A. Return from a foreign country. 從國外回來。

    B. Go to dinner and a movie. 去吃晚餐和看電影。

    C. Ask Kim out on a date. 約金出去約會。

    D. Make many friends. 交很多朋友。

    * **ask** sb. **out on a date** 約人出去約會

30. (**C**) Q: What does "went Dutch" mean?
　　　　　　　"went Dutch" 的意思是什麼?

    A. Refused to pay. 拒絕付錢。

    B. Covered the check. 支付支票。

C. Split the bill. 分開結帳。

D. Asked for a refund. 要求退款。

*refuse〔rɪˋfjuz〕v. 拒絕　　cover〔ˋkʌvɚ〕v. 支付
　check〔tʃɛk〕n. 支票　　split〔splɪt〕v. 使分裂；分攤
　bill〔bɪl〕n. 帳單　　refund〔ˋrifʌnd〕n. 退款

四、短文聽解

Questions 31 and 32 are based on the following report.

Studies suggest that optimistic, satisfied, and happy people have a lower risk of heart disease and stroke. Among the most optimistic individuals, risk was found to be 50 percent lower. While healthier people may tend to be happier people, researchers believe that a positive outlook can positively impact heart and cardiovascular health in a number of ways. Firstly, a sense of well-being could help lower blood pressure and cholesterol. In addition, people who are optimistic tend to be more inclined to engage in healthy behaviors like exercising and eating well.

研究顯示，樂觀、滿足、快樂的人，罹患心臟病及中風的風險較低。在最樂觀的人當中，風險相對低了百分之 50。雖然較健康的人也往往是比較開心的，研究人員相信，正向的人生觀透過某些方式對心血管健康有正面的影響。第一，幸福感能有助於降低血壓及膽固醇。此外，樂觀的人也比較容易參與健康的行為，像是運動及健康的飲食。

**

study〔ˋstʌdɪ〕n. 研究　　suggest〔səˋdʒɛst〕v. 顯示
optimistic〔ɑptɪˋmɪstɪk〕adj. 樂觀的

satisfied (ˈsætɪsˌfaɪd) *adj.* 滿足的　　risk (rɪsk) *n.* 風險
stroke (strok) *n.* 中風　　individual (ˌɪndəˈvɪdʒʊəl) *n.* 個人
positive (ˈpazətɪv) *adj.* 正面的；積極的
researcher (rɪˈsɝtʃɚ) *n.* 研究人員　　***tend to*** 易於；傾向於
outlook (ˈaʊtˌlʊk) *n.* 看法　　impact (ˈɪmˌpækt) *v.* 衝擊；影響
cardiovascular (ˌkardɪoˈvæskjələ) *adj.* 心血管的
sense (sɛns) *n.* 感覺　　well-being (ˈwɛlˈbiɪŋ) *n.* 幸福
lower (ˈloɚ) *v.* 降低　　***blood pressure*** 血壓
cholesterol (kəˈlɛstəˌrol) *n.* 膽固醇　　***in addition*** 此外
be inclined to V. 傾向於　　engage (ɪnˈgedʒ) *v.* 從事 < in >
behavior (bɪˈhevjɚ) *n.* 行為

31. (**D**) What is this talk mainly about? 這段談話主要是關於什麼？

    A. Money. 金錢。　　　　B. Psychology. 心理學。
    C. Society. 社會。　　　　D. Health. 健康。

    * psychology (saɪˈkalədʒɪ) *n.* 心理學
     society (səˈsaɪətɪ) *n.* 社會

32. (**B**) What is the main point of the talk?
    這段談話主要的重點是什麼？

    A. Healthy people have a more positive outlook on life.
       健康的人有更正面的人生觀。

    B. Happy people are less likely to develop heart
       disease. 快樂的人比較不會有心臟病。

    C. Optimistic people tend to eat more.
       樂觀的人容易吃得比較多。

    D. Healthy behavior directly influences a positive
       outlook. 健康的行為直接影響正向的人生觀。

    * ***be likely to*** 可能　　develop (dɪˈvɛləp) *v.* 罹患
     directly (dəˈrɛktlɪ) *adv.* 直接地
     influence (ˈɪnfluəns) *v.* 影響

Questions 33 and 34 are based on the following report.

Hundreds of students, teachers, police officers, city employees and volunteers spent last Friday cleaning up the 80-acre Yellow Pine Park so that it would be a more inviting place to visit. Jackson Middle School students partnered with the Morgan City Police Department and the Taylor County Park and Recreation Department to clean up the park. What a difference it made having the groups combine in an effort to clean the park. The group's effort was one of the most enthusiastic we have seen in some time around the Morgan City region, and it ended up showing a lot of results. We hope to see other efforts around Taylor County like the one last week. It is refreshing to have all the groups working together in unison as one community.

上百位學生、老師、警察、市府員工,及志工,上個禮拜五一起清理了 80 英畝的黃松公園,讓公園成為更吸引人參觀的地方。傑克森中學學生與摩根市警局、泰勒郡公園及休閒管理局一起來打掃公園。讓這些團體結合在一起,努力打掃公園,產生的影響相當大。這些團體的努力,是我們一段時間以來在摩根市地區所看到,最充滿熱忱行動之一,展現了許多的成果。我們希望在泰勒市能看到其他更多像上禮拜大家這麼努力。讓所有團體團結一致,共同合作,非常令人耳目一新。

**

police officer 警官　　employee〔ˋɪmplɔɪˏi〕*n.* 員工
volunteer〔ˏvɑlənˋtɪr〕*n.* 志工　　acre〔ˋekɚ〕*n.* 英畝
pine〔paɪn〕*n.* 松樹　　inviting〔ɪnˋvaɪtɪŋ〕*adj.* 吸引人的
middle school 中學　　partner〔ˋpɑrtnɚ〕*v.* 與⋯搭檔 < *with* >

recreation (ˌrɛkrɪˈəʃən) n. 休閒；娛樂
department (dɪˈpɑrtmənt) n. 部門；部；局
make a difference 產生重大影響　　combine (kəmˈbaɪn) v. 結合
in an effort to 企圖要　　enthusiastic (ɪnˌθjuzɪˈæstɪk) adj. 熱心的
region (ˈridʒən) n. 地區　　***end up + V-ing*** 最後…
refreshing (rɪˈfrɛʃɪŋ) adj. 令人耳目一新的
work together 合作　　***in unison*** 一起；同時
community (kəˈmjunətɪ) n. 社區

33. (**D**) Which was NOT involved in cleaning up the park?
　　　何者沒有參與打掃公園？
　　A. Jackson Middle School. 傑克森中學。
　　B. The Morgan City Police Department. 摩根市警局。
　　C. The Taylor County Park and Recreation Department.
　　　泰勒郡公園及休閒管理局。
　　D. The Committee to Save Yellow Pine Park.
　　　拯救黃松公園委員會。
　　* involved (ɪnˈvɑlvd) adj. 參與的　　save (sev) v. 拯救

34. (**A**) What was the main purpose of cleaning up the park?
　　　打掃公園的主要目的是什麼？
　　A. To make it a more inviting place to visit.
　　　讓公園成為一個更吸引人遊覽的地方。
　　B. To show community spirit. 展現社區精神。
　　C. To improve the reputation of Morgan City.
　　　改善摩根市的名聲。
　　D. To punish the students for poor grades.
　　　懲罰成績差的學生。
　　* improve (ɪmˈpruv) v. 改善
　　reputation (ˌrɛpjəˈteʃən) n. 名聲
　　punish (ˈpʌnɪʃ) v. 懲罰　　grade (gred) n. 成績

Questions 35 and 36 are based on the following report.

Edward Chen, the head of Taiwan's state electricity supplier, has resigned after a steep hike in utility rates prompted outrage, officials said. Taiwan Power Co. (Taipower) has lost $132.2 billion NT ($4.48 billion) since 2008, according to the island's economic ministry, and a 37 percent rise in electricity prices was meant to try to stem the cash outflow. But the public questioned its legitimacy and the company's operations, prompting the government to split the increase into three stages. Taiwan's major opposition party, the Democratic Progressive Party (DPP), has said it will hold a mass protest against the hikes this month, with tens of thousands expected to attend.

官員表示，台灣國家電力供應商負責人艾德華·陳，在電費爆漲造成民怨後，已經辭職。根據台灣經濟部的說法，自從 2008 年來，台電已經損失了一千三百二十二億台幣（即四十四億八千萬美元），漲了百分之三十七的電費，是為了要阻止資金流出。但是大眾質疑這項措施的正當性及公司的營運狀況，促使政府將分三階段漲價。台灣主要的反對黨——民進黨，已表示將會舉行大規模抗議活動，抗議這個月的數次調漲，預計將會有數萬人參加。

＊＊

head〔hɛd〕*n.* 負責人　　state〔stet〕*adj.* 國家的
electricity〔ɪ͵lɛk'trɪsətɪ〕*n.* 電力
supplier〔sə'plaɪ♭〕*n.* 供應商　　resign〔rɪ'zaɪn〕*v.* 辭職
steep〔stip〕*adj.* 陡峭的；（價錢）過高的
hike〔haɪk〕*n.*（薪資、物價等）提高；上漲
utility〔ju'tɪlətɪ〕*n.* 公用事業（鐵路、公車、瓦斯、電力、
　　自來水事業等）　　rate〔ret〕*n.* 費用；價格
prompt〔prɑmpt〕*v.* 促使　　outrage〔'aʊt͵redʒ〕*n.* 憤慨

official〔ə'fɪʃləl〕n. 官員　　lose〔luz〕v. 損失
billion〔'bɪljən〕n. 十億　　ministry〔'mɪnɪstrɪ〕n. 部
economic ministry 經濟部　　rise〔raɪz〕n. 上漲
be meant to 目的是為了　　stem〔stem〕v. 遏止
outflow〔'aut'flo〕n. 流出　　question〔'kwɛstʃən〕v. 質疑
legitimacy〔lɪ'dʒɪtəməsɪ〕n. 正當性
operation〔,ɑpə'reʃən〕n. 經營

split〔splɪt〕v. 使分開（成爲幾部份）
increase〔'ɪnkris〕n. 增加　　stage〔stedʒ〕n. 階段
major〔'medʒɚ〕adj. 主要的；較大的
opposition party 反對黨
Democratic Progress Party 民主進步黨
hold〔hold〕v. 舉行　　mass〔mæs〕adj. 大規模的
protest〔'protɛst〕n. 抗議　　***tens of thousands*** 數萬個
attend〔ə'tɛnd〕v. 參加

35. (**A**) According to the article, why did Chen resign?

依據本文，爲何陳先生要辭職？

A. In response to public outrage over utility rates.

爲了回應電費造成的民怨。

B. In an effort to save money. 爲了要省錢。

C. He was getting old. 他年紀越來越大了。

D. To satisfy the demands of the DPP.

爲了滿足民進黨的要求。

* ***in response to*** 爲了回應　　***in an effort to V.*** 爲了…

demand〔dɪ'mænd〕n. 要求

36. (**D**) What does the DPP plan to do this month?

民進黨這個月計劃要做什麼？

A. Split the utility hikes into three stages.

把電費分成三個階段來調漲。

B. Question the legitimacy of Taipower's finances.
質疑台電財務狀況的正當性。

C. Lose $132 billion NT. 損失一千三百二十億台幣。

D. Hold a public protest. 舉行民衆抗議活動。

* finance〔faɪˈnæns〕n. 財務

Questions 37 and 38 are based on the following report.

When I was a kid, I had an irrationally powerful fear of tsunamis. I swam in the ocean a lot when I was very young, so waves were a big part of my world. Yet I would fret about tsunamis whenever I was near the coast, and to this day I have occasional nightmares about a wave coming out of nowhere and sweeping me away. Looking back, part of what made tsunamis frightening was that I didn't know what they looked like, and my imagination ran wild filling in the gaps. I read what I could find about them. In particular, I remember being just old enough to work my way through this book, and carrying it around with me so I could read the tsunami section over and over.

當我小時候,我對海嘯有很不理性的強烈恐懼。我很小的時候常常在海裡游泳,所以海浪在我的生活中占很大的一部分。然而每當我一靠近海岸,我就會擔心海嘯,而且直到現在,我還是偶爾會做不知從哪來的海嘯把我沖走的惡夢。回顧過去,我會怕海嘯,有一部分是因爲我不了解海嘯是什麼樣子,於是我的想像力太過豐富,塡補了我不知道的部分。我讀了當時我所能找到的關於海嘯的資料。特別是當我夠大可以閱讀這一本書的時候,我把它帶在身邊,這樣我就能一遍又一遍地閱讀海嘯的章節。

** ───────────────────────

irrationally (ɪˈræʃənḷɪ) adv. 不理性地
powerful (ˈpaʊəfəl) adj. 強有大的;威力強大的
tsunami (tsuˈnɑmɪ) n. 海嘯　　　*a lot* 常常
fret (frɛt) v. 煩惱　　　coast (kost) n. 海岸
to this day 直到今天爲止　　　occasional (əˈkeʃənḷ) adj. 偶爾的
nightmare (ˈnaɪtˌmɛr) n. 惡夢
come out of nowhere 不知從何而來
sweep ~ away 把~沖走　　　*look back* 回顧;回想
frightening (ˈfraɪtṇɪŋ) adj. 可怕的
imagination (ɪˌmædʒəˈneʃən) n. 想像力
run wild 失去控制;不受約束　　　*fill in* 填補
gap (gæp) n. 裂縫;缺口　　　*in particular* 尤其;特別是
work one's way through 從頭到尾閱讀或做某事
around (əˈraʊnd) adv. 到處
section (ˈsɛkʃən) n. 部分　　　*over and over* 一再;反覆

37. (**A**) What is a tsunami? 什麼是海嘯?

　　A. An ocean wave. 一種海浪。
　　B. A tropical storm. 熱帶風暴。
　　C. A major earthquake. 大地震。
　　D. A Japanese book. 日文書。

　　* tropical (ˈtrɑpɪkḷ) adj. 熱帶的　　　major (ˈmedʒə) adj. 較大的

38. (**C**) What did the speaker do when he was young?
　　說話者小的時候做了什麼事?

　　A. He learned to surf. 他學衝浪。
　　B. He stayed away from the coast. 他遠離海岸。
　　C. He read everything he could about tsunamis.
　　　他讀了所有他找得到的有關海嘯的資料。
　　D. He stopped going to sleep. 他停止睡覺。

　　* surf (sɝf) v. 衝浪　　　*stay away from* 遠離

Questions 39 and 40 are based on the following report.

I'll be in Newport News, Virginia, this April 4th to give a talk at my old school, Christopher Newport University. I'm really looking forward to it! The chaos of the past year and a half didn't leave me with much time or energy for travel or events, so it'll be fun to get out and meet people again. I'm also looking forward to seeing the campus, which I hear has changed substantially since I left. The talk isn't limited to CNU students, so if you live nearby, you're welcome to come! Admission is free, but since space is limited, you'll need to reserve tickets. Hope to see you there!

四月四日維吉尼亞州的新港新聞節目中，將會播出我在我的母校克里斯多夫新港大學的演講。我真的很期待！過去一年半的混亂讓我沒有很多時間或精力去旅遊或參加大型活動，所以能再出去與人見面將會很有趣。我也很期待去看一看校園，我聽說校園從我離開後變了很多。這場演講並不侷限於克里斯多夫新港大學的學生，因此如果你住附近的話，很歡迎你來！不收入場費，但是因為空間有限，你必須要預先訂票。希望能在那裡見到你！

** ————————

Virginia〔 vəˋdʒɪnjə 〕n. 維吉尼亞州【位於美國東岸，與華盛頓特區相鄰】

give a talk 發表演說　　***look forward to + V-ing*** 期待

chaos〔ˋkeɑs 〕n. 混亂　　travel〔ˋtrævḷ 〕n. 旅行

event〔 ɪˋvɛnt 〕n. 事件；大型活動

fun〔 fʌn 〕n. 有趣的事　　campus〔ˋkæmpəs 〕n. 校園

substantially〔səb'stæʃəlɪ〕*adv.* 相當大地
be limited to 僅限於　　nearby〔'nɪr'baɪ〕*adv.* 在附近
admission〔əd'mɪʃən〕*n.* 入場費
free〔fri〕*adj.* 免費的　　space〔spes〕*n.* 空間
reserve〔rɪ'zɝv〕*v.* 預訂

39. (**B**) Why is the speaker looking forward to giving the talk?

爲什麼說話者很期待發表演說？

A. He needs the money. 他需要錢。

B. It's a chance to get out and meet people.

那是個出去與人見面的機會。

C. The money is good. 錢還蠻多的。

D. The campus hasn't changed.

校園並沒有改變。

* good〔gʊd〕*adj.* 令人滿意的；足夠的

40. (**A**) Who is welcome to attend the talk?

很歡迎誰來聽演講？

A. Anyone who lives nearby. 任何住在附近的人。

B. Only CNU students.

只有克里斯多夫新港大學的學生。

C. Paying customers. 付錢的顧客。

D. Only faculty of the university.

只有這所大學的教職員。

* paying〔'peɪŋ〕*adj.* 付款的
faculty〔'fækltɪ〕*n.* 教職員

高中英聽測驗模擬試題 ⑦ 詳解

一、看圖辨義：第一部分

For question number 1, please look at the four pictures.

1. (**B**) Kim and Roger just graduated. Polly is taking their picture. 金與羅傑剛畢業。波莉正在幫他們拍照。

       * graduate〔'grædʒu,et〕*v.* 畢業

For question number 2, please look at the four pictures.

2. (**A**) Carol is building a snowman. She's wearing striped pants. 卡蘿正在堆雪人。她穿著條紋褲。

       * snowman〔'sno,mæn〕*n.* 雪人
         striped〔straɪpt〕*adj.* 條紋的

For question number 3, please look at the four pictures.

3. (**D**) John is running late. His friends are irritated by having
to wait for him.

約翰快遲到了。他的朋友因為必須等他，而感到很生氣。

* ***run late*** 遲到　　irritated〔ˈɪrəˌtetɪd〕*adj.* 生氣的

For question number 4, please look at the four pictures.

4. (**D**) That's an interesting house. There's a heart-shaped
window above the front door.

那是間有趣的房子。在前門上有一個心形的窗戶。

* heart-shaped *adj.* 心形的　　***front door*** 前門

一、看圖辨義：第二部分

For question number 5, please look at picture 5.

5. (**A**、**B**) Which TWO of the following are true about the
picture? 關於這張圖片，下面哪兩項為真？

A. The teacher is asking a question.
這位老師正在問問題。

B. The girl with curly hair has
raised her hand.
這位捲髮的女孩舉起手來。

C. None of the students are willing to answer the
teacher's question.
沒有學生願意回答老師的問題。

D. All of the students want to answer the teacher's
question. 所有的學生都想要回答老師的問題。

* curly〔ˋkɝlɪ〕 *adj.* 捲的　　raise〔rez〕*v.* 舉起
none〔nʌn〕*pron.* 沒人　　willing〔ˋwɪlɪŋ〕*adj.* 願意的

For question number 6, please look at picture 6.

6. (**C**、**D**) Which TWO of the following are true about the
picture? 關於這張圖片，下面哪兩項為真？

A. Bob is using crutches.
鮑伯正在使用拐杖。

B. Bob has a cat.
鮑伯有一隻貓。

C. Bob is in a wheelchair. 鮑伯坐在輪椅上。

D. Bob has a dog. 鮑伯有一隻狗。

* crutch〔krʌtʃ〕 *n.* 枴杖　　wheelchair〔ˋwilˌtʃɛr〕*n.* 輪椅

For question number 7, please look at picture 7.

7. (**B、C**) Which TWO of the following are true about the
picture? 關於這張圖片，下面哪兩項為眞？

    A. The man is teaching his son how to ride a bike.
       這位男士正在敎他的兒子如何騎腳踏車。

    B. The man is teaching his son how to fix a bike.
       這位男士正在敎他的兒子如何修腳踏車。

    C. The bike is upside down.
       這台腳踏車上下顛倒。

    D. The bike is lying on its side.
       這台腳踏車倒在地上。

    * fix〔fɪks〕v. 修理　　*upside down* 上下顛倒
      lie on one's *side* 側躺

For question number 8, please look at picture 8.

8. (**A、D**) Which TWO of the following are true about the
picture? 關於這張圖片，下面哪兩項為眞？

    A. The man is waving to his
friends.
       這位男士在向他的朋友揮手。

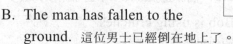

    B. The man has fallen to the
ground. 這位男士已經倒在地上了。

    C. There are five men in the picture.
       圖片中有五位男士。

    D. There are four men in the picture.
       圖片中有四位男士。

    * wave〔wev〕v. 揮手　　ground〔graʊnd〕n. 地面

For question number 9, please look at picture 9.

9. (**C、D**) Which TWO of the following are true about the
picture? 關於這張圖片，下面哪兩項爲眞？

A. Bill doesn't care for sports.
比爾不喜歡運動。

B. Bill can't read.
比爾不能閱讀。

C. Bill has his feet up on the bookcase.
比爾把腳放在書櫃上。

D. Bill is reading a sports magazine.
比爾正在看運動雜誌。

* *care for* 喜歡　　bookcase〔'buk,kes〕*n.* 書櫃
magazine〔,mæg'zin〕*n.* 雜誌
sports〔sports〕*adj.* 運動的

For question number 10, please look at picture 10.

10. (**A、D**) Which TWO of the following are true about the
picture? 關於這張圖片，下面哪兩項爲眞？

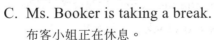

A. Ms. Booker is wearing gloves.
布客小姐正戴著手套。

B. Ms. Booker is doing laundry.
布客小姐正在洗衣服。

C. Ms. Booker is taking a break.
布客小姐正在休息。

D. Ms. Booker is doing yard work.
布客小姐正在整理院子。

* glove〔glʌv〕*n.* 手套　　laundry〔'lɔndrɪ〕*n.* 待洗的衣物
do laundry 洗衣服　　*take a break* 休息一下
yard〔jɑrd〕*n.* 院子

二、對答

11. (**C**) So what seems to be the problem, Kirk?
柯爾克，所以大概是哪裡有問題？

    A. They have a problem. 他們有問題。

    B. Kirk sent me. 柯爾克派我來。

    C. My knee hurts. 我的膝蓋痛。

    D. I need to see Kirk. 我必須見柯爾客。

    * seem〔sim〕v. 似乎　　knee〔ni〕n. 膝蓋
    hurt〔hɜt〕v. 痛

12. (**D**) How was your day? 你今天過得如何？

    A. I'm here every day. 我每天都在這裡。

    B. They never come out during the day.
他們白天絕不會出來。

    C. You should have been there. 你早該來這裡。

    D. Not bad. 不錯。

13. (**C**) Are you leaving soon? 你很快就要離開了嗎？

    A. It's late. 很晚了。

    B. I'm tired. 我很累。

    C. Yes, I am. 是的，我就快要走了。

    D. No, I can't see you. 不，我看不見你。

14. (**A**) What time is the meeting? 這個會議是什麼時候？

    A. It's at two o'clock. 是在兩點。

    B. You can come if you want. 如果你想的話，你可以來。

    C. It should last about an hour. 應該會持續約一個小時。

    D. Certainly, you should. 當然，你應該。

    * meeting〔'mitɪŋ〕n. 會議　　last〔læst〕v. 持續
    certainly〔'sɜtn̩lɪ〕adv. 當然

15. (**C**) Do you use computers at school?

你在學校有用電腦嗎？

A. My parents don't let us watch TV.

我的父母不讓我們看電視。

B. Yes, I'm studying biology. 是的，我正在研究生物學。

C. Yes. There are computers in every classroom.

每間教室都有電腦。

D. That's not nice. 那樣不好。

* biology〔baɪˈɑlədʒɪ〕*n.* 生物學

16. (**D**) Is Peter a good singer? 彼德是個好歌手嗎？

A. Ask for his autograph. 跟他要簽名。

B. All pop stars can dance. 所有流行歌星都會跳舞。

C. Why not me? 爲什麼不是我？

D. No, he's terrible. 不是，他很糟。

* ***ask for*** 要求　　autograph〔ˈɔtəgræf〕*n.* 親筆簽名
pop〔pɑp〕*adj.* 流行的　*n.* 流行歌曲
star〔stɑr〕*n.* 明星　　terrible〔ˈtɛrəbl̩〕*adj.* 可怕的；很糟的

17. (**C**) Does that coffee shop have wireless Internet access?

那間咖啡店有無線網路嗎？

A. I'll have a caramel latte. 我要喝焦糖拿鐵。

B. The coffee shop is closed. 咖啡店關了。

C. Yes, it does. 是的，它有。

D. Not where I come from. 那不是我來的地方。

* wireless〔ˈwaɪrlɪs〕*adj.* 無線的
Internet〔ˈɪntə‚nɛt〕*n.* 網際網路
access〔ˈæksɛs〕*n.* 接近或使用權
caramel〔ˈkærəml̩〕*n.* 焦糖　　latte〔ˈlɑte〕*n.* 拿鐵咖啡

18. (**A**) How's your term paper coming along?

你的學期報告進展得如何？

    A. Great! I'm almost finished.

       很順利！我快要完成了。

    B. You should try writing a term paper.

       你應該試著寫一份學期報告。

    C. It's due tomorrow. 明天就要交了。

    D. I won't be coming. 我不會來。

    * *come along* 進展　　*term paper* 學期報告

      finished（'fɪnɪʃt）*adj.* 完成的　　due（dju）*adj.* 到期的

19. (**B**) Are you studying Italian this semester?

你這學期是在學義大利文嗎？

    A. I love spaghetti! 我愛義大利麵！

    B. No, I'm studying German. 不是，我在學德文。

    C. I was in Rome last August.

       我去年八月人在羅馬。

    D. She's beautiful, isn't she? 她很漂亮，對不對？

    * Italian（ɪ'tæljən）*n.* 義大利文

      spaghetti（spə'gɛtɪ）*n.* 義大利麵

      German（'dʒɝmən）*n.* 德文　　Rome（rom）*n.* 羅馬

20. (**A**) Would you mind turning down your stereo?

你介不介意把你的音響關小聲一點？

    A. Sorry. I'll do it now. 很抱歉，我現在就關小聲。

    B. That's too bad. 真是糟糕。

    C. I never met him. 我從沒見過他。

    D. I'm watching television. 我正在看電視。

    * *Would you mind*…? 你介不介意…？　　*turn down* 關小聲

      stereo（'stɛrɪo）*n.* 立體音響

三、簡短對話

For question 21, you will listen to a short conversation.

> M：Excuse me, miss, but could we at least have some water brought to the table?
>
> 不好意思，小姐，能不能至少拿些水來我們這桌？
>
> W：Sorry, pal. I don't work here.
>
> 抱歉，朋友。我不在這工作。
>
> ** **at least** 至少　　pal〔pæl〕n. 夥伴；朋友*

21. (**C**)　Q：Why doesn't the woman do what the man asks?

　　　　　爲什麼這位女士沒有依照這位男士的請求來做？

　　　　A. She is already wet. 她已經淋濕了。

　　　　B. She doesn't need any water. 她不需要任何水。

　　　　C. She is also a diner. 她也是來吃飯的客人。

　　　　D. She can't hear him. 她聽不到他說的話。

　　　　* wet〔wɛt〕adj. 濕的　　diner〔'daɪnɚ〕n. 用餐者；吃飯的客人

For question 22, you will listen to a short conversation.

> M：I need a babysitter tonight. It's kind of a last-minute thing. 我今晚需要一個臨時保姆。眞的是事出突然。
>
> W：My cousin is looking to make a few extra bucks. How much will you pay her?
>
> 我表姐正在找賺更多錢的機會。你打算付她多少？
>
> M：I'll pay her $20 bucks an hour for five hours.
>
> 我會付她一小時 20 美元，總共五小時。

W：I'll watch your kids for a hundred bucks!

我決定為這一百美元幫你照顧小孩！

* babysitter〔'bebɪ,sɪtɚ〕n. 臨時保姆　　***kind of*** 有點
last-minute adj. 最後一分鐘的；緊急關頭的
extra〔'ɛkstrə〕adj. 額外的　　watch〔wɑtʃ〕v. 看護照顧
buck〔bʌk〕n.【口語】美元

22. (**D**) Q：What is true about the man? 關於這位男士何者為真？

A. He could use some quick cash. 他想要賺一些外快。

B. He wants to wait until the last minute.
他想要等到最後一分鐘。

C. He needs a cousin. 他需要一個表妹。

D. He is willing to pay someone to watch his kids.
他願意付錢給某人來幫他照顧小孩。

* ***could use*** 想要；需要　　***quick cash*** 外快

For question 23, you will listen to a short conversation.

W：Have you seen my younger sister?
你有看到我的妹妹嗎？

M：Yes, I saw her at the café about ten minutes ago.
有，我大約十分鐘前在咖啡餐廳看到她。

* café〔kə'fe〕n. 咖啡廳

23. (**B**) Q：When did the man last see the woman's sister?
這位男士最後一次看到這位女士的妹妹是什麼時候？

A. At the café. 在咖啡廳。

B. Ten minutes ago. 十分鐘前。

C. Yesterday. 昨天。

D. No, he didn't. 不是，他沒有。

For question 24, you will listen to a short conversation.

W：Did you drink my last beer in the fridge?

　　是你喝了我冰箱裡的最後一罐啤酒嗎？

M：Do I look stupid to you?　我看起來有那麼笨嗎？

　　* beer〔bɪr〕*n.* 啤酒　　fridge〔frɪdʒ〕*n.* 冰箱（= *refrigerator*）

24.（ **A** ）Q：What does the man mean?　這位男士的意思是什麼？

　　A. He wouldn't dare drink the woman's last beer.

　　　他不敢喝這位女士的最後一罐啤酒。

　　B. He drank the last beer and he's proud of it.

　　　他喝了最後一罐啤酒並且感到很驕傲。

　　C. He thinks the woman looks stupid.

　　　他認爲那位女士看起來很笨。

　　D. He has a learning disability.　他有學習障礙。

　　* dare〔dɛr〕*v.* 敢　　***be proud of*** 以～爲榮
　　disability〔ˌdɪsə'bɪlɪtɪ〕*n.* 無能力

For questions 25 and 26, you will listen to a short conversation.

W：Can you say it a little louder?　I can't hear you!

　　你可以說大聲一點嗎？我聽不見你說的話！

M：I said, what is that awful noise?

　　我說，那可怕的聲音是什麼？

W：I'm sorry, I can't hear you over the noise!

　　很抱歉，聲音這麼大我聽不到你說的話！

M：I think they are doing construction upstairs!

　　我想他們樓上正在施工！

W：It sounds like someone is doing construction upstairs!

聽起來像是有人在樓上施工！

M：That's what I said! 那就是我說的！

* awful〔'ɔfəl〕*adj.* 可怕的；糟糕的　　noise〔nɔɪz〕*n.* 噪音
construction〔kʌn'strʌkʃən〕*n.* 建造；施工
upstairs〔'ʌp'stɛrz〕*adv.* 在樓上

25. (**C**) Q：Why can't the woman hear the man?

為什麼這位女士聽不到這位男士說的話？

A. He is whispering. 他正在低聲說話。

B. He is talking too loud. 他講得太大聲。

C. There is too much noise. 有太多噪音。

D. She feels awful. 她覺得很糟。

* whisper〔'wɪspɚ〕*v.* 低聲說

26. (**C**) Q：What is happening upstairs? 樓上發生什麼事？

A. The conversation. 這段對話。

B. A rock band is performing.

一個搖滾樂團正在表演。

C. Construction work. 建築工程。

D. English lessons. 英文課。

* rock〔rak〕*n.* 搖滾樂　　perform〔pɚ'fɔrm〕*v.* 表演

For questions 27 and 28, you will listen to a short conversation.

W：That's the last time we invite the Hamiltons to dinner.

那是我們最後一次邀請漢米爾頓一家人來吃晚餐。

M：Why? I thought they were fine.

為什麼？我覺得他們人不錯呀。

W: Tom didn't even reach for his wallet when the check came. And Betty always orders the most expensive item on the menu. 帳單來的時候，湯姆連拿皮夾都不拿。貝蒂總是點菜單上最貴的項目。

M: In case you forgot, dear, we invited them to dinner. I didn't expect Tom to pay.

親愛的，說不定妳忘了，是我們邀請他們來吃晚餐。我並沒有期待湯姆會付錢。

W: I know, but he could have least made an effort to split the bill. 我知道，但他們至少可以努力分攤帳單。

M: Come on. What really bothers you about them?

算了吧。什麼才是讓妳對他們不開心的真正原因？

W: That's the third time we've taken them to dinner and they've never once returned the gesture.

那是我們第三次帶他們去吃晚餐，而他們從來都不曾禮尚往來。

M: I see your point. Tell you what, we won't ask them again and just wait for them to ask us. 我知道妳的意思。

我提個建議，我們就不要再邀請他們了，就等他們邀請我們吧。

---

* ***reach for*** 伸手去拿　　wallet〔ˈwɑlɪt〕 n. 皮夾
check〔tʃɛk〕 n. 帳單　　order〔ˈɔrdɚ〕 v. 點（餐）
tem〔ˈaɪtəm〕 n. 項目　　menu〔ˈmɛnju〕 n. 菜單
in case 以免；也許；說不定　　expect〔ɪkˈspɛkt〕 v. 期待
make an effort to V. 努力　　***split the bill*** 分攤帳單
bother〔ˈbɑðɚ〕 v. 使苦惱　　gesture〔ˈdʒɛstʃɚ〕 n.（心意的）表示
return the gesture 回禮　　see〔si〕 v. 知道；了解
point〔pɔɪnt〕 n. 要點；中心意思
(I'll) ***tell you what*** 我提個建議

27. (**D**) Q : Who are the speakers?　說話者是誰？

    A. Employer and employee.　雇主與員工。

    B. Tennis partners.　打網球的夥伴。

    C. Restaurant owners.　餐廳老闆。

    D. Husband and wife.　夫妻。

    * employer〔ɪm'plɔɪɚ〕 *n.* 雇主

    employee〔͵ɛmplɔɪ'i〕 *n.* 員工

    partner〔'pɑrtnɚ〕 *n.* 夥伴　　owner〔'onɚ〕 *n.* 所有人

28. (**B**) Q : What does the woman think of the Hamiltons?

    這位女士覺得漢米爾頓一家人如何？

    A. She thinks they are boring people.

      她覺得他們是無聊的人。

    B. She thinks they are cheap.　她覺得他們很小氣。

    C. She thinks they drink too much.

      她覺得他們喝太多了。

    D. She thinks they try too hard to be generous.

      她覺得他們太想表現得很慷慨。

    * cheap〔tʃip〕 *adj.* 小氣的；吝嗇的

    generous〔'dʒɛnərəs〕 *adj.* 慷慨的；大方的

For questions 29 and 30, you will listen to a short conversation.

    M : Why are you studying in the kitchen?

      為什麼你要在廚房讀書？

    W : It's too hot in my bedroom.　我的房間太熱了。

    M : Turn on the air conditioner.　要打開空調。

    W : It's not working.　空調壞了。

M：Did you tell the landlord? 你有跟房東說嗎？

W：Yes, he will buy a new one tomorrow.

　　有，他明天會買一台新的。

　　　* bedroom〔'bɛd,rum〕n. 臥室　　*turn on* 打開（電器）
　　　air conditioner 空調　　work〔wɝk〕v. 運作
　　　landlord〔'læn,lɔrd〕n. 房東

29. (**A**) Q：Where are these people? 這些人在哪裡？

　　　　A. They are at home. 他們在家。

　　　　B. They are in class. 他們在上課。

　　　　C. They are at work. 他們在工作。

　　　　D. They are on a bus. 他們在公車上。

30. (**D**) Q：What is true about the landlord?

　　　　　關於房東何者為真？

　　　　A. He is trying to study. 他想要讀書。

　　　　B. He is in the kitchen. 他在廚房裡。

　　　　C. He will turn on the air conditioner. 他會打開空調。

　　　　D. He will replace the air conditioner tomorrow.

　　　　　他明天會更換空調。

　　　　　* replace〔rɪ'ples〕v. 更換

四、短文聽解

Questions 31 and 32 are based on the following report.

　　　Well, a big question is how did the universe begin?
We cannot answer that question yet. Some people think
that the big bang is an explanation of how the universe

began. It is not. The big bang is a theory of how the universe evolved from a split second after whatever brought it into existence. Hopefully, one day we will be able to look right back at time zero, to figure out how it really began. I don't know how it'll affect your everyday life, but to me, if we really had a sense of how the universe really began, I think that would have a profound effect.

　　嗯，有個很重大的問題，那就是宇宙是如何開始的？我們至今仍無法回答這個問題。有的人認為，大爆炸理論是能解釋宇宙是如何開始的。但它不是。大爆炸理論是在某個東西讓宇宙開始後，宇宙如何在一瞬間開展的理論。希望有一天，我們能夠回頭看到宇宙的零點零分，來了解它究竟是如何開始的。我不知道這個問題會如何影響你的日常生活，但對我而言，如果我們真的了解宇宙究竟是如何開始的話，我覺得那將會有深遠的影響。

**

universe (ˈjunəˌvɜs) *n.* 宇宙　　　*big bang* 大爆炸
explanation (ˌɛkspləˈneʃən) *n.* 解釋
evolve (ɪˈvɑlv) *v.* 演化；開展　　*a split second* 一瞬間
existence (ɪgˈzɪstəns) *n.* 存在
bring…into existence 使…產生
hopefully (ˈhopfəlɪ) *adv.* 但願　　*look back at* 回顧
right (raɪt) *adv.* 正好；恰好　　zero (ˈzɪro) *n.* 零
time zero 時間計算起點；零點　　theory (ˈθiərɪ) *n.* 理論
figure out 了解　　affect (əˈfɛkt) *v.* 影響
have a sense of 認識　　profound (prəˈfaʊnd) *adj.* 深遠的
effect (ɪˈfɛkt) *n.* 影響

31. (**C**) How did the universe begin? 宇宙是如何開始的？
　　A. The big bang. 大爆炸。

B. At the beginning. 在一開始。

C. That question cannot be answered yet.
這問題現在仍無法回答。

D. Ask Einstein. 要問愛因斯坦。

* Einstein (ˈaɪnstaɪn) *n.* 愛因斯坦

32. (**C**) What is the big bang? 什麼是大爆炸理論？

A. Our place in the cosmos. 我們在宇宙中的地方。

B. Everyday life. 日常生活。

C. A theory of how the universe evolved.
宇宙如何演化的理論。

D. Time zero. 零點。

* cosmos (ˈkɑzməs) *n.* 宇宙

Questions 33 and 34 are based on the following report.

The New Testament of the Bible repeatedly stresses
the concept of forgiveness. "Bear with each other and
forgive whatever grievances you may have against one
another. Forgive as the Lord forgave you," says
Colossians 3:13. In Judaism, Yom Kippur— the Day
of Atonement——requires that Jews ask for forgiveness
from others whom they have sinned against, and grant
forgiveness to those who ask it. Anger and grudges
should be discarded: "Thou shalt not hate thy brother in
thy heart," says Leviticus 19:17.

新約聖經重複地強調原諒的重要。「彼此包容以及放下你對別
人的不滿。要像神饒恕你一般地去饒恕別人，」歌羅西書三章十三

節說：猶太敎裡的贖罪日，要求猶太人與他們所得罪的人尋求饒
恕，並且原諒那些請求原諒的人。憤怒與懷恨應該被丟棄：「你
們心裡不可恨你的弟兄，」利未記十九章十七節說。

**

the New Testament 新約聖經
repeatedly〔rɪˈpitɪdlɪ〕*adv.* 重複地
stress〔strɛs〕*v.* 強調　　concept〔ˈkɑnsɛpt〕*n.* 觀念
forgiveness〔fəˈgɪvnəs〕*n.* 原諒　　*bear with* 寬容
grievance〔ˈgrivəns〕*n.* 不滿　　*the Lord* 上帝
Colossian〔kəˈlɔʃən〕*n.* 歌羅西書【新約聖經中的一個書卷】
Judaism〔ˈdʒudəɪzəm〕*n.* 猶太敎　　*Yom Kippur* 贖罪日
atonement〔əˈtonmənt〕*n.* 贖罪
require〔rɪˈkwaɪr〕*v.* 要求
sin against 犯戒律；犯過失　　grant〔grænt〕*v.* 給予
grudge〔grʌdʒ〕*n.* 怨恨　　discard〔dɪsˈkɑrd〕*v.* 丟棄
thou〔ðaʊ〕*prop.* 你　　shalt〔ʃəlt〕*aux.* 必須；應該 (= *shall*)
thy〔ðaɪ〕*adj.* 你的
Leviticus〔ləˈvɪtɪkəs〕*n.* 利未記【舊約聖經中的一個書卷】

33. (**D**) What does the New Testament say about forgiveness?
　　關於饒恕新約聖經是怎麼說的？

　　A. It comes in handy every now and then. 偶爾很有用。

　　B. Forgive but never forget. 原諒但絕不忘記。

　　C. Your brother is the only one who will forgive you.
　　　　你的兄弟是唯一會原諒你的人。

　　D. Anger and grudges should be discarded.
　　　　生氣與怨恨應該被丟棄。

　　* *come in handy* 很有用；很方便
　　　　every now and then 偶爾

34. (**C**) What is Yom Kippur? 什麼是贖罪日？

    A. The concept of grievance. 不滿的概念。

    B. Leviticus's birthday. 利未的生日。

    C. A Jewish day of atonement. 一個猶太人的贖罪日。

    D. Colossians 3:13. 歌羅西書三章十三節。

Questions 35 and 36 are based on the following report.

All human laughter consists of variations on a basic form made of short, vowel-like notes repeated every 210 milliseconds. Laughter can be of the "ha-ha-ha" variety or the "ho-ho-ho" type but not a mixture of both. Other studies have confirmed that people are 30 times more likely to laugh in social settings than when they are alone. Scientific evidence also suggests that humans have a "detector" that responds to laughter by triggering other neural circuits in the brain, which, in turn, generates more laughter. This explains why laughter is contagious.

所有人類的笑聲都由基本形式變化組成，這基本的形式聲音很短，是每 210 毫秒重複一次，如同母音聲調一般。笑可以是「哈哈哈」或「呵呵呵」的類型，但卻不會是兩者的混合。其他研究已經證實，人們在社交場合比獨自自己一人時，會笑的可能性是三十倍。科學證據也顯示，人類有個偵測器，能透過激發腦內其他的神經迴路來回應笑聲，後來就會造成更多的笑聲。這解釋了為什麼笑是會傳染的。

** ————————————————

    laughter〔ˈlæftɚ〕*n.* 笑聲   ***consist of*** 由～組成；包含

    variation〔ˌvɛrɪˈeʃən〕*n.* 種類   basic〔ˈbesɪk〕*adj.* 基本的

form〔fɔrm〕*n.* 型式　　***be made of*** 由～做成
vowel〔ˈvauəl〕*n.* 母音　　note〔not〕*n.* 聲調
repeat〔rɪˈpit〕*v.* 重複
millisecond〔ˈmɪlɪˈsɛkənd〕*n.* 毫秒
variety〔vəˈraɪətɪ〕*n.* 種類　　type〔taɪp〕*n.* 類型
mixture〔ˈmɪkstʃə〕*n.* 混合　　confirm〔kənˈfɝm〕*v.* 確認
time〔taɪm〕*n.* 倍　　setting〔ˈsɛtɪŋ〕*n.* 環境；背景
social settings 社交場合　　alone〔əˈlon〕*adj.* 單獨的

evidence〔ˈɛvədəns〕*n.* 證據　　suggest〔səˈdʒɛst〕*v.* 顯示
detector〔dɪˈtɛktə〕*n.* 偵測器
respond〔rɪˈspɑnd〕*v.* 回應　　trigger〔ˈtrɪgə〕*v.* 引發
neural〔ˈnjurəl〕*adj.* 神經的
circuit〔ˈsɝkɪt〕*n.* 迴路；電路　　***neural circuit*** 神經迴路
in turn 結果；後來；轉而　　generate〔ˈdʒɛnəˌret〕*v.* 產生
explain〔ɪkˈsplen〕*v.* 解釋
contagious〔kənˈtedʒəs〕*adj.* 會傳染的；有感染力的

35.（**C**）What is true about laughter? 關於笑聲，何者為眞？

　　A. People are 210 times more likely to laugh when they are at work.

　　　　當人們在工作時，會笑的可能性是 210 倍。

　　B. It is always a combination of "ha-ha-ha" and "ho-ho-ho."

　　　　笑聲總是「哈哈哈」與「呵呵呵」的結合。

　　C. People are 30 times more likely to laugh in social settings. 人們在社交場合中，笑的可能性是 30 倍。

　　D. It is repeated every millisecond.

　　　　它每毫秒重複一次。

　　* combination〔ˌkɑmbəˈneʃən〕*n.* 結合

36. (**C**) Why is laughter contagious? 為何笑聲是有傳染性的？

    A. Germs are everywhere. 到處都是病菌。

    B. Funny situations have poor hygiene.
        好笑情境的衛生條件不好。

    C. Humans have a "detector" that responds to laughter.
        人類有回應笑聲的「偵測器」。

    D. The brain doesn't have protection against humor.
        頭腦無法預防幽默。

    * germ〔dʒɝm〕*n.* 病菌　　funny〔'fʌnɪ〕*adj.* 好笑的
      hygiene〔'haɪdʒin〕*n.* 衛生　　***have protection against*** 預防
      humor〔'hjumɚ〕*n.* 幽默

Questions 37 and 38 are based on the following report.

    The advance of technology and the Internet may have made our lives easier, but together they have wiped out an array of traditional industries. The video rental business is dead. Why head to the local Blockbuster when NetFlix will deliver or offer for download any film you want?—— and that's not even mentioning the hundreds of movies available on cable TV. Digital cameras and online image sharing make your local photo developer obsolete. Consumers also no longer need to pay to develop 20 pictures of squinting relatives to get one decent image.

    科技的先進與網路可能已經使我們的生活更輕鬆，但它們也已經除掉了許多傳統產業。影帶出租業沒有生意。當 NetFlix 可以傳送或提供下載你所想要的任何影片時，為何還要跑去附近的百事達呢？——更不用提可以看到數百部電影的有線電視。數位相機與網路圖片分享使你家附近的相片沖洗藥水變得落伍過時。消費者也不用再爲了一張不錯的照片，而花錢洗出 20 張有親戚半閉眼睛的照片。

**————————————————

advance〔əd'væns〕n. 進步　　technology〔tɛk'nɑlədʒɪ〕n. 科技

easy〔'izɪ〕adj. 容易的；輕鬆的　　**wipe out** 除掉

array〔ə're〕n. 一長排（物品）；一大群（人）

traditional industry 傳統產業

video rental business 影帶出租業

dead〔dɛd〕adj. 無活力的；沒有生意的　　**head to** 前往

local〔'lokḷ〕adj. 當地的　　Blockbuster〔'blɑk,bʌstə〕n. 百事達

NetFlix〔'nɛt'flɪks〕n. 一家美國當紅網路串流隨選播放媒體公司
名稱　　deliver〔dɪ'lɪvə〕v. 傳送　　offer〔'ɔfə〕v. 提供

download〔'daun,lod〕n. 下載　　mention〔'mɛnʃən〕v. 提到

available〔ə'veləbḷ〕adj. 可獲得的　　**cable TV** 有線電視

digital〔'dɪdʒɪtḷ〕adj. 數位的　　**digital camera** 數位相機

online〔'ɑn,laɪn〕adj. 線上的　　image〔'ɪmɪdʒ〕n. 影像

develop〔dɪ'vɛləp〕adj. 沖洗（相片）

photo developer 相片沖洗藥水

obsolete〔'ɑbsə,lit〕adj. 過時的　　squint〔skwɪnt〕v. 眯眼

relative〔'rɛlətɪv〕n. 親戚　　decent〔'disṇt〕adj. 不錯的

37. (**B**) What has technology and the Internet done to certain traditional industries?

科技與網路對一些傳統產業造成了什麼影響？

A. Knocked them up. 使他們筋疲力盡。

B. Wiped them out. 除掉他們。

C. Voted them in. 投票選出他們。

D. Held them down. 壓迫他們。

* **knock up** 使累垮；使筋疲力盡　　**vote in** 投票選出
hold down 壓迫

38. (**C**) What caused the local photo developer to become obsolete? 什麼使當地的相片沖洗藥水變得過時？
   A. Blockbuster. 百事達。　　B. Cable TV. 有線電視。
   C. Digital cameras and online image sharing.
   　數位相機及網路照片分享。
   D. Netflix. 美國知名網路隨選播放公司。

Questions 39 and 40 are based on the following report.

In my junior year of high school I had a part-time job working as the assistant property manager for a luxury high-rise condominium. It was only a couple hours every evening and fairly simple. My job was to walk around the common areas and confirm that everything was in working order. If I saw something wrong, I'd call one of the maintenance guys to come up and fix it. The head property manager made it clear that my job was strictly observation, and I was not to offer help to anybody——resident or maintenance staff——under any condition.

在我高二時，我有份兼差的工作，擔任豪華公寓大樓物業經理的助理。這只有花晚上幾個小時的時間，並且很簡單。我的工作是在公共區域到處走，並且確認所有的東西都正常運作。如果我看到哪裡有問題，我會叫其中一個維修人員來修理。物業主任經理很清楚地說明，我的工作就只是觀察——在任何情況下，我都不必協助任何人——不論是住戶或是維修人員。

** ————————————————————

junior year of high school　高二
part-time (ˋpɑrt͵taɪm) *adj.* 兼差的　　***work as*** 擔任
assistant (əˋsɪstənt) *adj.* 助理的　　property (ˋprɑpətɪ) *n.* 物業

manager〔'mænɪdʒə〕 *n.* 經理　　luxury〔'lʌkʃərɪ〕 *adj.* 豪華的

high-rise *n.* 大樓　　condominium〔,kɑndə'mɪnɪəm〕 *n.* 公寓

a couple 幾個；兩個　　fairly〔'fɛrlɪ〕 *adv.* 相當地

common area 公共區域　　confirm〔kən'fɝm〕 *v.* 確認

in working order 能正常發揮作用

maintenance〔'mentənəns〕 *n.* 維修　　guy〔gaɪ〕 *n.* 人；傢伙

come up 來　　head〔hɛd〕 *adj.* 居首位的

make it clear 說清楚　　strictly〔'strɪktlɪ〕 *adv.* 嚴格地；完全地

observation〔,ɑbzɚ'veʃən〕 *n.* 觀察　　*be not to V.* 不必～

resident〔'rɛzədənt〕 *n.* 居民　　staff〔stæf〕 *n.* 全體工作人員

condition〔kən'dɪʃən〕 *n.* 情況

39. (**D**) What was the speaker's part-time job title?

　　說話者的兼職工作頭銜是什麼？

　　A. Resident assistant. 住戶助理。

　　B. Chief maintenance officer. 維修主任。

　　C. Guest relations agent. 客戶關係專員。

　　D. Assistant property manager. 物業經理的助理。

　　* *chief…officer* 總監…　　guest〔gɛst〕 *n.* 客人

　　relation〔rɪ'leʃən〕 *n.* 關係　　agent〔'edʒənt〕 *n.* 代理人；專員

40. (**D**) What was the speaker specifically instructed NOT to do?

　　說話者被特別指示不用去做什麼？

　　A. Confirm that everything was in working order.

　　　確認所有東西都正常運作。

　　B. Work more than six hours every evening.

　　　每晚工作超過六小時。

　　C. Call one of the maintenance guys. 叫維修人員。

　　D. Offer to help residents or the maintenance staff.

　　　協助住戶或維修人員。

　　* specifically〔spɪ'sɪfɪklɪ〕 *adv.* 明確地

　　instruct〔ɪn'strʌkt〕 *v.* 指導；指示

高中英聽測驗模擬試題 ⑧ 詳解

一、看圖辨義：第一部分

For question number 1, please look at the four pictures.

1. (**A**) Jane works out in the gym every day.　Today she is jogging on the treadmill.

　珍每天在體育館裡運動鍛鍊。今天她在跑步機上慢跑。

　　* ***work out*** 運動　　gym〔dʒɪm〕*n.* 健身房
　　jog〔dʒɑg〕*v.* 慢跑　　treadmill〔'trɛ,mɪl〕*n.* 跑步機

For question number 2, please look at the four pictures.

2. (**B**) The washing machine is broken.　The technician will fix it.

　洗衣機壞掉了。技術人員將會修理它。

　　* broken〔'brokən〕*adj.* 損壞的
　　technician〔tɛk'nɪʃən〕*n.* 技術人員；技師　　fix〔fɪks〕*v.* 修理

For question number 3, please look at the four pictures.

3. (**D**) Susan is having a dinner party tonight. The main course
will be seafood.

蘇珊今晚將要舉行晚餐派對。主菜將會是海鮮。

　　 * *main course* 主菜　　 seafood〔'si,fud〕*n.* 海鮮

For question number 4, please look at the four pictures.

4. (**D**) There is a fishbowl and a plant on the counter. The plant
is to the left of the fishbowl.

有一個魚缸和一株植物在櫃台。這株植物在魚缸的左邊。

　　 * fishbowl〔'fɪʃ,bol〕*n.* 玻璃魚缸
　　　counter〔'kaʊntɚ〕*n.* 櫃台
　　　to the left of 在…的左邊

一、看圖辨義：第二部分

For question number 5, please look at picture 5.

5. (**A** 、 **B**) Which TWO of the following are true about the
picture? 關於這張圖片，下列哪兩項為真？

   A. Gordon keeps his personal belongings in a chest.
高登把他的個人物品放在一個箱子裡。

   B. Gordon has many toys. 高登有很多玩具。

   C. Steve is impressed with the book.
史帝夫對這本書感到印象深刻。

   D. Steve is wearing a long sleeve
shirt. 史帝夫正穿著長袖襯衫。

  * personal〔ˈpɝsṇḷ〕*adj.* 個人的
belongings〔bɪˈlɔŋɪŋz〕*n. pl.* 財產；物品
chest〔tʃɛst〕*n.* 箱子；櫃子
impressed〔ɪmˈprɛst〕*adj.* 印象深刻的
sleeve〔sliv〕*n.* 袖子

For question number 6, please look at picture 6.

6. (**B** 、 **C**) Which TWO of the following are true about the
picture? 關於這張圖片，下列哪兩項為真？

   A. Grandma broke her arm.
祖母的手斷了。

   B. Grandma broke her leg.
祖母的腿斷了。

   C. Grandma's leg is in a cast. 祖母的腿打著石膏。

   D. Grandma's arm is in a sling.
祖母的手臂用吊腕帶吊掛著。

  * break〔brek〕*v.* 折斷　　cast〔kæst〕*n.* 石膏
sling〔slɪŋ〕*n.*【醫】吊腕帶

For question number 7, please look at picture 7.

7. (**A**、**C**) Which TWO of the following are true about the
picture? 關於這張圖片，下列哪兩項為眞？

A. Helen works as a cashier in a supermarket.
海倫在一間超市當收銀員。

B. Helen works as a waitress in a restaurant.
海倫在一間餐廳當女服務生。

C. Helen is wearing an apron.
海倫穿著一件圍裙。

D. Helen is rude to customers.
海倫對顧客很粗魯。

* ***work as*** 擔任　cashier〔kæ'ʃɪr〕*n.* 收銀員
supermarket〔'supə,markɪt〕*n.* 超市
waitress〔'wetrɪs〕*n.* 女服務生　apron〔'eprən〕*n.* 圍裙
rude〔rud〕*adj.* 粗魯的；無禮的

For question number 8, please look at picture 8.

8. (**B**、**C**) Which TWO of the following are true about the
picture? 關於這張圖片，下列哪兩項為眞？

A. The teacher is excited. 老師感到興奮。
B. The man is excited. 男士感到興奮。
C. The man is wearing a tie.
男士打著一條領帶。

D. The teacher is not wearing
glasses. 老師沒有戴眼鏡。

* excited〔ɪk'saɪtɪd〕*adj.* 興奮的
tie〔taɪ〕*n.* 領帶　glasses〔'glæsɪz〕*n. pl.* 眼鏡

For question number 9, please look at picture 9.

9. (**A**、**B**) Which TWO of the following are true about the
picture? 關於這張圖片，下列哪兩項為眞？

A. These two guys don't really get along.
這兩個人眞的不太合。

B. The guy on the left has an unpleasant expression on his face.
在左邊的那個人臉上有著不愉快的表情。

C. These two guys are best friends.
這兩個人是最好的朋友。

D. The guy on the right has a look of concern on his face. 在右邊的那個人臉上看起來很擔心。

* guy〔gaɪ〕n. 人；傢伙　　***get along*** 和睦相處
unpleasant〔ʌn'plɛzn̩t〕adj. 不愉快的
expression〔ɪk'sprɛʃən〕n. 表情
look〔lʊk〕n. 表情　　concern〔kən'sɝn〕n. 擔心

For question number 10, please look at picture 10.

10. (**B、C**) Which TWO of the following are true about the picture? 關於這張圖片，下列哪兩項爲眞？

A. The boys are having an argument.
男孩們正在爭論。

B. The girls are gossiping about another student.
女孩們正在閒聊另一個學生。

C. The girl on the left is carrying a book.
在左邊的女孩正拿著一本書。

D. The girl in the middle is on her knees.
在中間的女孩正跪著。

* argument〔'ɑrgjəmənt〕n. 爭執
gossip〔'gɑsəp〕v. 閒聊　　carry〔'kærɪ〕v. 拿著
middle〔'mɪdl̩〕n. 中間　　knee〔ni〕n. 膝蓋
on** one's **knees 跪著

二、對答

11. (**C**) In what part of town do you live? 你住在城鎮裡的哪一區？

    A. My apartment. 我的公寓。

    B. The rent is too high. 租金太高。

    C. I live on the north side. 我住在北邊。

    D. Take a left turn on Main Street. 在緬恩街左轉。

    * apartment〔ə'pɑrtmənt〕*n.* 公寓
    rent〔rɛnt〕*n.* 租金　　***take a left turn*** 左轉

12. (**A**) Excuse me, I think this is yours. It fell out of your purse. 不好意思，我想這是你的。這從你的錢包掉出來。

    A. Oh, thank you so much! 喔，非常謝謝你！

    B. Wow, that's a lot! 哇，那很多！

    C. See, I told you! 你看吧，我早就跟你說過了！

    D. Serves you right! 你活該！

    * ***fall out of*** 從…掉出　　purse〔pɝs〕*n.* 錢包
    (It) ***serves you/sb. right!*** 你活該！

13. (**C**) Jerry is the most handsome man I've ever met.
    傑瑞是我遇過最英俊的男人。

    A. He certainly is a funny guy. 他一定是個很好笑的人。

    B. I'm handy around the house, too.
       我也在這間房子附近。

    C. I don't find him attractive at all.
       我一點都不覺得他有吸引力。

    D. Give me a hand, will you? 幫我一個忙，好嗎？

    * funny〔'fʌnɪ〕*adj.* 好笑的　　guy〔gaɪ〕*n.* 人；傢伙
    handy〔'hændɪ〕*adj.* 手邊的；附近的
    attractive〔ə'træktɪv〕*adj.* 有吸引力的
    not…at all 一點也不　　***give sb. a hand*** 幫某人一個忙

14. (**B**) Do you practice or follow any type of religion?
　　　你有信奉任何一種宗教嗎？

　　A. I'm a vegetarian. 我是個素食主義者。

　　B. I'd rather not answer that. 我寧可不要回答這個問題。

　　C. I've been practicing. 我一直在練習。

　　D. I'm not following you. 我沒聽懂你說的。

　　* practice ('præktɪs) v. 實踐；實行；（反覆的）練習
　　　follow ('falo) v. 信奉；聽懂　　type (taɪp) n. 類型
　　　religion (rɪ'lɪdʒən) n. 宗教
　　　vegetarian (ˌvɛdʒə'tɛrɪən) n. 素食主義者

15. (**B**) My son is learning to crawl. 我的兒子正在學爬。

　　A. My kids are getting poor grades, too.
　　　我的孩子也是成績不好。

　　B. Next thing you know, he'll be walking.
　　　下一件事，你知道的，他將會走路。

　　C. It's a short walk. 只要走很短的距離。

　　D. Mine is better than yours. 我的比你的好。

　　* crawl (krɔl) v. 爬行　　grade (gred) n. 成績
　　　walk (wɔk) n. 步行距離；路程

16. (**A**) My next-door neighbor is getting married this Saturday.
　　　我隔壁鄰居這星期六要結婚。

　　A. Will you attend the ceremony? 你會去參加婚禮嗎？

　　B. I'm divorced. 我離婚了。

　　C. On Saturday. 在星期六。

　　D. Thanks, but I'm busy. 謝謝，但我很忙。

　　* next-door ('nɛkstˌdor) adj. 隔壁的
　　　neighbor ('nebɚ) n. 鄰居　　***get married*** 結婚
　　　attend (ə'tɛnd) v. 參加　　ceremony ('sɛrəˌmonɪ) n. 典禮
　　　divorced (də'vɔrst) adj. 離婚的

17. (**D**) Listen! They're playing your favorite song.
你聽！他們正播放著你最喜歡的歌。

    A. Maybe, if you want. I can't sing very well.
也許，如果你想要的話。我不是很會唱歌。

    B. Yes, we can play all your favorites. Name a few.
是的，我們可以播放所有你喜歡的歌。說一些你喜歡的歌。

    C. Sure, they're free. Take one anytime.
當然，它們是免費的。隨時可以拿一個。

    D. No, you must be thinking of someone else. I hate
that song. 不，你一定是想到別人了。我討厭那首歌。

    * favorite〔'fevərɪt〕adj. 最喜歡的 n. 最喜歡的人或物
name〔nem〕v. 說出…的名稱

18. (**A**) In Taiwan, is it considered impolite to ask someone how
much they make?
在台灣，問某人賺多少錢會被認爲是不禮貌的嗎？

    A. Yes, it is. 是的，是不禮貌的。

    B. No, they aren't. 不，他們不會。

    C. Maybe I will. 或許我會。

    D. Sure, they can. 當然，他們可以。

    * consider〔kən'sɪdə〕v. 認爲
impolite〔,ɪmpə'laɪt〕adj. 無禮的 **make money** 賺錢

19. (**B**) If I don't get the promotion, I'm going to resign.
如果我沒有得到升遷，我將會辭職。

    A. I can't right now. Ask the receptionist to do it.
我現在不行。要求接待員去做。

    B. Don't make any rash decisions. You might regret it.
不要做任何輕率的決定。你可能會後悔。

    C. Good luck with your next project.
祝你下一個企畫能有好運。

D. Times are tough. I need money too.

時間很緊急。我也需要錢。

* promotion〔 prə'moʃən 〕n. 升遷
resign〔 rɪ'zaɪn 〕v. 辭職
receptionist〔 rɪ'sɛpʃənɪst 〕n. 接待員
rash〔 ræʃ 〕adj. 輕率的　　regret〔 rɪ'grɛt 〕v. 後悔
project〔 prɑ'dʒɛkt 〕n. 計畫；企劃
tough〔 tʌf 〕adj. 艱難的
Times are tough. 日子很不好過。(= *Times are hard.*)

20. (**C**) When will we be taking off? Why are we still sitting on the runway? 我們什麼時候要起飛？為什麼我們還在跑道上？

A. Relax. You can do it. 放輕鬆。你可以做到的。

B. Not now. I need to sit down. 不要現在。我需要坐下。

C. Calm down. The captain said there will be a brief delay. 冷靜。機長說會有短暫的延遲。

D. Knock it off. They'll hear us. 別鬧了。他們會聽見。

* **take off** (飛機) 起飛
runway〔'rʌn,we 〕n. (機場的) 跑道　　**calm down** 平靜下來
captain〔'kæptən 〕n. (飛機的) 機長
brief〔 brif 〕adj. 短暫的　　delay〔 dɪ'le 〕n. 延遲；耽擱
knock it off 別吵了；別鬧了

(三) 簡短對話

For question 21, you will listen to a short conversation.

W : Would you mind lending me some cash until we get back to the hotel? 你介不介意借我一些現金，直到我們回到飯店？

M : How much? I might need to hit an ATM as well.

多少？我可能也需要去自動提款機。

W : Fifty bucks, if you have that much, but twenty should cover me.

五十美元，如果你有那麼多的話，但是二十應該就夠了。

* lend〔lɛnd〕*v.* 借（出）
  get back to 回到　　hit〔hɪt〕*v.* 到達
  ATM *n.* 提款機；自動櫃員機（= *automated-teller machine*）
  buck〔bʌk〕*n.* 一美元
  cover〔'kʌvɚ〕*v.*（錢）足夠付；對⋯夠用

21. (**B**) Q : What does the woman want?　這位女士想要什麼？
    A. She wants to go back to the hotel.　她想要回飯店。
    B. She wants to borrow money from the man.
       她想要跟那位男士借錢。
    C. She wants to find an ATM.　她想找到一台提款機。
    D. She wants her money back.　她想要要回她的錢。

    * borrow〔'baro〕*v.* 借（入）

For question 22, you will listen to a short conversation.

M : Do you remember the first time you ever kissed a boy?
    妳記得妳第一次親男孩的時候嗎？

W : Yes, I was 16. His name was Josh. What about you?
    Do you remember the first time you kissed a girl?
    是的，我十六歲。他的名字是喬許。那你呢？你記得你第一次
    親女孩的時候嗎？

M : I didn't even hold hands with a girl until I was 18.
    My first kiss came sometime after that, while I was
    in college. I couldn't tell you her name though.
    我到十八歲時才和女生牽手。我的初吻大概是在那之後，當時
    我還在念大學。然而我沒有辦法告訴你她的名字。

22. (**A**) Q：What does the man imply? 這位男士暗示什麼？

　　A. He has a vague memory of his first kiss.
　　　他對他的初吻有著模糊的記憶。

　　B. He was lonely in college. 他在大學時是寂寞的。

　　C. He is a good kisser. 他是個接吻高手。

　　D. He was a good student. 他是個好學生。

　　* ***hold hands*** 牽手　　sometime〔ˈsʌmˌtaɪm〕*adv.* 某時
　　though〔ðo〕*adv.*【置於句尾】不過　　imply〔ɪmˈplaɪ〕*v.* 暗示
　　vague〔veg〕*adj.* 模糊的　　memory〔ˈmɛmərɪ〕*n.* 記憶
　　lonely〔ˈlonlɪ〕*adj.* 寂寞的　　kisser〔ˈkɪsɚ〕*n.* 接吻的人

For question 23, you will listen to a short conversation.

　　M：Hi, Elaine.　What are you doing?
　　　嗨，依蓮。妳正在做什麼？

　　W：I'm trying to figure out how to use my new camera.
　　　我正在摸索如何使用我的新相機。

　　M：Don't you have the instruction manual?
　　　你沒有操作指南手冊嗎？

　　W：I do, but it's only written in Chinese!
　　　我有，但只有中文說明！

　　　* ***figure out*** 了解　　camera〔ˈkæmərə〕*n.* 照相機
　　instruction〔ɪnˈstrʌkʃən〕*n.* 使用說明；操作指南
　　manual〔ˈmænjuəl〕*n.* 手冊

23. (**A**) Q：What problem does the woman have with her
　　　camera? 這位女士在使用她的相機上有什麼問題？

　　A. She can't read the instruction manual.
　　　她看不懂操作指南手冊。

　　B. There are too many buttons. 有太多按鈕了。

C. The battery is dead. 電池沒電。

D. It won't take pictures. 相機無法拍照。

* button〔ˋbʌtn̩〕 n. 按鈕　　battery〔ˋbætərɪ〕 n. 電池
dead〔dɛd〕 adj. 無電流的；不通電的　　***take pictures*** 拍照

For question 24, you will listen to a short conversation.

W：Did you call a plumber? 你打電話給水管工人了嗎？

M：Yes. He'll be here at 5:00 p.m.
有。他將會在下午五點到這裡。

W：But that's too late! I have to leave for work at 4:00.
但是那樣就太晚了！我必須在下午四點去工作。

M：No problem. I'll cut out of work early to be here.
沒問題。我會早點結束工作到這裡來。

* plumber〔ˋplʌmɚ〕 n. 水管工人
leave for 動身前往　　***cut out of*** sth. 停止

24. (**B**) Q：What kind of problem do the speakers most likely
have? 說話者很可能遇到什麼問題？

A. Their roof is leaking. 他們的屋頂正在漏水。

B. Their pipes are clogged. 他們的水管堵塞。

C. Their walls need painting. 他們的牆需要粉刷。

D. Their windows are broken. 他們的窗戶破掉了。

* roof〔ruf〕 n. 屋頂　　leak〔lik〕 v. 漏水
pipe〔paɪp〕 n. 水管　　clog〔klɑg〕 v. 堵塞
paint〔pent〕 v. 油漆

For questions 25 and 26, you will listen to a short conversation.

W：How long were you in Paris? 你在巴黎待多久？

M : Long enough to see the sights and get out of there.
久到足以看完景點再離開。

W : Oh, I take it you didn't enjoy your visit?
喔，我就當作你不喜歡你這次的旅行？

M : You can say that again.　妳說的沒錯。

* sights 〔 saɪts 〕 *n. pl.* 名勝；觀光景點
visit 〔 'vɪzɪt 〕 *n.* 參觀；拜訪

25. (**D**) Q : How long was the man in Paris?
這位男士在巴黎待多久？

    A. Two days. 兩天。　　　B. One week. 一星期。
    C. A month. 一個月。
    D. It is impossible to say. 無法得知。

26. (**C**) Q : What does the man imply? 這位男士暗示什麼？

    A. He can't wait to go back to Paris. 他等不及要回到巴黎。
    B. He is excited about his trip to Paris.
他對於他的巴黎之旅感到興奮。
    C. Paris did not appeal to him. 巴黎不吸引他。
    D. The woman isn't speaking clearly.
這位女士沒有說清楚。

* imply 〔 ɪm'plaɪ 〕 *v.* 暗示　　*appeal to* 吸引

For questions 27 and 28, you will listen to a short conversation.

M : Hi, Sue. What do you know about computers?
嗨，蘇。妳對電腦了解多少？

W : Not much, Alan. I know how to turn one on and check
my e-mail. That's about it. Why? What's your
problem?

不多，艾倫。我知道如何開啓和檢查我的電子郵件。大概就這
樣。為什麼這樣問？你的問題是什麼？

M : Oh, I can't get this program to work properly. It keeps
freezing up. 喔，我無法讓這個程式正常運作。它一直動不了。

W : You should talk to Meredith. She's a genius when it
comes to these things.

你應該跟梅樂蒂斯說。當提到這些事時，她是個天才。

* ***turn on*** 打開（電源）　***That's about it.*** 大致如此。
program〔'progræm〕 *n.* 程式　　work〔wɜk〕 *v.* 運作
properly〔'prɑpəlɪ〕 *adv.* 適當地；正確地　***freeze up*** 凍結
genius〔'dʒinjəs〕 *n.* 天才　　***when it comes to*** 一提到

27. (**B**) Q : What is the man's problem? 這位男士的問題是什麼？

A. He can't access his e-mail. 他無法存取他的電子郵件。

B. A computer program doesn't work properly.
有個電腦程式無法正常運作。

C. He can't get a hold of Meredith.
他無法聯絡上梅樂蒂斯。

D. Sue turned off his computer without asking.
蘇沒有問過就把他的電腦關機。

* access〔'æksɛs〕 *v.* 存取（資料）
get a hold of *sb.* 聯繫上某人　　***turn off*** 關掉（電源）

28. (**C**) Q : What does the woman suggest? 這位女士建議什麼？

A. That the man reinstall the program.
建議這位男士重新安裝該程式。

B. That the man get a new computer.
建議這位男士買個新電腦。

C. That the man talk to Meredith.
建議這位男士跟梅樂蒂斯談一談。

D. That the man take a computer class.
　　建議這位男士去上電腦課。

* suggest〔sə'dʒɛst〕v. 建議　　reinstall〔͵riɪn'stɔl〕v. 重新安裝
get〔gɛt〕v. 買　　***take a…class*** 上…課

For questions 29 and 30, you will listen to a short conversation.

W : What's wrong, Carl?　You look worried.
　　怎麼了，卡爾？你看起來很擔心。

M : I spilled red wine on Gloria's new couch.　She's going to
kill me. 我把紅酒灑在葛洛莉雅的新沙發上。她會殺了我。

W : You mean that little spot?　She'll never notice that.
　　你是說那一小點嗎？她絕對不會注意到的。

M : You don't know Gloria.　She doesn't miss a thing.
　　妳不了解葛洛莉雅。她什麼都會注意到。

* worried〔'wɝɪd〕adj. 擔心的　　spill〔spɪl〕v. 灑出
wine〔waɪn〕n. 葡萄酒　　couch〔kautʃ〕n. 長沙發
spot〔spat〕n. 斑點　　notice〔'notɪs〕v. 注意到
miss〔mɪs〕v. 錯過；沒注意到

29. (**D**) Q : What did the man do?　這位男士做了什麼？

A. He upset Gloria. 他讓葛洛莉雅不開心。
B. He shot and killed someone. 他射殺了某人。
C. He came home late last night. 他昨晚很晚才回家。
D. He spilled wine on Gloria's new couch.
　　他把酒灑在葛洛莉雅的新沙發上。

* shoot〔ʃut〕v. 射擊

30. (**B**) Q : What does the man imply?　這位男士暗示什麼？

A. Gloria is very careless. 葛洛莉雅非常粗心。

B. Gloria is very observant. 葛洛莉雅觀察力非常敏銳。

C. Gloria is very worried. 葛洛莉雅非常擔心。

D. Gloria is very pushy. 葛洛莉雅非常強勢。

* careless〔ˈkɛrlɪs〕adj. 粗心的
  observant〔əbˈzɝvənt〕adj. 觀察力敏銳的
  pushy〔ˈpuʃɪ〕adj. 強勢的；強人所難的

四、短文聽解

Questions 31 and 32 are based on the following report.

Murder is wrong. Since childhood we have been taught this indisputable truth. Ask yourself, then, what is capital punishment? In its simplest form, capital punishment is defined as one person taking the life of another. Coincidentally, that is the definition of murder. There are 36 states with the death penalty, and they must change. These states need to abolish it on the grounds that it carries a dangerous risk of punishing the innocent, it is unethical and barbaric, and it is an ineffective deterrent of crime versus the alternative of life in prison without parole.

謀殺是錯誤的，我們從小就被教導這個不爭的事實。那麼，問問你自己，什麼是死刑？死刑最簡單的定義，就是一個人奪走另一個人的生命。巧合的是，這就是謀殺的定義。有 36 州有死刑，而他們必須改變。這些州需要廢除死刑，因為死刑是有風險的，可能會懲罰無辜的人，死刑是不道德，而且野蠻的，而且和終身監禁不得假釋這項替代方案對比之下，死刑對於遏阻犯罪是無效的。

** ───────────────

murder〔'mɝdə 〕n. 謀殺　childhood〔'tʃaɪld,hʊd 〕n. 童年時期
indisputable〔,ɪndɪ'spjutəbḷ 〕adj. 無可爭論的
truth〔truθ 〕n. 事實　*capital punishment* 死刑
form〔fɔrm 〕n. 形式　define〔dɪ'faɪn 〕v. 下定義
take sb's life 殺死某人
coincidentally〔ko,ɪnsə'dɛntḷɪ 〕adv. 碰巧的是；巧合地
definition〔,dɛfə'nɪʃən 〕n. 定義；釋義　state〔stet 〕n. 州

with〔wɪθ 〕prep. 有　penalty〔'pɛnḷtɪ 〕n. 刑罰
death penalty 死刑　abolish〔ə'bolɪsh 〕v. 廢除
on the grounds of 因為　carry〔'kærɪ 〕v. 具有
risk〔rɪsk 〕n. 風險　innocent〔'ɪnəsṇt 〕adj. 無罪的；清白的
unethical〔ʌn'ɛθɪkḷ 〕adj. 不道德的
barbaric〔bɑr'bærɪk 〕adj. 野蠻的
ineffective〔,ɪnə'fɛktɪv 〕adj. 無效的

deterrent〔dɪ'tɝrənt 〕n. 威懾力量；制止物
versus〔'vɝsəs 〕prep. …對…
alternative〔ɔl'tɝnətɪv 〕n. 供選擇的東西；替代方案
prison〔'prɪzṇ 〕n. 監獄
life in prison 終生監禁（ = *life imprisonment* ）
parole〔pə'rol 〕n. 假釋

31. (**A**) What is another term for capital punishment?
　　　capital punishment 的另一個說法是什麼？

　　A. The death penalty. 死刑。
　　B. The kiss of death. 死亡之吻。
　　C. The spice of life. 生活趣味。
　　D. The National Anthem. 國歌。

　　* term〔tɝm 〕n. 名詞；用語
　　　spice〔spaɪs 〕n. 趣味；風味；香料
　　　anthem〔'ænθəm 〕n. 頌歌；國歌　*national anthem* 國歌

32. (**B**) What is the speaker's opinion of capital punishment?
說話者對死刑的看法是什麼？

  A. It is highly effective in fighting crime.
   死刑對打擊犯罪是非常有效的。

  B. It is wrong and should be stopped.
   死刑是錯的而且應該停止。

  C. It is the truth.　死刑是眞理。

  D. It is a fitting punishment for murderers.
   死刑對殺人犯而言是一項適當的懲罰。

  * opinion〔ə'pɪnjən〕n. 意見；看法
   highly〔'haɪlɪ〕adv. 非常　　fitting〔'fɪtɪŋ〕adj. 適當的
   murderer〔'mɝdərə〕n. 謀殺犯；兇手

Questions 33 and 34 are based on the following report.

  U.S. intelligence agencies recently broke up a plot to bomb an airliner and have seized an explosive device that is similar to ones previously used by Al Qaeda, officials said Monday.　The plot was discovered before it threatened any Americans, and no airliners were at risk, one U.S. official said.　A plastic explosive device like the one used in the failed attempt to bomb a Detroit-bound jet in 2009 was recovered, the official said, adding that it was meant for use by a suicide bomber.　A spokesman for the Department of Homeland Security said authorities have "no specific, credible information regarding an active terrorist plot against the U.S. at this time," although they continue to monitor efforts to carry out such attacks.

  官員在週一時表示，美國情報機構最近破解一樁想炸毀客機的陰謀，並且起獲一個類似蓋達組織先前所使用的爆炸裝置。該陰謀在任何美國人被威脅之前就被發現，也沒有一架客機處於危險之中，一位美國官員說。該負責人說，這個塑膠爆破性裝置就像 2009 年企圖轟炸一架飛往底特律的噴射機的攻擊一樣被發現，他還說，此裝置是一名自殺炸彈客想使用的。美國國土安全部發言人說，當局表示雖然目前並沒有「關於對付美國的活躍的恐怖陰謀之具體、可信的資訊」，但是他們仍將繼續監控進行此類攻擊的活動。

** ────────────────────

intelligence〔ɪnˋtɛlədʒəns〕*n.* 情報

agency〔ˋedʒənsɪ〕*n.* 行政機構（局、署、處、社）

break up 打破；粉碎；中止　　plot〔plɑt〕*n.* 陰謀

bomb〔bɑm〕*v.* 轟炸　　airliner〔ˋɛr͵laɪnɚ〕*n.* 大型客機；班機

seize〔siz〕*v.* 沒收；扣押　　explosive〔ɪkˋsplosɪv〕*adj.* 爆炸的

device〔dɪˋvaɪs〕*n.* 裝置　　previously〔ˋprivɪəslɪ〕*adv.* 先前

Al Qaeda *n.* 阿爾・蓋達基地組織【由奧薩瑪・賓拉登所領導的全球
　　恐怖網路】　　official〔əˋfɪʃəl〕*n.* 官員

threaten〔ˋθrɛtn̩〕*v.* 威脅　　***at risk*** 有危險

plastic〔ˋplæstɪk〕*adj.* 塑膠的　　failed〔feld〕*adj.* 失敗的

attempt〔əˋtɛmpt〕*n.* 企圖；攻擊

Detroit〔dɪˋtrɔɪt〕*n.* 底特律【美國城市名】

bound〔baʊnd〕*adj.*【常構成複合字】往…的

jet〔dʒɛt〕*n.* 噴射機　　recover〔rɪˋkʌvɚ〕*v.* 恢復；發現

add〔æd〕*v.* 又說　　***be meant for*** 目的；是為了

suicide〔ˋsuə͵saɪd〕*adj.* 自殺的　　bomber〔ˋbɑmɚ〕*n.* 用炸彈的人

spokesman〔ˋspoksmən〕*n.* 發言人

Department of Homeland Security *n.* 美國國土安全部【為美國
　　政府在九一一事件之後設立的一個聯邦行政部門，負責國內安全及防
　　止恐怖行動】　　authorities〔əˋθɔrətɪz〕*n. pl.* 當局

specific〔spɪˋsɪfɪk〕*adj.* 特定的；明確的

credible〔ˋkrɛdəbl̩〕*adj.* 可信的

regarding〔rɪˋgɑrdɪŋ〕*prep.* 關於（= *about*）

active〔ˋæktɪv〕*adj.* 活躍的　　terrorist〔ˋtɛrərɪst〕*n.* 恐怖分子

monitor〔əˋθɔrətɪ〕*v.* 監控　　effort〔ˋɛfɚt〕*n.* 努力；活動

carry out 實行；執行　　attack〔əˋtæk〕*n.* 攻擊

33. (**D**)　Where did this report most likely take place?
　　　　這份報告最有可能在哪裡發表？

　　　　A.　At a sporting event.　在一場體育活動中。

　　　　B.　In a church.　在一間教堂裡。

　　　　C.　During a rock concert.　在一場搖滾演唱會中。

　　　　D.　On television.　在電視上。

　　　　* *take place* 發生　　sporting〔'spɔrtɪŋ〕*adj.* 運動的
　　　　event〔ɪ'vɛnt〕*n.* 大型活動
　　　　rock〔rɑk〕*n.* 搖滾樂（= *rock and roll*）
　　　　concert〔'kɑnsət〕*n.* 音樂會；演唱會

34. (**C**)　What happened?　發生了什麼事？

　　　　A.　The U.S. bombed al Qaeda.　美國轟炸蓋達組織基地。

　　　　B.　The U.S. issued a terror warning.　美國發布恐怖警告。

　　　　C.　The U.S. broke up a plot to bomb a plane.
　　　　　　美國破解一樁轟炸飛機的陰謀。

　　　　D.　The U.S. recovered from a terrorist attack.
　　　　　　美國從一場恐怖份子攻擊中恢復。

　　　　* issue〔'ɪʃju〕*v.* 發出　　terror〔'tɛrə〕*n.* 恐怖主義；恐怖活動

Questions 35 and 36 are based on the following report.

　　　　Music is a powerful thing. It evokes feelings and
has the power to bring people together. Music is also a
way for people to express themselves and share ideas,
whether through poetic lyrics or throbbing anthems.
But today, artists are not known for their music, but for
how extravagant their outfits are and how many times
their wealthy relatives can get them out of jail. And thus
music is lost. Pop and rap music has evolved into a shallow,

image-obsessed industry that conforms to what the public
wants to hear and see, eliminating the focus on the actual
music. Mainstream music is no longer composed of
emotion, but instead of themes of money, sex, and fame.

　　音樂的力量很強大。它能喚起情感，並且具有把人們聚在一起
的力量。音樂也是一種人們表達自我和分享想法的方式，無論是透
過具有詩意的抒情作品，或是撼動人心的頌歌。但現在，藝人們不
是因為他們的音樂而出名，而是因為他們服裝是如何的奢華，以及
富有的親戚可以讓他們從拘留所出來多少次。然後音樂就這樣消失
了。流行音樂和饒舌音樂，逐步演變成符合大眾所希望聽到和看到
的，膚淺且過分關注形象的產業，不再聚焦在實質的音樂上。主流
音樂不再是由情感所組成，取而代之的是金錢、性和名聲的題材。

** ────────────────

powerful〔'pauɚfəl〕*adj.* 強有力的　　evoke〔ɪ'vok〕*v.* 喚起
feelings〔'filɪŋz〕*n. pl.* 感覺；感情　　***bring together*** 使團結
express〔ɪk'sprɛs〕*v.* 表達
poetic〔po'ɛtɪk〕*adj.* 詩情畫意的　　lyrics〔'lɪrɪks〕*n. pl.* 歌詞
throbbing〔'θrɑbɪŋ〕*adj.* 有節奏地跳動的；激動的
anthem〔'ænθəm〕*n.* 頌歌；國歌
artist〔'ɑrtɪst〕*n.* 藝術家；藝人
extravagant〔ɪk'strævəgənt〕*adj.* 奢華的
outfit〔'aut,fɪt〕*n.* 服裝　　wealthy〔'wɛlθɪ〕*adj.* 有錢的

relative〔'rɛlətɪv〕*n.* 親戚　　jail〔dʒel〕*n.* 監獄；拘留所
lost〔lɔst〕*adj.* 消失了的　　pop〔pɑp〕*adj.* 流行的
rap〔ræp〕*n.* 說唱；饒舌　　evolve〔ɪ'vɑlv〕*v.* 逐漸發展
shallow〔'ʃælo〕*adj.* 膚淺的　　image〔'ɪmɪdʒ〕*n.* 形象
obsessed〔əb'sɛst〕*adj.* 著迷的
image-obsessed *adj.* 過分關注形象的
industry〔'ɪndəstrɪ〕*n.* 產業
conform〔kən'fɔrm〕*v.* 符合 < *to* >
eliminate〔ɪ'lɪmə,net〕*v.* 除去　　focus〔'fokəs〕*n.* 焦點

actual (ˈæktʃuəl) *adj.* 眞正的　　mainstream (ˈmenˌstrim) *n.* 主流
no longer 不再　　***be composed of*** 由⋯組成
emotion〔ɪˈmoʃən〕*n.* 情緒；情感
instead〔ɪnˈstɛd〕*adv.* 取而代之
theme〔θim〕*n.* 主題；題材　　fame〔fem〕*n.* 名聲

35. (**D**) What is the speaker's attitude toward popular music
　　　today? 說話者對現在流行音樂的態度是什麼？
　　　A. Envious. 嫉妒的。　　　B. Emotional. 情緒化的。
　　　C. Respectful. 尊敬的。　　D. Disappointed. 失望的。

　　* envious (ˈɛnvɪəs) *adj.* 嫉妒的；羨慕的 < of >
　　　emotional〔ɪˈmoʃənḷ〕*adj.* 情緒化的
　　　respectful〔rɪˈspɛktfəl〕*adj.* 恭敬的
　　　disappointed〔ˌdɪsəˈpɔɪntɪd〕*adj.* 失望的

36. (**B**) What does the speaker think about today's pop and rap
　　　music? 說話者認爲現在的流行及饒舌音樂如何？
　　　A. It is fresh and exciting. 新穎且令人興奮的。
　　　B. It is shallow and vain. 膚淺且虛榮的。
　　　C. It is powerful and throbbing.
　　　　強有力且節奏感十足的。
　　　D. It is slow and boring. 緩慢且無聊的。

　　* fresh〔frɛʃ〕*adj.* 新鮮的　　vain〔ven〕*adj.* 虛榮的

Questions 37 and 38 are based on the following report.

　　　It seems like every holiday season we have to go
through the same routine. For whatever reason, people
need to be reminded that drinking and driving is dangerous,
and worst of all, often deadly. The holiday season is
supposed to be a special time for celebrating with friends
and family, but every year we hear the same stories. A

family of four is killed in a head-on collision with a drunk driver. Seven pedestrians are severely injured when a drunk driver jumps the curb and mows them down on the sidewalk. Alcohol is involved in 38 percent of fatal automobile accidents nationwide. Every 30 minutes someone is killed by a drunk driver. Everybody knows this. It's common knowledge. Don't drink and drive. Why should the holiday season be any different?

似乎每個節慶假期我們都要經歷同樣的例行程序。無論基於何種原因，人們都需要被提醒酒後駕車是危險的，而且最糟糕的是，往往是致命的。節慶假期應該是個與家人朋友慶祝的特別時刻，但每年我們卻聽到相同的故事。一家四口在一場與酒醉駕駛的司機迎面撞上而身亡。七位行人被酒醉駕駛的司機衝過邊欄、撞上人行道而受重傷。全國致命車禍中，有38％與酒駕有關。每30分鐘就有一人因酒駕而死亡。每個人都知道這一點。這是眾所皆知的事。喝酒不開車。爲何節慶假期應該有所不同呢？

** ————————————————

season〔'sizn〕 *n.* 時期
the holiday season 休假期【耶誕節、復活節、八月等】
go through 經歷　　routine〔ru'tin〕 *n.* 例行公事
whatever〔hwɑt'ɛvɚ〕 *adj.* 不論⋯的
remind〔rɪ'maɪnd〕 *v.* 提醒
drinking〔'drɪŋkɪŋ〕 *n.* 喝酒　　***worst of all*** 最糟的是
deadly〔'dɛdlɪ〕 *adj.* 致命的　　***be supposed to*** 應該
celebrate〔'sɛlə,bret〕 *v.* 慶祝　　***be killed*** 死亡
head-on〔'hɛd'ɑn〕 *adj.* 迎面的　　collision〔kə'lɪʒən〕 *n.* 相撞
pedestrian〔pə'dɛstrɪən〕 *n.* 行人
drunk〔drʌŋk〕 *adj.* 喝醉的　　severely〔kə'vɪrlɪ〕 *adv.* 嚴重地
injure〔'ɪndʒɚ〕 *v.* 使受傷　　jump〔dʌmp〕 *v.* 跳躍；躍過
curb〔kɝb〕 *n.* （人行道旁的）邊石；邊欄

> ***jump the curb*** 開上人行道　　mow〔mo〕*v.* 割（草）
> ***mow down*** 掃射；殺死；摧毀
> sidewalk〔'saɪd‚wɔk〕*n.* 人行道　　alcohol〔'ælkə‚hɔl〕*n.* 酒
> ***be involved in*** 和…有關　　fatal〔'fetḷ〕*adj.* 致命的
> nationwide〔'neʃən‚waɪd〕*adv.* 在全國
> ***drink and drive*** 酒醉駕車　　***common knowledge*** 眾所皆知

37. (**C**) What does the speaker imply? 說話者暗示什麼？

A. The holiday season is a time for celebration.
節慶假期是個歡慶的時刻。

B. The holiday season is a well-worn story.
節慶假期是個陳腐的故事。

C. The holiday season is not an excuse to drink and
drive. 節慶假期不是酒駕的藉口。

D. The holiday season is the best time to drink and
drive. 節慶假期是酒駕最好的時間。

* well-worn〔'wɛl'worn〕*adj.* 用舊了的；陳腐的；平凡的
excuse〔ɪk'skjus〕*n.* 藉口

38. (**A**) What does the speaker complain about? 說話者抱怨什麼？

A. Having to remind people that drinking and driving
is dangerous. 要提醒人們酒醉駕車是危險的。

B. Having to explain himself during the holiday season.
要在節慶假期中為自己的行為做出解釋。

C. Having to avoid drinking during the holiday season.
必須在節慶假期中避免飲酒。

D. Having to drive his drunken friends home.
必須開車載他喝醉的朋友回家。

* complain〔kəm'plen〕*v.* 抱怨
explain *oneself* 把自己的意思解釋清楚；解釋自己的行為
drive *sb.* ***home*** 開車載某人回家

Questions 39 and 40 are based on the following report.

In a country that is searching for answers as to why its children are not reaching their academic potential, it seems fairly obvious that one of those answers may be found in the time at which they start their school day. For any parent who has looked with pity upon their teenage children as they drag themselves, glassy-eyed, and bedraggled, out of bed at 6:00 a.m. each day, there is a way to help. Be pro-active and approach your school board with well-researched pleas for a later start to the high school day. Not only will our students be healthier and more successful at tasks in school, they will become nicer individuals.

在一個正一直在尋找關於孩子爲什麼沒有發揮他們的學術潛力的解答的國家，很明顯的是，這問題的答案之一，可能在他們開始上學的時間就可以發現。對於心疼地看著自己十幾歲的小孩，每天拖著沈重的腳步、眼睛無神、邋裡邋遢地在清晨六點起床的父母而言，有一種方法可以幫助他們。要積極主動，並且經過詳細研究，來與教育委員們商量，懇求他們讓孩子唸高中時晚一點上學。這樣不僅我們的學生會更健康，而且在學校的課業的表現會更成功，他們也將成爲更好的人。

** ——————————————————————

search for 尋找　　**as to** 關於
academic〔͵ækə'dɛmɪk〕adj. 學術的
potential〔pə'tɛnʃəl〕n. 潛力
reach one's **potential** 發揮潛力（= achieve one's potential）
fairly〔'fɛrlɪ〕adv. 相當地　　obvious〔'ɑbvɪəs〕adj. 明顯的
look upon 看著（= look on）　　pity〔'pɪtɪ〕n. 可憐；同情
teenage〔'tin͵edʒ〕adj. 青少年的；十幾歲的
drag〔dræg〕v. 拖著　　**drag** oneself 拖著沈重的腳步

glassy-eyed〔'glæsɪ'aɪd〕 *adj.* 目光呆滯的
bedraggled〔bɪ'drægld〕 *adj.* 不整潔的
pro-active〔pro'æktɪv〕 *adj.* 積極的；主動的
approach〔ə'protʃ〕 *v.* 找…商量
board〔bord〕 *n.* 董事會；委員會　　***school board*** 教育委員會
well-researched *adj.* 經過詳細研究的
plea〔pli〕 *n.* 請求；懇求　　individual〔ˌɪndə'vɪdʒuəl〕 *n.* 個人

39. (**B**) What is the speaker's main point? 說話者的重點是什麼？

   A. Students have too much homework.
      學生們有太多的回家作業。

   B. Students have to get up too early in the morning.
      學生早上必須太早起床。

   C. Teachers need to be more understanding.
      老師們需要更通情達理。

   D. The school board doesn't care about the students.
      教育委員會並不在意學生。

   * ***main point*** 要點　　***get up*** 起床
   　understanding〔ˌʌndə'stændɪŋ〕 *adj.* 能諒解的

40. (**D**) What is said about students in this country?
   關於這個國家的學生本文提到什麼？

   A. They are doing just fine. 他們都做得很好。

   B. They are more successful than students from other
      countries. 他們比其他國家的學生都要成功。

   C. They are ignored by the school board.
      他們被教育委員會忽視。

   D. They are not reaching their potential.
      他們沒有發揮他們的潛能。

   * just〔dʒʌst〕 *adv.* 真地；完全
   　be doing fine 做得不錯；做得好　　ignore〔ɪg'nor〕 *v.* 忽視

高中英聽測驗模擬試題 ⑨ 詳解

一、看圖辨義：第一部分

For question number 1, please look at the four pictures.

1. (**A**) Rex plays tennis.　He's our school champion.

　　雷克斯打網球。他是我們學校的冠軍。

　　　　* tennis ('tɛnɪs) *n.* 網球　　champion ('tʃæmpɪən) *n.* 冠軍

For question number 2, please look at the four pictures.

2. (**D**) Todd is a good older brother.　He walks his little sister to school every day.

　　陶德是一位好哥哥。他每天陪他妹妹走路上學。

For question number 3, please look at the four pictures.

3. (**A**)　Janet is not a morning person.　She never feels fully
　　　rested after a night's sleep.　珍妮特不是個早起的人。
　　　她從來都不覺得睡一晚之後有充分的休息。

　　　　　* fully〔ˈfʊlɪ〕adv. 完全地；十分地　　　rested〔ˈrɛstɪd〕adj. 休息

For question number 4, please look at the four pictures.

4. (**A**)　They had a wonderful time at the seashore.　It was a
　　　perfect day to enjoy a barbeque.　他們在海邊玩得很愉快。
　　　那是很適合享受烤肉的日子。

　　　　　* wonderful〔ˈwʌndəfəl〕adj. 很棒的
　　　　　　seashore〔ˈsiˌʃor〕n. 海岸
　　　　　　perfect〔ˈpɝfɪkt〕adj. 完美的；最合適的
　　　　　　barbecue〔ˈbɑrbɪˌkju〕n. 烤肉

一、看圖辨義：第二部分

For question number 5, please look at picture 5.

5.（**A、B**）Which TWO of the following are true about the
picture? 關於這張圖片，下列哪兩項爲眞？

A. Kevin is doing his homework.
凱文正在做他的家庭作業。

B. Kevin is writing with a pencil.
凱文正在用他的鉛筆寫字。

C. Kevin is reading a newspaper.
凱文正在看報紙。

D. Kevin is eating a sandwich. 凱文正在吃三明治。

* newspaper〔'nuz͵pepɚ〕*n.* 報紙
sandwich〔'sændwɪtʃ〕*n.* 三明治

For question number 6, please look at picture 6.

6.（**C、D**）Which TWO of the following are true about the
picture? 關於這張圖片，下列哪兩項爲眞？

Λ. The man is sitting at a desk.
那男人正坐在書桌前。

B. The boy is learning to crawl.
那男孩正在學習爬行。

C. The man is running alongside the boy.
那男人正跑在男孩旁邊。

D. The boy is learning how to ride a bicycle.
那男孩正在學習如何騎腳踏車。

* crawl〔krɔl〕*v.* 爬
alongside〔ə'lɔŋ'saɪd〕*prep.* 在…旁邊

For question number 7, please look at picture 7.

7. (**C、D**) Which TWO of the following are true about the picture? 關於這張圖片，下列哪兩項為真？

    A. Some people are playing chess. 有些人正在下西洋棋。

    B. Some people are flying kites. 有些人正在放風箏。

    C. Some people are playing basketball. 有些人正在打籃球。

    D. Some people are swimming. 有些人正在游泳。

    * chess〔tʃɛs〕n. 西洋棋　　kite〔kaɪt〕n. 風箏
    fly a kite 放風箏

For question number 8, please look at picture 8.

8. (**A、C**) Which TWO of the following are true about the picture? 關於這張圖片，下列哪兩項為真？

    A. The man is leaning over the car's engine. 那男人正傾身靠近車子的引擎。

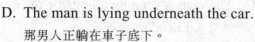

    B. The man is a dentist. 那男人是位牙醫。

    C. The man is a mechanic. 那男人是一位技工。

    D. The man is lying underneath the car. 那男人正躺在車子底下。

    * lean〔lin〕v. 傾身 < over >　　engine〔'ɛndʒən〕n. 引擎
    dentist〔'dɛntɪst〕n. 牙醫
    mechanic〔mə'kænɪk〕n. 技工；機械工人
    lie〔laɪ〕v. 躺　　underneath〔ˌʌndə'niθ〕prep. 在⋯下面

For question number 9, please look at picture 9.

9. (**C、D**) Which TWO of the following are true about the
picture? 關於這張圖片，下列哪兩項為眞？

A. Garrett is hard at work.
嘉瑞特工作時很嚴格。

B. It's raining.
現在正在下雨。

C. Garrett is relaxing. 嘉瑞特正在放鬆。

D. It's a sunny day. 今天是陽光普照的一天。

* hard〔 hɑrd 〕adj. 嚴厲的；嚴格的
at work 在工作
relax〔 rɪ'læks 〕v. 放鬆
sunny〔 'sʌnɪ 〕adj. 陽光充足的

For question number 10, please look at picture 10.

10. (**A、D**) Which TWO of the following are true about the
picture? 關於這張圖片，下列哪兩項為眞？

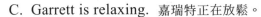

A. The men are having a meal.
男士們正在吃飯。

B. The men are playing a game.
男士們正在玩一個遊戲。

C. The men are sitting side-by-side.
男士們正肩並肩地坐著。

D. The men are sitting across from one another.
男士們正坐在彼此的對面。

* have〔 hæv 〕v. 吃　　meal〔 mil 〕n. 一餐
side-by-side adv. 肩並肩地；一起
across from 在…的對面

二、對答

11. (**A**) Are you still planning to drop out of school?
    你仍然計畫要休學嗎？

  A. No, I've had second thoughts. 不，我要重新考慮。

  B. No, they will give you a second chance.
   不，他們會給你第二次機會。

  C. No, I wouldn't give her a second look.
   不，我不會再看她一眼。

  D. No, unless he gets a second wind.
   不，除非他再恢復體力。

  * plan 〔 plæn 〕 v. 計畫；打算　　***drop out of school*** 輟學
  thought 〔 θɔt 〕 n. 想法；考慮
  have second thoughts 重新考慮
  a second 另一個 (= *another*)　　chance 〔 tʃæns 〕 n. 機會
  second wind 恢復體力

12. (**C**) Elaine is always checking herself in the mirror.
    伊蓮總是會檢查鏡子裡的自己。

  A. That's a good quality in a friend.
   那是朋友身上很好的特質。

  B. Ask for the check. 去要帳單。

  C. She must be very vain. 她一定很虛榮。

  D. Do you see your reflection? 你看到你自己的影像了嗎？

  * check 〔 tʃɛk 〕 v. 檢查　n. 帳單；支票
  quality 〔 'kwɑlətɪ 〕 n. 特質；特性　　***ask for*** 請求 (給予)
  vain 〔 ven 〕 adj. 虛榮心強的
  reflection 〔 rɪ'flɛkʃən 〕 n. 倒影；影像

13. (**C**) Have you ever been to the top of Taipei 101?
    你有到過台北 101 的頂端嗎？

  A. They're at the top of their game. 他們的表現很優秀。

B. The game is tied 1-1. 比賽是一比一平手。

C. Not yet, but I'm planning on it. 還沒，但我正在計畫。

D. Everyone knows Taipei 101. 大家都知道台北 101。

* top〔tɑp〕n. 頂端　　***at the top of*** one's game　表現優異的
tied〔taɪd〕adj. 打成平手的　　***not yet***　尚未；還沒
plan on　擬定…的計畫

14. (**B**) Have you ever been in a fist fight? 你有用拳頭鬥毆過嗎？

A. He was knocked unconscious. 他被打到失去意識。

B. No, I'm not a violent person. 沒有，我不是個暴力的人。

C. You started it. 是你先開始的。

D. See this fist? 看到這拳頭了嗎？

* fist〔fɪst〕n. 拳頭　　knock〔nɑk〕v. 敲；擊；打
unconscious〔ʌn'kɑnʃəs〕adj. 不省人事的；失去知覺的
violent〔'vaɪələnt〕adj. 暴力的

15. (**D**) Today's special is spaghetti with tomato sauce and garlic bread. 今日特餐是義大利麵佐蕃茄醬汁和大蒜麵包。

A. Just put it over there. It's nothing special.
就放在那裡吧。沒有什麼特別的。

B. It's making a strange sound. 它正發出奇怪的聲音。

C. Thanks, but I don't drink. 謝謝，但我不喝酒。

D. Sounds delicious. I'll have that.
聽起來很美味。我要吃那個。

* special〔'spɛʃəl〕n. 特餐　　spaghetti〔spə'gɛtɪ〕n. 義大利麵
tomato〔tə'meto〕n. 蕃茄　　sauce〔sɔs〕n. 醬汁
garlic〔'gɑrlɪk〕adj. 以蒜調味的

16. (**C**) What do you do for a living? 你以什麼維生？

A. I'm an atheist. 我是無神論者。

B. I'm Chinese and French. 我是中法混血兒。

C. I'm a teacher. 我是一位老師。

D. I'm running late. 我快遲到了。

* living〔'lɪvɪŋ〕 n. 生計；生存　　atheist〔'eθɪɪst〕 n. 無神論者
Chinese and French 中法混血兒
be running late 快要遲到了

17. (**A**) How did you sleep last night? 你昨晚睡得如何？

A. Not very well. 不太好。

B. We won't know for a while. 我們暫時還不清楚。

C. I'm not sleepy yet. 我還不想睡。

D. I was sleeping when you called last night.
你昨晚打電話給我的時候，我正在睡覺。

* **for a while** 暫時；一會兒　　sleepy〔'slipɪ〕 adj. 想睡的

18. (**D**) Is Jim staying for dinner? 吉姆要留下來吃晚餐嗎？

A. It's hot in here. 這裡好熱。

B. I'll take you to dinner. 我會帶你去吃晚餐。

C. Yes, that's my watch. 是的，那是我的錶。

D. Let me ask him. 讓我問他。

19. (**A**) Why do you want to attend Harvard? 你為什麼想唸哈佛？

A. It has an excellent reputation. 它有很好的名聲。

B. They offer retirement benefits. 他們提供退休福利。

C. I've been unemployed for a year. 我已經失業一年了。

D. My graduation is next week. 我的畢業典禮是下個星期。

* attend〔ə'tɛnd〕 v. 上（學）
Harvard〔'hɑrvəd〕 n. 哈佛大學【常被直接稱為哈佛，是一所私立研
究型大學因歷史、學術地位等因素而獲評為世上最享負盛名的學府】
excellent〔'ɛkslənt〕 adj. 優秀的
reputation〔ˌrɛpjə'teʃən〕 n. 名聲　　offer〔'ɔfə〕 v. 提供
retirement〔rɪ'taɪrmənt〕 n. 退休

benefits〔'bɛnəfɪts〕*n. pl.* 津貼；獎金；福利
unemployed〔ˌʌnɪm'plɔɪd〕*adj.* 失業的
graduation〔ˌgrædʒu'eʃən〕*n.* 畢業；畢業典禮

20.（**A**）Would you mind helping me with this box?
　　你介意幫忙我搬這個箱子嗎？

　　A. Sure.　Where would you like me to put it?
　　　　好。你要我把它放在哪裡？

　　B. Put it in the box.　把它放進箱子裡。

　　C. No, they don't need it any more.　不，他們不再需要它。

　　D. It completely slipped my mind.　我完全忘記了。

　　* ***help*** *sb.* ***with*** *sth.* 幫助某人某事　***not…any more*** 不再…
　　completely〔kəm'plitlɪ〕*adv.* 完全地
　　sth. ***slip*** *one's* ***mind*** 某人忘記某事

三、簡短對話

For question 21, you will listen to a short conversation.

M : Please read the directions carefully, Miss Smith.　There
　　are 20 tablets and you can get no refills.
　　請仔細閱讀使用方法，史密斯小姐。這裡是 20 個藥片，而且妳
　　不能用此次處方再配藥。

W : You mean I'll have to get a new prescription after these?
　　What a bother!　你的意思是在吃完這 20 個藥片後，我必須要
　　取得另一張新處方。真麻煩！

　　* directions〔də'rɛkʃəns〕*n. pl.* 使用方法
　　tablet〔'tæblɪt〕*n.* 藥片　　refill〔'rifɪl〕*n.* 處方的再配
　　prescription〔prɪ'skrɪpʃən〕*n.* 處方
　　bother〔'baðɚ〕*n.* 使人煩惱的人或事物

21. (**A**) Q : Where does this conversation take place?

這段對話發生在哪裡？

    A. At a pharmacy. 在藥局。

    B. At a supermarket. 在超市。

    C. At a fire station. 在消防站。

    D. At a library. 在圖書館。

    * ***take place*** 發生；舉行   **pharmacy**〔ˈfɑrməsɪ〕*n.* 藥房；藥局
    fire station 消防站   **library**〔ˈlaɪˏbrɛrɪ〕*n.* 圖書館

For question 22, you will listen to a short conversation.

W : I never seem to be able to get all my chores done.

我似乎永遠都沒辦法把我的家事做完。

M : That's because you're always taking breaks.

那是因為妳總是在休息。

    * chores〔tʃorz〕*n. pl.* 家庭雜務；家事   ***get sth. done*** 完成某事
    take a break 休息一下

22. (**B**) Q : What problem is the woman having?

這位女士有什麼麻煩？

    A. She doesn't want to take breaks. 她不想休息。

    B. She cannot finish her chores. 她無法把家事做完。

    C. She doesn't have enough chores to do.

      她沒有足夠的家事要做。

    D. The man wants her to take breaks. 那位男士要她休息。

For question 23, you will listen to a short conversation.

W : Marshal, are you doing anything special for your presentation in political science tomorrow?

馬歇爾，你要為明天政治學報告特別做些什麼嗎？

M : Not really. Because the class so often turns into a discussion, I've decided to play it by ear.

沒有。因為這堂課太常變成討論，所以我決定到時候再說。

* presentation〔͵prɛzn̩'teʃən〕 *n.* 報告
  political science 政治學　　***not really*** 並沒有；並不是
  turn into 變成　　discussion〔dɪ'skʌʃən〕 *n.* 討論
  play it by ear 見機行事；隨機應變

23. (**C**) Q : What does Marshal plan to do? 馬歇爾計畫要做什麼？
    A. Wait and take the class next year. 等待明年修這門課。
    B. Become a musician. 成為一位音樂家。
    C. Give his presentation without a plan.
       毫無計畫地上台報告。
    D. Discuss the presentation with the professor.
       和他的教授討論他的報告。

    * ***take a class*** 修一門課
      give a presentation 報告 (= *make a presentation*)

For question 24, you will listen to a short conversation.

M : How can I cut down on my spending?
    我如何減少我的支出？

W : Why don't you keep track of everything you buy?
    你何不記錄你買的所有東西？

    * ***cut down on*** 減少　　spending〔'spɛndɪŋ〕 *n.* 開銷；花費；支出
      keep track of 記錄

24. (**B**) Q : What is the woman's advice? 這位女士的忠告是什麼？
    A. The man should deposit his money into a bank
       account. 這位男士應該將他的錢存入銀行帳戶。

B. He should write down all his purchases.
　　他應該寫下他所有購買的物品。

C. He should buy more things.　他應該買更多東西。

D. He should buy less.　他應該買少一點。

*　advice〔əd'vaɪs〕n. 忠告　　deposit〔dɪ'pɑzɪt〕v. 存（錢）
　　account〔ə'kaʊnt〕n. 帳戶
　　purchase〔'pɝtʃəs〕n. 購買（的東西）

For questions 25 and 26, you will listen to a short conversation.

W : My steak is undercooked.　How about yours?
　　我的牛排沒熟。你的如何？

M : Mine is overcooked.　我的是太老了。

W : Maybe the waiter switched them up.　Is yours
　　medium-well?　This one is medium-rare.　可能服務生
　　把牛排調換過了。你的是七分熟嗎？這一個是三分熟的。

M : I'm going to call the waiter over.　我要叫服務生過來。

*　undercooked〔'ʌndə‚kʊkt〕adj. 尚未煮熟的
　　overcooked〔‚ovə'kʊkt〕adj. 煮得過熟的
　　switch〔swɪtʃ〕v. 調換；交換
　　medium-well　adj.（牛排）七分熟
　　medium-rare　adj.（牛排）三分熟　　*call sb. over* 叫某人過來

25. (**C**) Q : Where are the speakers?　說話者在哪裡？

　　A. In a subway station.　在地鐵站裡。

　　B. In a cooking class.　在烹飪課中。

　　C. In a restaurant.　在餐廳裡。

　　D. In a television studio.　在電視攝影棚裡。

*　studio〔'stjudɪ‚o〕n. 工作室；攝影棚

26. (**A**) Q：What does the woman think happened?
　　　　　這位女士認為發生了什麼事情？

　　A. The waiter made a mistake. 服務生弄錯了。

　　B. The steaks were dropped on the floor.
　　　　牛排掉到地上了。

　　C. The steaks were overcooked. 牛排煎太熟了。

　　D. The man forgot his wallet. 這位男士忘了他的皮夾。

　　* **made a mistake** 犯錯　　drop〔drɑp〕v. 使掉落
　　　wallet〔'wɑlɪt〕n. 皮夾

For questions 27 and 28, you will listen to a short conversation.

　　M：Rumor has it that you might drop out at the end of the
　　　　semester.　I hope it's not true.
　　　　有傳言說妳將會在學期末休學。我希望不是真的。

　　W：Unfortunately, it's very likely to happen.　My mother
　　　　has been diagnosed with cancer and I need to be closer
　　　　to home. 很遺憾，傳言很有可能會發生。我媽已被診斷出罹
　　　　患癌症，我必須離家近。

　　M：I'm so sorry to hear that.　Is she going to be OK?
　　　　聽到這個消息我很難過。她會沒事吧？

　　W：We don't know yet. 我們目前還不知道。

　　* rumor〔'rumɚ〕n. 謠言　　**Rumor has it that** 謠傳說
　　drop out 輟學　　semester〔sə'mɛstɚ〕n. 學期
　　unfortunately〔ʌn'fɔrtʃənɪtlɪ〕adv. 不幸地；遺憾地
　　diagnose〔ˌdaɪəg'noz〕v. 診斷　　cancer〔'kænsɚ〕n. 癌症
　　not…yet 尚未；還沒

27. (**D**) Q：What might happen at the end of the semester?
　　　　　學期末可能會發生什麼事？

A. The man might transfer to a different school.
　這位男士會轉去別的學校。

B. The man might get married. 這位男士可能會結婚。

C. The woman might change her major.
　這位女士可能會改變她的主修科目。

D. The woman might drop out of school.
　這位女士可能會休學。

* transfer〔træns'fɜ〕v. 轉學　　major〔'medʒɚ〕n. 主修科目

28. (**C**) Q : Why might this happen? 爲什麼這件事可能會發生？

A. The man has poor grades. 這位男士的成績不好。

B. The man will graduate. 這位男士將要畢業。

C. The woman's mother is ill. 這位女士的母親生病了。

D. The woman's family will come to visit.
　這位女士的家人會來拜訪她。

* grade〔gred〕n. 成績　　graduate〔'grædʒu‚et〕v. 畢業
ill〔ɪl〕adj. 生病的　　***come to visit*** 來訪

For questions 29 and 30, you will listen to a short conversation.

M : Can you recommend a decent restaurant in the area?
　你可以推薦這一區的一家還不錯的餐廳嗎？

W : That depends on what you'd like to eat.
　這就要看你想要吃什麼了。

M : I'm open to just about anything, as long as it's good.
　我幾乎任何食物都接受，只要是好的。

W : There's an Italian place just up the street called Luna's.
　That's where I would go if I were you. 在街的那頭有一家
　義大利餐廳叫露娜的店。如果我是你，我就會去那裡。

* recommend〔‚rɛkə'mɛnd〕v. 推薦

decent〔'disn̩t〕*adj.* 相當不錯的　　***depend on*** 視⋯而定
open〔'opən〕*adj.* 開放的　　***be open to*** 樂意接受；願意考慮
as long as 只要　　Italian〔ɪ'tæljən〕*adj.* 義大利的　*n.* 義大利文
place〔ples〕*n.* 餐廳　　up〔ʌp〕*prep.* 在⋯的較遠處；沿⋯而去
up the street 在街那邊的

29. (**B**) Q：What does the man want to do? 這位男士想做什麼？

    A. Get some rest. 休息一下。

    B. Get something to eat. 找東西吃。

    C. Learn to speak Italian. 學說義大利文。

    D. Find a decent hotel. 找一間不錯的飯店。

    * ***get some rest*** 休息一下

30. (**D**) Q：What does the woman imply? 這位女士暗示什麼？

    A. Luna's is the worst restaurant in the area.
       露娜的店是這一區最糟的餐廳。

    B. Luna's is the most expensive restaurant in the area.
       露娜的店是這一區最貴的餐廳。

    C. Luna's is the only restaurant in the area.
       露娜的店是這一區唯一的一家餐廳。

    D. Luna's is her favorite restaurant in the area.
       露娜的店是這一區她最喜歡的餐廳。

    * imply〔ɪm'plaɪ〕*v.* 暗示　　favorite〔'fevərɪt〕*adj.* 最喜愛的

四、短文聽解

Questions 31 and 32 are based on the following report.

    A well-known brand name can be valuable, but it requires constant attention. Brand values can rise or fall on management decisions, changes in the competitive environment or the belief that the brand has aged beyond its useful lifetime. Often, the true cause of a decline in a brand's value is folly and arrogance. Even the most powerful brand cannot survive poor marketing decisions. A brand derives its value from several factors, the most obvious being how much money it earns. Some brands have grown on fantastic claims, only to fail when those claims were not realized.

　　一個廣為人知的名牌可能是很有價值的，但是它需要持續的關注。品牌可能會因為管理決策、競爭環境的改變，或者認為這個品牌已經老化，超出其使用壽命，而使其價值上升或下降。通常，在品牌價值下降的真正原因，會是愚蠢和傲慢。即使是最強而有力的品牌，也無法在差勁的行銷決策中存活。一個品牌的價值，源自幾個因素，其中最明顯的，就是這個品牌可以賺多少錢。有些以夢幻般訴求而成長的品牌，當這些訴求沒有實現時，只能失敗。

** ─────────────

well-known〔'wɛl'non〕adj. 有名的　　***brand name*** 名牌
valuable〔'væljuəbl̩〕adj. 有價值的
require〔rɪ'kwaɪr〕v. 需要
constant〔'kɑnstənt〕adj. 不斷的；持續的
attention〔ə'tɛnʃən〕n. 注意　　value〔'vælju〕n. 價值
rise〔raɪz〕v. 上升　　fall〔fɔl〕v. 下降
on〔ɑn〕prep. 根據　　management〔'mænɪdʒmənt〕n. 管理
decision〔dɪ'sɪʒən〕n. 決定
competitive〔kəm'pɛtətɪv〕adj. 競爭的
environment〔ɪn'vaɪrənmənt〕n. 環境
belief〔bɪ'lif〕n. 相信；看法；信念　　age〔edʒ〕v. 變老
lifetime〔'laɪf,taɪm〕n. 壽命　　***useful lifetime*** 使用壽命
cause〔kɔz〕n. 原因　　decline〔dɪ'klaɪn〕n. 衰退
folly〔'fɑlɪ〕n. 愚蠢　　arrogance〔'ærəgəns〕n. 自大；傲慢
powerful〔'pauəfəl〕adj. 強大的；強而有力的
survive〔sə'vaɪv〕v. 自…中生還
marketing〔'mɑrkɪtɪŋ〕n. 行銷

derive〔 dəˈraɪv 〕*v.* 得到；源自　　factor〔ˈfæktɚ〕*n.* 因素
obvious〔ˈɑbvɪəs〕*adj.* 明顯的　　earn〔 ɜn 〕*v.* 賺
fantastic〔 fænˈtæstɪk 〕*adj.* 異想天開的；不切實際的；很棒的
claim〔 klem 〕*n.* 主張；訴求　　realize〔ˈrɪəˌlaɪz〕*v.* 實現

31. (**B**)　Where is this talk most likely being given?
　　　這段對話最有可能在哪裡進行？
　　　A. At a weight-loss clinic. 在一家減重診所。
　　　B. At a business convention. 在一場商務會議。
　　　C. At a law seminar. 在一場法律研討會。
　　　D. At an art gallery. 在一間藝廊。

　　　＊weight-loss *adj.* 減重的　　clinic〔ˈklɪnɪk〕*n.* 診所
　　　convention〔 kənˈvɛnʃən 〕*n.* 代表大會；定期會議
　　　seminar〔ˈsɛməˌnɑr〕*n.* 研討會　　gallery〔ˈgælərɪ〕*n.* 畫廊

32. (**A**)　What does "fantastic" mean in this context?
　　　"fantastic" 在本文中是什麼意思？
　　　A. Unlikely. 不太可能的。　　B. Credible. 可信的。
　　　C. Modest. 謙虛的。　　　　D. Luxurious. 奢侈的。

　　　＊context〔ˈkɑntɛkst〕*n.* 上下文
　　　unlikely〔 ʌnˈlaɪklɪ 〕*adj.* 不可能的
　　　credible〔ˈkrɛdəbḷ〕*adj.* 可信的
　　　modest〔ˈmɑdɪst〕*adj.* 謙虛的
　　　luxurious〔 lʌgˈʒurɪəs 〕*adj.* 奢侈的；豪華的

Questions 33 and 34 are based on the following report.

　　Parents always say that if schools had uniforms, everything would be so much easier. We wouldn't get caught up in looks and would learn the skills we need. I disagree with this. I think that school uniforms would put a restriction on our creativity. We dress the way we do for a certain reason. Clothes let us express ourselves. The first impression we get of people is usually clothes, facial expression and language. If we all wear the same thing, we don't get to really see what people are like on the inside. Usually girly girls wear pink and frilly things. Skaters wear baggy pants and Goths usually wear black. Clothes don't distract us from learning; they inspire our imaginations and light up our world.

父母總是說，如果學校有制服，一切都會容易得多。我們不會執著於外表，並會學習我們所需要的技能。我不同意這一點。我認為學校制服會限制我們的創造力。我們的穿著方式一定有某種原因。衣服讓我們能表達自己。我們對人的第一印象，通常是來自衣服、臉部表情，和語言。如果我們都穿同樣的衣服，我們就無法真正了解別人的內在。通常很少女的女孩會穿著粉紅色的和有花邊的衣服。玩滑板的人，穿寬大的褲子，而哥德人一般穿黑色。衣服不會分散我們學習的注意力；衣服能激發我們的想像力，而且照亮我們的世界。

** ——————

uniform〔'junə,fɔrm〕 n. 制服　　***be caught up in*** 受…吸引
looks〔lʊks〕 n. pl. 外表
disagree〔,dɪsə'gri〕 v. 不同意 < *with* >
restriction〔rɪ'strɪkʃən〕 n. 限制
creativity〔,krie'tɪvətɪ〕 n. 創造力　　certain〔'sɝtn̩〕 adj. 某種的
express〔ɪk'sprɛs〕 v. 表達　　impression〔ɪm'prɛʃən〕 n. 印象
facial〔'feʃəl〕 adj. 臉部的　　expression〔ɪk'sprɛʃən〕 n. 表情
get to V. 得以～　　inside〔'ɪn'saɪd〕 n. 內部
girly〔'gɝlɪ〕 adj. 女孩的；少女的　　frilly〔'frɪlɪ〕 adj. 滿是褶邊的
skater〔'sketɚ〕 n. 溜冰者；參加滑板運動的人
baggy〔'bægɪ〕 adj. 袋狀的；寬鬆下垂的
Goth〔gɑθ〕 n. 哥德人【Goth 是指一些黑暗、氣氛音樂和服裝元素，其追隨者則被稱為「哥德人」】
distract〔dɪ'strækt〕 v. 使分心　　inspire〔ɪn'spaɪr〕 v. 激勵
imagination〔ɪ,mædʒə'neʃən〕 n. 想像力　　***light up*** 照亮

33. (**C**)　Who is speaking?　說話者是誰？

　　　A. A parent.　一位家長。　　B. A teacher.　一位老師。
　　　C. A student.　一位學生。　　D. A coach.　一位教練。
　　　* coach〔kotʃ〕n. 教練

34. (**B**)　What does the speaker think about the idea of school
　　　uniforms?　說話者對學校制服有何看法？

　　　A. Uniforms promote a positive learning environment.
　　　　制服能促進一個正向的學習環境。
　　　B. Uniforms restrict creativity.　制服限制創造力。
　　　C. Uniforms make things easier.　制服讓事情更容易。
　　　D. Uniforms are for girly girls.　制服適合很少女的女生。
　　　* promote〔prə'mot〕v. 促進　　restrict〔rɪ'strɪkt〕v. 限制

Questions 35 and 36 are based on the following report.

　　　The United States may be a wealthy, privileged,
industrialized nation, but when it comes to being an ideal
place to raise a family, it ranks well below several
European countries. Most of the countries in the top 10 are
in Europe, where paid maternity leave is the norm,
breastfeeding is widely accepted, and government-backed
support programs for new parents abound. With high
levels of female education, women in politics, and one of
the most generous family leave policies in the developed
world, Norway took top honors. Take into account
parental leave policies, low preschool enrollment rates,
and high teen-pregnancy rates, and the U.S. rank falls even
further. Overall, the U.S. ranks 25th out of 165 countries.

That's up six spots from its 31st place showing last year, largely thanks to improvements in education rates for girls.

　　美國可能是一個富裕的、幸運的、工業化的國家，但當談到作爲成家的理想地點時，它的排名遠低於一些歐洲國家。排名於前 10 位的國家，大多在歐洲，在這些國家帶薪產假是常態，母乳餵養被廣泛接受，政府對於新手父母的財力支援計劃比比皆是。女性教育水準高的、有女性從政，以及在已開發國家中最慷慨的家務假政策，挪威獲得了最高榮譽。如果考慮到產假政策，低學前教育入學率，和高青少年懷孕率，使美國的排名跌幅更大。整體來看，美國在 165 個國家中排名第 25 位。美國已從去年的第 31 名上升了 6 名，主要是因爲女性受教育的比率有改善。

**

wealthy〔ˋwɛlθɪ〕*adj.* 有錢的
privileged〔ˋprɪvɪlɪdʒd〕*adj.* 有特權的；幸運的；得天獨厚的
industrialized〔ɪnˋdʌstrɪəlˏaɪzd〕*adj.* 工業化的
When it comes to 一提到　　raise〔rez〕*v.* 養育
family〔ˋfæməlɪ〕*n.* 子女；孩子
rank〔ræŋk〕*v.* 位居　　*n.* 排名
well below 還低於的　　paid〔ped〕*adj.* 有薪水的
maternity〔məˋtɜnətɪ〕*adj.* 孕婦的　　leave〔liv〕*n.* 休假
maternity leave 產假　　norm〔nɔrm〕*n.* 標準；規範
breastfeeding〔ˋbrɛstˏfidɪŋ〕*n.* 餵母乳
government-backed〔ˋgʌvənməntˋbækt〕*adj.* 有政府財力支援的
support〔səˋport〕*n.* 支持；援助
program〔ˋprogræm〕*n.* 計劃　　abound〔əˋbaʊnd〕*v.* 大量存在
family leave（雇員爲照顧嬰兒或生病家屬的）家務假；家庭
　　（照顧）假　　developed〔dɪˋvɛləpt〕*adj.* 已開發的
take…into account 考慮到…
preschool〔ˋpriˋskul〕*adj.* 就學前的
enrollment〔ɪnˋrolmənt〕*n.* 入學　　rate〔ret〕*n.* 比率
teen〔tin〕*adj.* 青少年的　　pregnancy〔ˋprɛgnənsɪ〕*n.* 懷孕
further〔ˋfɝðə〕*adv.* 更進一步地
overall〔ˋovəˏɔl〕*adv.* 整體而言；大體上

up〔ʌp〕*adv.* 向更高處；朝上方
spot〔spɑt〕*n.* (序列等中的)位置　***thanks to*** 由於
improvement〔ɪm'pruvmənt〕*n.* 改善

35. (**A**) What is the speaker mainly talking about?
說話者主要在談論什麼？
A. Good places to raise a family. 成立家庭的好地方。
B. Family leave policies in Europe. 歐洲的家務假政策。
C. Norway's quality of life. 挪威的生活品質。
D. Breastfeeding. 餵母乳。

36. (**C**) According to the speaker, which of the following
statements is true? 根據說話者的說法，下列敘述何者爲眞？
A. The U.S. has low teen-pregnancy rates.
美國的青少年懷孕率很低。
B. The U.S. has high preschool enrollment rates.
美國的學前教育入學率很高。
C. The U.S. ranks 25th out of 165 countries overall.
整體而言，美國在 165 個國家中排名第 25 位。
D. The U.S. is a good place to raise a family.
美國是個成家的好地方。

Questions 37 and 38 are based on the following report.

Technology changes the way we live, and within the
last 100 years things have changed rapidly and
dramatically. Personally, I applaud the advances in
technology which have occurred since my grandmother
was a child. We now have electricity, air conditioning, cars,
indoor plumbing, television, computers, home phones and
cell phones! Like everything else, cell phones

are both a blessing and a curse.　That being said, I've been
trying to go through life the last year and a half without a
cell phone.　I tell you... that's hard in this day and age.
People expect you to have a phone.　I miss school calls
telling me my kids are sick.　I miss doctors calling back
with important information.　Cell phones are an important
piece of technology if you are to live in this world today.

　　科技改變了我們的生活方式，並且在過去的 100 年間，情況
有了迅速和極大的改變。就我個人而言，我很讚賞從我祖母小時
候開始就有的科技進步。我們現在有電力、空調、汽車、室內管
線、電視、電腦、家用電話，和手機！就像其他事物一樣，手機
既是幸福也是詛咒。話雖如此，過去的一年半裡，我一直在努力
過著沒有手機的生活。我告訴你…在這個時代是非常困難的。人
們預期你會有手機。我漏接學校告訴我，我孩子生病了的電話。
我錯過醫生回電話給所要通知我的重要訊息。如果你要生活在現
在這個世界，那手機就是一個很重要的科技配備。

**　━━━━━━━━━━━━━━━━━━━━━━━━━━━

technology〔tɛk'nɑlədʒɪ〕*n.* 科技
within〔wɪð'ɪn〕*prep.* 在…之內　　　things〔θɪŋz〕*n. pl.* 情況
rapidly〔'ræpɪdlɪ〕*adv.* 快速地
dramatically〔drə'mætɪklɪ〕*adv.* 戲劇性地；相當大地
personally〔'pɝsn̩lɪ〕*adv.* 就個人而言
applaud〔ə'plɔd〕*v.* 贊成　　advance〔əd'væns〕*n.* 進步
occur〔ə'kɝ〕*v.* 發生　　electricity〔ɪˏlɛk'trɪsətɪ〕*n.* 電力
air conditioning 空調　　indoor〔'ɪnˏdor〕*adj.* 室內的
plumbing〔'plʌmɪŋ〕*n.* 水電工程；配管（工程）
cell phone 手機　　blessing〔'blɛɪŋ〕*n.* 祝福
curse〔kɝs〕*n.* 詛咒　　***that being said*** 話雖如此
go through 經歷　　day〔de〕*n.* 時代　　age〔edʒ〕*n.* 時代
expect〔ɪk'spɛkt〕*v.* 預料；預期　　miss〔mɪs〕*v.* 錯過
piece〔pis〕*n.* 一件　　***be to V.*** 預定…；必須…

37. (**D**) Which of the following is NOT mentioned by the speaker? 說話者沒有提到下列何者？

A. Air conditioning. 空調。

B. Indoor plumbing. 室內配管工程。

C. Television. 電視。　　D. The Internet. 網路。

* Internet〔'ɪntə,nɛt〕*n.* 網際網路

38. (**C**) What is the speaker's attitude toward cell phones? 說話者對於手機有何看法？

A. Cell phones are a blessing. 手機是個祝福。

B. Cell phones are a curse. 手機是個詛咒。

C. Cell phones are important in the modern world. 手機在現代生活中很重要。

D. Cell phones are only for entertainment purposes. 手機只是爲了娛樂的目的。

* attitude〔'ætə,tjud〕*n.* 態度；看法
toward〔tord〕*prep.* 對於
entertainment〔,ɛntə'tenmənt〕*n.* 娛樂
purpose〔'pɝpəs〕*n.* 目的；用途

Questions 39 and 40 are based on the following report.

How much water should you drink each day? It's a simple question with no easy answer. Studies have produced varying recommendations over the years, but in truth, your water needs depend on many factors, including your health, how active you are and where you live. Although no single formula fits everyone, knowing more about your body's need for fluids will help you estimate how much water to drink each day.

　　你每天應該喝多少水？這是一個簡單問題，但卻沒有簡單的答案。這些年來，研究產出不同的建議，但事實上，水的需求取決於許多因素，包括你的健康，你的活動量，和你居住地點。雖然沒有適合每個人的單一公式，但多了解你身體對液體的需求，會幫助你估計自己每天要喝多少水。

** ────────────────────

study〔ˈstʌdɪ〕*n.* 研究　　produce〔prəˈdjus〕*v.* 製造；產生
varying〔ˈvɛrɪŋ〕*adj.* 不同的
recommendation〔ˌrɛkəmɛnˈdeʃən〕*n.* 推薦；建議
in truth 事實上（= *in fact*）　　need〔nid〕*n.* 需求
depend on 視…而定；取決於
active〔ˈæktɪv〕*adj.* 活動的；活潑的　　single〔ˈsɪŋgḷ〕*adj.* 單一的
formula〔ˈfɔrmjələ〕*n.* 公式　　fit〔fɪt〕*v.* 適合
fluid〔ˈfluɪd〕*n.* 液體　　estimate〔ˈɛstəˌmet〕*v.* 估計

39. (**D**) What is the speaker mainly talking about?
   說話者主要在談論什麼？
   A. Economics. 經濟學。　　B. Education. 教育。
   C. Politics. 政治學。　　　D. Health. 健康。
   * economics〔ˌikəˈnɑmɪks〕*n.* 經濟學

40. (**A**) What will the speaker most likely talk about next?
   說話者接下來最有可能談論什麼？
   A. The health benefits of water. 水對健康的好處。
   B. The cost of recycling wastewater.
      廢水回收處理的費用。
   C. The formula of making water. 製造水的公式。
   D. The amount of water wasted in an average day.
      平常一天當中浪費了多少水。
   * benefit〔ˈbɛnəfɪt〕*n.* 利益；好處的
   recycling〔riˈsaɪkḷɪŋ〕*n.* 回收再利用
   wastewater〔ˈwestˌwɔtɚ〕*n.*（工廠的）廢水；污水
   amount〔əˈmaunt〕*n.* 數量
   average〔ˈævərɪdʒ〕*adj.* 一般的；普通的

高中英聽測驗模擬試題⑩詳解

一、看圖辨義：第一部分

For question number 1, please look at the four pictures.

1. (**A**) Sparky and Tina are sitting on a park bench. They are
blowing bubbles.

斯派奇和蒂娜正坐在公園的長椅上。他們正在吹泡泡。

* bench〔bɛntʃ〕*n.* 長椅　　blow〔blo〕*v.* 吹
bubble〔'bʌbḷ〕*n.* 泡泡

For question number 2, please look at the four pictures.

2. (**D**) Greg is riding his bicycle. Frank is walking his dog.

格瑞克正騎著他的腳踏車。法蘭克正在遛狗。

* walk〔wɔk〕*v.* 遛（狗）

For question number 3, please look at the four pictures.

3. (**D**)　Today is our class field trip.　We're going to the zoo.

　　　　今天是我們班上校外教學。我們要去動物園。

　　　　　* ***field trip*** 實地考察旅行

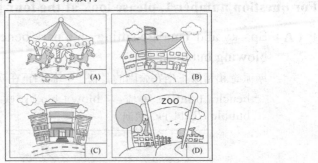

For question number 4, please look at the four pictures.

4. (**C**)　Frank did well on the entrance exam.　To celebrate, he went out for ice cream.

　　　　法蘭克入學考試考得不錯。為了慶祝，他出去吃冰淇淋。

　　　　　* ***do well*** （考試）考得好　　　entrance〔ˋɛntrəns〕*n.* 入學

一、看圖辨義：第二部分

For question number 5, please look at picture 5.

5. (**A、D**) Which TWO of the following are true about the
picture?　關於這張圖片，下列哪兩項為真？

A. Mick is exercising.　米克正在運動。

B. Mick is resting.　米克正在休息。

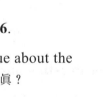

C. Mick is having a casual
workout.　米克正在隨意的運動。

D. Mick is trying as hard as he
can.　米克正試著盡他所能地努力。

* rest〔rɛst〕v. 休息
casual〔'kæʒʊəl〕adj. 隨便的；漫不經心的
workout〔'wɜk,aʊt〕n. 運動
as…as one can 盡可能… (= *as…as possible*)

For question number 6, please look at picture 6.

6. (**C、D**) Which TWO of the following are true about the
picture?　關於這張圖片，下列哪兩項為真？

A. They received identical grades.
他們得到相同的成績。

B. The student on the left
received an F.
左邊的學生得到一個 F。

C. The student on the left received a D.
左邊的學生得到一個 D。

D. The student on the right received an A.
右邊的學生得到一個 A。

* receive〔rɪ'siv〕v. 收到；接到；得到

identical〔aɪˈdɛntɪkḷ〕*adj.* 完全相同的
grade〔gred〕*n.* 成績

For question number 7, please look at picture 7.

7.（**A、C**）Which TWO of the following are true about the
picture? 關於這張圖片，下列哪兩項為眞？

   A. They are using a computer.
     她們正在使用電腦。

   B. They are preparing a meal.
     她們正在準備餐點。

   C. The girl is typing on the keyboard.
     女孩正在用鍵盤打字。

   D. The woman is resting her hands on the girl's
     shoulders. 那女士正把她的手放在女孩的肩膀上。

* prepare〔prɪˈpɛr〕*v.* 準備　　type〔taɪp〕*v.* 打字
keyboard〔ˈkiˌbord〕*n.* 鍵盤
rest〔rɛst〕*v.* 把⋯靠在；把⋯放在

For question number 8, please look at picture 8.

8.（**B、D**）Which TWO of the following are true about the
picture? 關於這張圖片，下列哪兩項為眞？

   A. They are in a bar.
     他們在一家酒吧。

   B. They are in a chemistry lab.
     他們在一間化學實驗室。

   C. They are having a drink. 他們正在喝飲料。

   D. They are conducting an experiment.
     他們正在做實驗。

* bar〔bar〕*n.* 酒吧　　chemistry〔ˈkɛmɪstrɪ〕*n.* 化學

lab〔læb〕n. 實驗室（＝laboratory）
have〔hæv〕v. 喝　　conduct〔kən'dʌkt〕v. 做；進行
experiment〔ɪk'spɛrəmənt〕n. 實驗

For question number 9, please look at picture 9.

9. (**A** 、 **C**) Which TWO of the following are true about the
picture? 關於這張圖片，下列哪兩項為眞？

A. Mr. Walker has a moustache.
沃克先生有留八字鬍。

B. Mr. Walker is blind.
沃克先生是盲的。

C. Mr. Walker is mowing the lawn.
沃克先生正在割草坪的草。

D. Mr. Walker is planting a tree. 沃克先生正在種樹。

* moustache〔məs'tæʃ〕n. 八字鬍
blind〔blaɪnd〕adj. 盲的　　mow〔mo〕v. 割（草）
lawn〔lɔn〕n. 草坪；草地　　plant〔plænt〕v. 栽種

For question number 10, please look at picture 10.

10. (**C** 、 **D**) Which TWO of the following are true about the
picture? 關於這張圖片，下列哪兩項為眞？

A. They both have straight hair.
她們兩個都是直髮。

B. They both are wearing pants.
她們兩個都穿褲子。

C. Martha has invited Chloe to have a seat.
瑪莎邀請克洛依坐下。

D. Chloe will probably sit next to Martha.
克洛依可能將會坐在瑪莎旁邊。

* straight〔stret〕*adj.* 直的　　pants〔pænts〕*n. pl.* 褲子
  have a seat 坐下　　***next to*** 在⋯旁邊

二、對答

11. (**A**) Don't you just love ice cream? What's your favorite
    flavor?　你不愛冰淇淋嗎？你最喜愛的口味是什麼？

    A. Strawberry. 草莓。　　　B. Leather. 皮革。
    C. Hard. 堅硬的。　　　　　D. Warmth. 溫暖。

    * strawberry〔'strɔ,bɛrɪ〕*n.* 草莓　　leather〔'lɛðɚ〕*n.* 皮革
      hard〔hɑrd〕*adj.* 堅硬的　　warmth〔wɔrmθ〕*n.* 溫暖

12. (**B**) Would you mind if I joined you? The cafeteria is so
    crowded today.

    你介意我和你一起坐嗎？今天自助學生餐廳好擁擠。

    A. There's plenty in back. 後面有很多。
    B. No, I wouldn't mind at all. 不，我完全不介意。
    C. My friend won't be coming. 我的朋友不會來。
    D. It can't be moved. 它不能被移動。

    * mind〔maɪnd〕*v.* 介意　　cafeteria〔,kæfə'tɪrɪə〕*n.* 自助餐廳
      crowded〔'kraʊdɪd〕*adj.* 擁擠的
      plenty〔'plɛntɪ〕*n.* 豐富；多量　　***in back*** 在後面
      not⋯at all 一點也不　　move〔muv〕*v.* 移動

13. (**B**) Do you know how to swim? 你知道怎麼游泳嗎？

    A. No. I'm type A. 不，我是 A 型。
    B. I never learned how. 我從來沒有學過。
    C. Let me get you a towel. 讓我幫你拿個毛巾。
    D. The water is too cold. 水太冷了。

    * type〔taɪp〕*n.* 類型　　towel〔'tauəl〕*n.* 毛巾

14. (**A**) Hi, Jane. Why are you so cheerful today?
　　　嗨，珍。妳今天爲什麼這麼開心？

　　　A. It's my birthday! 今天是我的生日！
　　　B. I don't feel very well. 我覺得不太舒服。
　　　C. Yesterday. 昨天
　　　D. It doesn't bother me. 這不會困擾我。

　　　* cheerful〔'tʃɪrfəl〕*adj.* 高興的　　well〔wɛl〕*adj.* 健康的
　　　bother〔'bɑðɚ〕*v.* 困擾

15. (**D**) We're out of soft drinks. Would you like a beer instead?
　　　我們沒有清涼飲料了。你要不要改成啤酒？

　　　A. Just a little off the sides. 只要修一下兩邊的頭髮。
　　　B. Sure enough, he ate the carrot. 他果然吃胡蘿蔔。
　　　C. Black. 黑色的。
　　　D. OK. Sounds good. 好的。聽起來不錯。

　　　* *be out of* 用完；沒有
　　　soft drink 清涼飲料；不含酒精的飲料
　　　beer〔bɪr〕*n.* 啤酒　　instead〔ɪn'stɛd〕*adv.* 作爲替代
　　　Just a little off the sides. 只要修一下兩邊的頭髮。
　　　sure enough 果然；果眞　　carrot〔'kærət〕*n.* 胡蘿蔔
　　　Sounds good. 聽起來不錯。(= *It sounds good*.)

16. (**A**) Do you remember where we parked the car?
　　　你記得我們把車停在哪裡嗎？

　　　A. Don't worry. I remember. 不要擔心。我記得。
　　　B. Close the door. It's cold. 把門關上。很冷。
　　　C. It's OK. They can't hear us.
　　　　沒關係。他們聽不見我們說話。
　　　D. Oh no! He has a gun! 喔，糟糕！他有槍！

　　　* park〔pɑrk〕*v.* 停（車）　　gun〔gʌn〕*n.* 槍

17. (**A**) That was quite a party last night. What time did you leave? 昨天晚上的派對真的很特別。你什麼時候離開的？

    A. I left around midnight. 我大概是午夜左右離開。

    B. He was the life of the party. 他是派對上最活躍的人。

    C. It was like that when I got there.
       當我到達的時候就是那樣。

    D. I went to a party. 我去參加一場派對。

    * *quite a* 異常的；出眾的   around〔ə'raʊnd〕*prep.* 大約
      midnight〔'mɪd,naɪt〕*n.* 半夜；午夜
      life〔laɪf〕*n.* 活力的泉源；活躍氣氛的人（或事物）
      the life of the party 派對上最活躍的人

18. (**C**) Who are those kids? I've never seen them before.
    那些孩子是誰？我以前從來沒看過他們。

    A. That's too bad. 真糟糕。

    B. My brother. 我兄弟。

    C. I don't know. I've never seen them before either.
       我不知道。我以前也從來沒見過他們。

    D. Kids will be kids. 孩子終歸是孩子。

19. (**C**) It's almost noon and time for lunch, Bobby. What would you like to eat?
    快到中午，是該吃午餐的時候了，巴比。你想吃什麼？

    A. Greetings. 大家好。

    B. I feel so fortunate. 我覺得很幸運。

    C. I'm in the mood for a cheeseburger. 我想吃起司漢堡。

    D. You never liked me anyway. 反正你從未喜歡過我。

    * noon〔nun〕*n.* 中午
      greetings〔'gritɪŋz〕*interj.*【問候語】大家好
      fortunate〔'fɔrtʃənɪt〕*adj.* 幸運的   mood〔mud〕*n.* 心情
      be in the mood for 有心情做…   anyway〔'ɛnɪ,we〕*adv.* 反正

20. (**B**)　Hi, Toby. How do you like your new school?

嗨，托比。你喜不喜歡你的新學校？

A. Probably math. 可能是數學。　　B. I love it. 我愛它。

C. I prefer used things. 我比較喜歡舊的事物。

D. I like you. 我喜歡你。

*　*How do you like* ~ ?* 你喜不喜歡~？；你覺得怎麼樣~？

prefer〔prɪ′fɜ〕*v.* 比較喜歡

used〔juzd〕*adj.* 舊的；用舊了的

三、簡短對話

For question 21, you will listen to a short conversation.

M：I'd like to mail this package. 我想寄這個包裹。

W：Overnight, second-day air, or regular ground service?

隔日寄達、航空郵件兩天到、或者一般的平信寄送服務？

M：That depends. What are the rates? 看情況。費用是多少？

*　mail〔mel〕*v.* 郵寄　　package〔′pækɪdʒ〕*n.* 包裹

overnight〔′ovɚ′naɪt〕*adj.* 持續整夜的；隔日寄達的【在美國有所

謂的「隔日寄達」，所以很多最速件都用 overnight 表示】

air〔ɛr〕*n.* 天空；空中【在郵務用語中，air 通常表示航空郵件】

regular〔′rɛgjələ〕*adj.* 普通的；一般的

ground〔graʊnd〕*adj.* 地面的；基本的

depend〔dɪ′pɛnd〕*v.* 視…而定；取決於＜*on*＞

That depends. 要看情況。　　rate〔ret〕*n.* 費用；價格

21. (**D**)　Q：Where are the speakers? 說話者在哪裡？

A. At the airport. 在機場。

B. At the bus station. 在巴士站。

C. At the train station. 在火車站。

D. At the post office. 在郵局。

For question 22, you will listen to a short conversation.

W : Good afternoon, Mr. Franklin.　How was your trip?
　　午安，富蘭克林先生。你的旅行如何？

M : It was fine, Mary, thanks.　Any messages while I was
　　away?　旅行很好，瑪麗，謝謝。我不在的時候有任何訊息嗎？

W : Yes, quite a few of them.　I put them on your desk.
　　有，訊息還不少。我把它們放在你的桌上了。

　　* *quite a few* 很多

22. (**C**)　Q : Where did Mary put Mr. Franklin's messages?
　　　　　　　瑪麗把富蘭克林先生的訊息放在哪裡？

　　A. In a computer file.　在電腦的檔案夾裡。
　　B. On the bulletin board.　在佈告欄上。
　　C. On Mr. Franklin's desk.　在富蘭克林先生的桌上。
　　D. He doesn't have any messages.　他沒有任何的訊息。

　　* file〔faɪl〕*n.* 檔案　　bulletin〔'bʊlətn̩〕*n.* 佈告
　　board〔bord〕*n.* 木板　　***bulletin board*** 佈告欄

For question 23, you will listen to a short conversation.

M : I'm back, Jill.　I got the stuff you wanted from the store.
　　我回來了，吉兒。我從商店把妳要的東西買回來了。

W : Oh, great!　I noticed you didn't bring the list with you.
　　噢，太棒了！我注意到你沒有帶清單。

M : No, I didn't need it.　I've got a photographic memory.
　　是的，我不需要它。我有過目不忘的記憶力。

　　* get〔gɛt〕*v.* 買　　stuff〔stʌf〕*n.* 東西

notice〔'notɪs〕*v.* 注意到   list〔lɪst〕*n.* 清單
photographic〔ˌfotə'græfɪk〕*adj.* 攝影（術）的；攝影用的
memory〔'mɛmərɪ〕*n.* 記憶；記憶力
photographic memory 照相般清晰的記憶力；過目不忘的能力

23. (**A**) Q：What does the man imply? 這位男士暗示什麼？

    A. He has a good memory. 他有很好的記憶力。

    B. He is good with money. 他很會處理金錢。

    C. He is handy with a camera. 他很擅長玩相機。

    D. He has a list of things to talk about.

        他有一長串的事情可以談論。

    * ***be good with*** 擅長於   ***be handy with*** 擅長於
    camera〔'kæmərə〕*n.* 照相機

For question 24, you will listen to a short conversation.

M：Why is Rita wearing a mask? Is she ill?

    為什麼麗塔戴著口罩？她生病了嗎？

W：No. But a couple of her classmates are sick and she's
    afraid she'll catch something.

    不。但是她的一些同學生病了，她害怕她會被感染。

M：Well, it is the cold and flu season.

    嗯，現在是感冒和流感的季節。

    * mask〔mæsk〕*n.* 口罩   ill〔ɪl〕*adj.* 生病的
    a couple of 幾個；數個   catch〔kætʃ〕*v.* 感染
    cold〔kold〕*n.* 感冒   flu〔flu〕*n.* 流行性感冒（= *influenza*）

24. (**B**) Q：What do we know about Rita?

    關於麗塔我們可以知道什麼？

    A. She is ill. 她生病了。

B. She is a student. 她是個學生。

C. She is careless. 她是很粗心。

D. She is late for school. 她上學遲到。

* careless ('kɛrlɪs) adj. 粗心的

For questions 25 and 26, you will listen to a short conversation.

M : Oh, look at the line. There must be a dozen people
waiting for a table.

噢，妳看那排隊伍。一定有許多人在等桌子。

W : Let's go somewhere else. I'm starving and don't feel
like waiting. 我們去別的地方吧。我餓死了而且我不想等。

M : Me too. Let's try the Indian place around the corner.
我也是。我們去轉角那家印度餐廳吧。

* dozen ('dʌzn̩) n. 一打；十二個   *a dozen* 一打；相當多
starving ('stɑrvɪŋ) adj. 很餓的；飢餓的
feel like 想要   Indian ('ɪndɪən) adj. 印度的
place (ples) n. 餐廳   *around the corner* 就在轉角

25. (**C**) Q : Where is this conversation taking place?
這段對話發生在哪裡？

A. At an airport. 在機場。

B. At a bank. 在銀行。

C. At a restaurant. 在餐廳。

D. At a movie theater. 在電影院。

26. (**C**) Q : What will the speakers most likely do next?
說話者接下來最有可能做什麼？

A. Continue to wait. 繼續等。

B. Make a reservation.　預先訂位。

C. Go somewhere else.　去別的地方。

D. Ask for the check.　要求帳單。

* next〔nɛkst〕*adv.* 接下來　　reservation〔‚rɛzə‘veʃən〕*n.* 預訂
make a reservation 預訂　　　***ask for*** 要求
check〔tʃɛk〕*n.*（餐廳的）帳單

For questions 27 and 28, you will listen to a short conversation.

W：Excuse me, but could you tell me which bus goes to
　　Taipei 101 from here?　不好意思，可以請你告訴我，哪
　　一台公車可以從這裡到台北 101 嗎？

M：There are two, the 15 and the 20, both of which stop
　　here.　有兩台，15 號和 20 號公車，這兩台都會在這裡停靠。

W：Do you know how often they run?
　　你知道它們多久來一台嗎？

　　* run〔rʌn〕*v.*（車、船）行駛

27.（**A**）Q：Where does the woman want to go?
　　　　　　　這位女士想去哪裡？

A. Taipei 101.　台北 101。

B. The Taipei Flora Exhibition.　台北花博。

C. The National Palace Museum.　國立故宮博物院。

D. New Taipei City.　新北市。

* flora〔‘florə〕*n.* 所有植物
exhibition〔‚ɛksə‘bɪʃən〕*n.* 展覽會　　palace〔‘pælɪs〕*n.* 宮殿

28.（**D**）Q：How often do the buses run?　公車多久來一台？

A. Every 15 minutes.　每 15 分鐘。

B. Every 20 minutes. 每 20 分鐘。

C. Every hour. 每小時。

D. We don't know. 我們不知道。

For questions 29 and 30, you will listen to a short conversation.

W : It was so nice of you to give me the gift, Oscar, but I
can't accept it.

奧斯卡，你送我禮物眞的很貼心，但是我不能接受。

M : Why not? It's your birthday! 爲什麼不？今天是妳的生日！

W : My boyfriend is very jealous. He'll think there's
something going on between us.

我的男朋友很會吃醋。他會覺得我們兩個之間有什麼。

* jealous〔'dʒɛləs〕adj. 嫉妒的；吃醋的

29. (**B**) Q : What do we know about the woman?

關於這位女士，我們知道什麼？

A. She is a secretary. 她是位秘書。

B. She has a boyfriend. 她有個男朋友。

C. She is 30 years old today. 她今天 30 歲。

D. She is interested in dating Oscar.

她有興趣和奧斯卡約會。

* secretary〔'sɛkrə,tɛrɪ〕n. 祕書　　date〔det〕v. 和…約會

30. (**C**) Q : Why did the woman reject the man's gift?

這位女士爲什麼拒絕這位男士的禮物？

A. She already has a boyfriend. 她已經有男朋友了。

B. She's not interested in him. 她對他沒有興趣。

C. Her boyfriend would not approve.
她的男朋友不會同意。

D. She is allergic to chocolate. 她對巧克力過敏。

* reject〔rɪ'dʒɛkt〕*v.* 拒絕　　approve〔ə'pruv〕*v.* 贊成；同意
allergic〔ə'lɝdʒɪk〕*adj.* 過敏的<*to*>
chocolate〔'tʃɔklɪt〕*n.* 巧克力

四、短文聽解

Questions 31 and 32 are based on the following report.

　　The relation between older and younger generations can be compared to that of a freshman and senior in high school. The senior has just experienced all there is to high school. The freshman is new to the system and unaware of what to expect in the coming years. As the older individual in the situation, the senior is responsible for teaching the freshman; in return, the freshman shows appreciation and respect. Likewise, it is important to remember that without the sacrifices made by the previous generations, we would have no way of understanding history and what to expect in the coming years of life.

　　較老一代和較年輕一代之間的關係，可以比喻為高中校園裡的高一新生和高三學長姐。高三的前輩剛剛經歷了所有高中生活會發生的事。高中校園體制對高一新生來說是陌生的，而且他們不知道該對未來幾年有什麼期待。身為在此情況下資歷較老的人，高三生必須負責教新生；高一新生則是要以感激與尊重作為回報。同樣地，要記住一個要點，但如果沒有前面世代所做的犧牲，我們就沒辦法了解歷史，而且沒有辦法預期未來。

**　**

relation〔rɪ'leʃən〕n. 關係；關聯
generation〔͵dʒɛnə'reʃən〕n. 世代
compare〔kəm'pɛr〕v. 比較；比喻 < to >
freshman〔'frɛʃmən〕n. 一年級；新生
senior〔'sinjə〕n. 前輩；學長；大四學生；高三學生
experience〔ɪk'spɪrɪəns〕v. 經歷；體驗
new〔nju〕adj. 不熟悉的　　*be unaware of* 不知道；沒察覺到
expect〔ɪk'spɛkt〕v. 預期　　coming〔'kʌmɪŋ〕adj. 即將來臨的
individual〔͵ɪndə'vɪdʒuəl〕n. 個人
situation〔͵sɪtʃu'eʃən〕n. 情況　　*be responsible for* 要對…負責
in return 作爲回報　　appreciation〔ə͵priʃɪ'eʃən〕n. 感激
respect〔rɪ'spɛkt〕n. 尊敬　　likewise〔'laɪk͵waɪz〕adv. 同樣地
sacrifice〔'sækrə͵faɪs〕n. 犧牲
previous〔'privɪəs〕adj. 以前的

31.（**D**）To what does the speaker compare the generation gap?
說話者主要在談論什麼？

　　A. The Great Depression. 大蕭條。
　　B. Fortune telling. 算命。
　　C. Old people. 老人。
　　D. High school. 高中。

　　* mainly〔'menlɪ〕adv. 主要地
　　　depression〔dɪ'prɛʃən〕n. 不景氣；蕭條
　　　the Great Depression 經濟大蕭條【是指 1929 年至 1933 年之間
　　　全球性的經濟大衰退。大蕭條是第二次世界大戰前最爲嚴重的世界
　　　性經濟衰退】　　fortune telling〔'fɔrtʃən͵tɛlɪŋ〕n. 算命
　　　gap〔gæp〕n. 隔閡；差距　　*generation gap* 代溝

32.（**B**）What does the speaker imply? 說話者暗示什麼？

　　A. You never know what to expect.
　　　你永遠不知道要期待什麼。
　　B. We should respect our elders. 我們應該要尊重長輩。

C. High school is challenging. 高中生活很有挑戰性。

D. Seniors know everything. 前輩知道任何事情。

* elder 〔ˈɛldɚ〕 *n.* 前輩;長輩

  challenging 〔ˈtʃælɪndʒɪŋ〕 *adj.* 有挑戰性的

Questions 33 and 34 are based on the following report.

I consider myself lucky to have had Tom Watson as my basketball coach. From Coach Watson, I learned that the phrase "I can't" needed to be removed from my vocabulary. He made me and the other players realize our potential was beyond what we thought we could do. He taught me that the way you play basketball is the way you live your life. If you play hard and give everything you have on the basketball court, then you should do the same in life. Never say "I can't." His passion and love for the game became contagious for me and every other player on the team. Every time I play basketball now, I think about Coach Watson and how much he taught me about basketball and life.

我認為自己很幸運,能有湯姆・華森當我的籃球教練。從華森教練那裡,我學到了「我不能」這句話,需要從我的用字中刪除。他使我和其他的球員了解,我們的潛力是超出我們認為自己可以做到的。他教導我,打籃球的方式,就是生活的方式。如果你在籃球場上會努力打球,而且盡全力,那麼你也應該在生活中這麼做。永遠不要說「我不能」。他對籃球比賽的熱情和熱愛逐漸感染我,以及隊上其它的球員。現在,每當我在打籃球時,我都會想到華森教練,和他教過我多少關於籃球和生活的事。

** ─────────────────

consider〔kən'sɪdə〕v. 認為　　coach〔kotʃ〕n. 教練
phrase〔frez〕n. 片語　　remove〔rɪ'muv〕v. 除去
vocabulary〔və'kæbjə,lɛrɪ〕n. 字彙；用字範圍
player〔'pleə〕n. 球員；選手　　realize〔'rɪə,laɪz〕v. 領悟；了解
potential〔pə'tɛnʃəl〕n. 潛力
give everything one **have** 盡全力
court〔kort〕n.（籃球、網球）球場　　passion〔'pæʃən〕n. 熱情
contagious〔kən'tedʒəs〕adj. 具感染力的　　team〔tim〕n. 隊

33. (**B**) Who is Tom Watson? 湯姆・華森是誰？

A. A basketball player. 一個籃球員。
B. A basketball coach. 一位籃球教練。
C. A language instructor. 一位語言教師。
D. A motivational speaker. 一位激勵人心的演講者。

* instructor〔ɪn'strʌktə〕n. 教員；指導者
motivational〔,motə'veʃənəl〕adj. 激勵人心的
speaker〔'spekə〕n. 說話者；演講者

34. (**C**) What phrase needed to be removed from the speaker's
vocabulary? 哪一句話需要從說話者的用字中去除？

A. Just do it. 做就對了。
B. Easy come, easy go. 來得容易，去得快。
C. I can't. 我不能。
D. Yes, I can. 是的，我可以。

Questions 35 and 36 are based on the following report.

The Earth's oceans are among the most mysterious
places on the planet, but scientists now have at least figured
out how deep the oceans are and just how much water they
hold. A group of scientists used satellite measurements to

get new estimates of these values, which turned out to be 1.3 billion cubic kilometers for the volume of the oceans and 3,682 meters for the average ocean depth. Both of these numbers are less than many previous estimates of the ocean's volume and depth. The researchers report that the world's total ocean volume is less than the most recent estimates by a volume equivalent to about five times the Gulf of Mexico, or 500 times the Great Lakes. While that might seem a lot at first glance, it is only about 3 percent lower than the estimates of 30 years ago.

　　地球的海洋是在這個星球上最神秘的地方，但科學家現在至少算出海洋有多深，和海洋容納了多少水。有一群科學家利用人造衛星，測量得到一個新的估計數值，結果海洋的體積是十三億立方公里，而海洋的平均深度為 3,682 公尺。這兩個海洋體積與深度的數據，都比以前估計的小。研究人員報告指出，全世界海洋總體積小於最近的估計值，其體積約五倍墨西哥灣，或五大湖區的 500 倍。雖然這乍看之下似乎很多，但這個數值比 30 年前的估計值只低 3％左右。

** ————————————————

Earth〔ɝθ〕*n.* 地球　　ocean〔'oʃən〕*n.* 海洋
mysterious〔mɪs'tɪrɪəs〕*adj.* 神祕的
planet〔'plænɪt〕*n.* 行星　　***at least*** 至少
figure out 算出；了解　　satellite〔'sætḷ,aɪt〕*n.* 人造衛星
measurement〔'mɛʒəmənt〕*n.* 測量；測定
estimate〔'ɛstəmɪt〕*n.* 估計值　　value〔'væljʊ〕*n.* 數值
turn out to be 結果是　　billion〔'bɪljən〕*n.* 十億
cubic〔'kjubɪk〕*adj.* 立方的　　kilometer〔'kɪlə,mitə〕*n.* 公里
volume〔'vɑljəm〕*n.* 體積　　meter〔'mitə〕*n.* 公尺
average〔'ævərɪdʒ〕*adj.* 平均的　　depth〔dɛpθ〕*n.* 深度；厚度

previous〔'priviəs〕*adj.* 先前的
researcher〔rɪ'sɜtʃɚ〕*n.* 研究人員
total〔'totl̩〕*adj.* 全體的；總計的
equivalent〔ɪ'kwɪvələnt〕*adj.* 相等的＜ *to* ＞
time〔taɪm〕*n.* 倍數   gulf〔gʌlf〕*n.* 海灣
the Gulf of Mexico 墨西哥灣【是北美洲南部大西洋的一海灣，北
　　爲美國，南、西爲墨西哥，東經佛羅里達海峽與大西洋相連】
or〔ɔr〕*conj.* 也就是   lake〔lek〕*n.* 湖
the Great Lakes 五大湖【是位於加拿大與美國交界處的幾座大型
　　淡水湖泊，按面積從大到小分別爲：蘇必略湖（Lake Superior）、
　　休倫湖（Lake Huron）、密西根湖（Lake Michigan）、伊利湖
　　（Lake Erie）和安大略湖（Lake Ontario）】
while〔hwaɪl〕*conj.* 雖然   glance〔glæns〕*n.* 看一眼
at first glance 乍看之下   percent〔pɚ'sɛnt〕*n.* 百分之…

35. (**A**) What is this talk mainly about? 這篇演講主要是關於什麼？

　　A. The Earth's oceans. 地球上的海洋。

　　B. The Gulf of Mexico. 墨西哥灣。

　　C. The moon. 月球。

　　D. Thirty years ago. 三十年前。

36. (**D**) According to the new estimates, how deep are the oceans? 根據新的估計，海洋有多深？

　　A. 500 times the Great Lakes. 五大湖的 500 倍。

　　B. 1.3 billion cubic kilometers. 13 億立方公里。

　　C. 3 percent deeper than 30 years ago.
　　　　比 30 年前的估計値還深了 3%。

　　D. About 3,700 meters on average.
　　　　平均大約 3,700 公尺。

　　* *on average* 平均而言

Questions 37 and 38 are based on the following report.

Moore's law is a <u>rule of thumb</u> in computer science whereby the capability of technology doubles approximately every two years. The capabilities of many digital electronic devices are strongly linked to Moore's law: processing speed, memory capacity, sensors and even the number and size of pixels in digital cameras. All of these are improving at roughly the same rate. This improvement has dramatically enhanced the impact of digital electronics in nearly every segment of the world economy. Moore's law describes a driving force of technological and social change in the late 20th and early 21st centuries.

摩爾定律是計算機科學的經驗法則，而科技的性能大約每隔兩年就會加倍。許多數位電子設備的性能，和摩爾定律是密切相關的：處理速度、記憶體容量、感應器，甚至是數位相機中像素的數量和大小。所有的這些都以大致相同的速率在進步。這樣的進步大大地增強了數位電子產品對幾乎每一個環節的世界經濟產生衝擊。摩爾定律描述 20 世紀末和 21 世紀初技術和社會變遷的驅動力。

** ——————————————————

law〔lɔ〕*n.* 法律；定律

Moore's law 摩爾定律【摩爾定律是指：IC 上可容納的電晶體數目，約每隔 18 個月便會增加一倍，性能也將提升一倍】

rule〔rul〕*n.* 規則　　thumb〔θʌm〕*n.* 大拇指

rule of thumb 用拇指的測量法；經驗法則【根據經驗而不根據理論的做法】

whereby〔hwɛrˈbaɪ〕*adv.* 藉以

capability〔͵kepəˈbɪlətɪ〕*n.* 能力；性能

technology〔tɛk'nɑlədʒɪ〕*n.* 技術　　double〔'dʌbḷ〕*v.* 加倍

approximately〔ə'prɑksəmɪtlɪ〕*adv.* 約

digital〔'dɪdʒɪtḷ〕*adj.* 數位的

electronic〔ɪ,lɛk'trɑnɪk〕*adj.* 電子的

device〔dɪ'vaɪs〕*n.* 裝置；設備

strongly〔'strɔŋlɪ〕*adv.* 強烈地；堅固地　　link〔lɪŋk〕*v.* 使連結

be linked to 和…有關連　　processing〔'prɑsɛsɪŋ〕*n.* 處理

memory〔'mɛmərɪ〕*n.* 記憶裝置　　capacity〔kə'pæsətɪ〕*n.* 容量

sensor〔'sɛnsə〕*n.* 感應器　　pixel〔'pɪksəl〕*n.* 像素

digital camera 數位相機　　improve〔ɪm'pruv〕*v.* 改善

roughly〔'rʌflɪ〕*adv.* 大約　　rate〔ret〕*n.* 速率

improvement〔ɪm'pruvmənt〕*n.* 改善；增進

dramatically〔drə'mætɪkḷɪ〕*adv.* 大大地

enhance〔ɪn'hæns〕*v.* 提高；增強　　impact〔'ɪmpækt〕*n.* 衝擊

electronics〔ɪ,lɛk'trɑnɪks〕*n. pl.* 電子設備

segment〔'sɛgmənt〕*n.* 部分　　economy〔ɪ'kɑnəmɪ〕*n.* 經濟

describe〔dɪ'skraɪb〕*v.* 敘述　　driving〔'draɪvɪŋ〕*adj.* 驅使的

force〔fors〕*n.* 力量

technological〔tɛknə'lɑdʒɪkḷ〕*adj.* 技術（學）的

late〔let〕*adj.* 末期的　　early〔'ɝlɪ〕*adj.* 初期的

century〔'sɛntʃərɪ〕*n.* 世紀

37. (**C**) What is this talk mainly about? 這段談話主要是關於什麼？

　　A. Law. 法律。　　　　　B. Economics. 經濟學。

　　C. Technology. 科技。　　D. Social change. 社會的變遷。

38. (**A**) What is a <u>rule of thumb</u>? 「經驗法則」是什麼？

　　A. A practical rule not based on science or exact
　　　measurement.
　　　一項不是基於科學或精確測量的實用法則。

　　B. A series of laws based on traditional lengths of
　　　measure. 一系列根據傳統測量長度的法則。

C. An outdated way of measuring by using your thumb.
一種用大拇指測量的過時方式。

D. A modern way of saying "Do unto others."
一種「對待別人」的現代說法。

* practical〔'præktɪkḷ〕adj. 實際的
exact〔ɪg'zækt〕adj. 精確的　　a series of 一系列的
based on 根據　　traditional〔trə'dɪʃənḷ〕adj. 傳統的
length〔lɛŋθ〕n. 長度　　measure〔'mɛʒɚ〕n. v. 測量
outdated〔'aʊt'detɪd〕adj. 過時的
unto〔'ʌntə〕prep.【古】【詩】對；給；於【全句為：Do unto
others as you would have them do unto you. (想要別人怎麼
對你，你就要怎麼對待別人。) 】

Questions 39 and 40 are based on the following report.

If you're a bird lover, then there's no question that
you've seen some of the adorable videos both online and
on television of parrots and other types of pet birds dancing
their tails off to popular music. One of the funniest and
easiest tricks to teach your bird, dancing comes naturally to
many of our feathered friends. If you'd like to teach your
bird how to dance, I can teach you how to encourage your
pet to try out a few moves. Not only will teaching your bird
to dance be entertaining, it will offer your pet some extra
exercise, which can improve its overall health.

如果你是個鳥類愛好者，那毫無疑問地，你在網路和電視上
一定已經看過一些鸚鵡和其他類型的寵物鳥，配合流行音樂大秀
舞蹈的可愛影片。跳舞是可以敎你的鳥，最有趣、最簡單的把戲

之一，跳舞對我們許多有羽毛的朋友是天生自然的。如果你想教你的鳥如何跳舞，我可以教你如何鼓勵你的寵物去嘗試一些動作。教你的鳥跳舞不僅具有娛樂效果，也能提供你的寵物，一些額外的運動，以增進其整體健康。

**　　——————————————————

adorable〔ə'dorəbḷ〕adj. 可愛的　　video〔'vɪdɪo〕n. 影片
online〔'ɑn‚laɪn〕adv. 在線上；在網路上
parrot〔'pærət〕n. 鸚鵡　　pet〔pɛt〕adj. 作為寵物的　n. 寵物
tail〔tel〕n. 尾巴
dance one's tail off 拼命跳舞【*work one's tail off* 拼命工作】
to〔tu〕prep. 配合著　　funny〔'fʌnɪ〕adj. 好笑的
trick〔trɪk〕n. 把戲
naturally〔'nætʃərəlɪ〕adv. 天生地；自然地
come naturally to sb. （做某事）對某人很容易
featured〔'fɛðəd〕adj. 有羽毛的
encourage〔ɪn'kɝɪdʒ〕v. 鼓勵　　*try out* 試用；試驗
move〔muv〕n. 動作；移動　　*not only…but also* 不僅…而且~
entertaining〔‚ɛntə'tenɪŋ〕adj. 使人得到娛樂的；使人愉快的
extra〔'ɛkstrə〕adj. 額外的　　overall〔'ovə‚ɔl〕adj. 整體的

39. (**B**) Who would most likely be interested in this talk?
誰最有可能會對這段談話感興趣？

　　A. Dancers. 舞者。　　　　B. Bird owners. 擁有鳥的人。
　　C. Musicians. 音樂家。　　D. Parrots. 鸚鵡。

40. (**B**) What does the speaker say he can do?
說話者說他能夠做什麼？

　　A. Teach your bird to speak. 教你的鳥說話。
　　B. Teach your bird to dance. 教你的鳥跳舞。
　　C. Teach your bird to fly. 教你的鳥飛。
　　D. Teach your bird to make videos. 教你的鳥製作影片。